Well Played

Well Played

A Christian Theology of Sport and the Ethics of Doping

Michael R. Shafer

Foreword by
Robert Song

The Lutterworth Press

The Lutterworth Press
P.O. Box 60
Cambridge
CB1 2NT
United Kingdom

www.lutterworth.com
publishing@lutterworth.com

ISBN: 978 0 7188 9433 7

British Library Cataloguing in Publication Data
A record is available from the British Library

First published by The Lutterworth Press, 2016

Copyright © Michael R. Shafer, 2015

Published by arrangement
with Pickwick Publications

Contents

Foreword

SPORT IS EVERYWHERE. FROM massive global spectacles such as the Olympic Games or the World Cup to everyday dramas on the school playing field or in the park down the street, from the back pages of newspapers to the heart of many people's leisure activities, sport is a major preoccupation of the modern world. Sports stadia are routinely described as the cathedrals of our time, sports stars receive adulation as demi-gods, and sports teams generate passions and allegiances that are quasi-religious in nature. Yet from a casual scan of the topics which Christian ethicists take it upon themselves to deliberate about, it would not be easy to tell that sport was of much human or moral significance. To be sure, the matters to which ethicists do attend are scarcely unimportant—sex and death, life and love, money and power, war and peace, people and planet. But the fact that pervasive cultural phenomena such as sport are not probed with the same level of theological seriousness as is routinely devoted to social and political ethics, bioethics, sexual ethics or environmental ethics, is something so striking as itself to be worthy of investigation. To be sure, other reflective disciplines have begun to take up the challenge, and there are burgeoning literatures not least on the philosophy and sociology of sport. But theological thinking in the area is only just beginning to gather momentum. Clearly there is plenty of work to be done.

Sport ought also to be of particular interest to Christian ethicists because of what it tells us about the nature and limits of human capacities. This is evident when we turn to think about which ways of enhancing human physical and mental capacities we regard as legitimate, and which ways we find questionable. It is one of the striking facts about contemporary sport that just at a time when there seem to be fewer and fewer justifications for

vii

questioning performance enhancements within the terms of our dominant philosophical traditions, nevertheless the public culture still remains profoundly sceptical of doping in sport. In cycling, athletics, weightlifting and a whole host of other sports, doping is widely regarded as cheating. Yet in the face of some contemporary accounts of morality, it might be tempting to dismiss such attitudes as atavistic relics of intellectually unsustainable distinctions between normal and enhanced bodies. Unsurprisingly a number of philosophers are inclined towards this conclusion. But equally we might consider working the argument in the opposite direction, using the conflict between popular instinct and philosophical reasoning as a locus for examining the cogency of our theoretical commitments. We might analyse what lies behind our revulsion against doping, and see what this tells us about our fundamental understandings of what it is to be human.

Michael Shafer's book is therefore just the kind of exploration we need. Michael is a passionate enthusiast for sport, both as a participant and as a spectator: he is a bottomless fund of information about a whole range of sports, from track and field to motor racing, from basketball to mixed martial arts. (He is even willing to indulge the English preoccupation with cricket, a game that goes on so much longer than baseball that George Bernard Shaw was led to quip that the English, not being a very spiritual people, invented cricket to give them some idea of eternity.) However, much more than that, he is passionate about Jesus, and about bringing Christian thinking to bear on sport. When he embarked on this project, he intended to address particular questions about the ethics of biotechnological enhancements in sport, as a case study within the broader field of human technological enhancement. But he soon discovered how the theological study of sport is a field in its infancy. So he had to do a lot of background foundational work on the nature of sport, its relationship to play, to competition, and to leisure, as well as on the history of Christian attitudes towards sport. Only when that had been done was he in a position to address the questions with which he had started out. The result is a highly instructive and very welcome theological exploration of what our everyday concerns about doping tell us about the nature of sport, and beyond that, of what our care about sport tells us about our own nature as human beings—as those who are cheered on by the watching crowds to run with perseverance the race marked out before us and so to win the prize for which we are called.

Robert Song
Durham University

Acknowledgments

AT THE RISK OF sounding like so many of the disingenuous athletes I have observed over the years I want to first thank my Lord and Savior for blessing me with the ability to reach this accomplishment. It was his love and grace that gave me purpose to pursue this qualification which will further prepare and equip me to be more like Christ in all future ministry endeavors.

Then there are numerous people I wish to thank who have contributed in some way to this accomplishment. Let me begin by thanking my primary supervisor, Robert Song. His pointed intellect and clear thinking have challenged and sharpened my own intellectual development but it is his enduring patience and warm heartedness that I have the most respect for. Never once did he express any frustration or irritation (though he must have felt some) as he walked me through years of progress and multiple revisions to get this work where it is today. Robert has become a good friend and I am grateful for our relationship which extends beyond my academic pursuits. We have enjoyed meals together with our families and we even attended a Premier League football match (which given the subject matter of my thesis we considered a joint research project!)

Other academic acknowledgements include my secondary supervisor, Chris Insole for his assistance on Aquinas, natural law, and many other aspects of my research. Michael Sleasman also helped me clarify my thoughts on numerous points throughout the thesis. During my PhD program at Durham I had the privilege of spending four months back home in the States in another Durham, this time in North Carolina. I am grateful for the three faculty members of Duke University's Department of Religion from whom I had the privilege of learning. Amy Laura Hall, Stanley Hauerwas, and Allen Verhey were most gracious during my time there as they helped me develop my thinking on issues that extend beyond the scope of my writing in these pages.

C. Ben Mitchell's guidance though my Master's degree and subsequent advice on pursuing a doctoral degree cannot go without notice. Much like Robert, Ben has also become a good friend and a reliable source of wisdom and counsel.

I would be remiss if I did not thank certain family members and friends who's constant support and encouragement was present at all the right times. Will and Jackie Dunaway, as well as Bob and Tina Shafer, have provided emotional, financial, spiritual, and moral support throughout this entire process. Eric and Rosa Bryant have been the truest of friends, visiting us all over the world, bringing a sense of the familiar to wherever we happened to be. My daughter Regin has provided a neverending source of joy and laughter which has been a constant reminder of how precious life is and how fast time passes us by.

More than any other, I am grateful for my amazing wife, Whitney. None of this would have been possible without the support of the greatest woman in the world. She was willing to leave everything behind to help me achieve this goal. With a one year old child she sold everything and moved half-way around the world because she believed in me. The most difficult moments in life are made bearable by her love and wisdom while the best parts are enriched by her friendship and humor. She has patiently tolerated my incessant love of sport (again, research) and has sacrificed many things to see this goal achieved. For more than a decade she has been an example of a godly life and has kept my eye on the prize. My prayer is that our daughter grows up to be just like her. She deserves praise for this accomplishment more than I do. Therefore, it is with great honor that I dedicate this work to her.

Introduction

EVERY DAY MILLIONS OF people around the world concern themselves with sport. They watch it on television, read about it in various media outlets, and in many cases participate in it themselves. From young to old, sport has captured the hearts, minds, and bodies of people the world over. It is a worldwide phenomenon that is no respecter of age, race, gender, nationality, or socio-economic status. Sport is everywhere. Which is why it is interesting that one is not likely to find many Christian theological treatments of sport. It seems to be a reality that theologians tend to be as uninterested in the ideas of sport as athletes are about the finer points of Christian doctrine.

Yet, it is my assumption that Christians are to be actively engaged in the culture around them and so the absence of Christian thought in the sports world signals a failure of the Church to be salt and light to the world.[1] Sport is an activity of growing importance in many cultures and therefore merits serious theological reflection. My goal is to challenge Christian athletes and spectators to gain a richer understanding of how their faith offers formative principles to guide their attitudes and behaviors as well as provide spiritually meaningful reasons for participating in sport. In doing so I hope to offer a theological contribution to the burgeoning field of sports ethics and open the door to further theological inquiries of sport.[2] As an example of practical application I will give particular reference to the ethics of doping. The theological conversation about sport presented in this thesis will

1. Matt 5:13–16.

2. I do not intend for 'sport' to be perceived as any particularly defined athletic activity except where I am using specific examples. By sport I am going to mean very generally the idea of sport as it encompasses all forms of athletic competition.

1

contribute an alternative viewpoint to the current ways of approaching the ethics of enhancing athletes.

Throughout this book I will demonstrate how the prohibitionists rightly reject doping but could strengthen the argument against it by incorporating a theologically informed understanding of sport. The first chapter will discuss the three key arguments as they are typically expressed in attempts to show the problematic nature of biotechnological enhancements in sport. These common challenges include the notions that doping is a form of cheating, a means of coercing other athletes, and unjustifiable based on the health risks presented to the athletes.

Doping proponents believe they have sufficient answers for each of these arguments and thus believe they have won the debate. However, my contention in this chapter is that if proponents of doping win this battle, it is not because their arguments are stronger, but in part due to the thin structure of the debate itself.

It has been argued by proponents of doping that the disquiet over the biotechnological enhancement of athletes as currently expressed is reducible to a bioethical concern for the health of the athlete. Prohibiting such enhancements will no longer be a justifiable position when the health risks are minimized.

However, this places the debate over performance enhancing substances firmly under the jurisdiction of medical ethics and has nothing to say about sports, per se. What is needed, I will suggest, is a consideration sport's fundamental purpose. Therefore, in addition to highlighting the major points of contention in the debate I will call for a more detailed examination of the nature of sport and the goods being sought therein. It is here that we find a starting point for addressing the deep-seated divide that exists between those who wish to allow doping in sport and those who do not. The purpose of the first chapter is to demonstrate that the current theoretical framework for considering ethical issues in sport is insufficiently prepared to address the deeper problems facing the contemporary sports culture.

Chapter 2 begins the inquiry into the nature of sport by discussing different ways in which the basic values of sport have been understood. In other words, is sport purely a subjective value, where its meaning is created by and for only those participating in the sport, or does sport contain some transcendent value(s) identifiable by all rational beings? Much contemporary philosophy of sport literature seeking to answer this question draws heavily on the work of one of two philosophers. The community-based theories of Alasdair MacIntyre and Richard Rorty, respectively, have been the most influential in identifying and contrasting values within competing societies. Each promotes an interpersonal relationship with other participants to arrive at a moral perspective of social activities such as sport but, as we will see, they are marked by extreme differences.

On one hand sport may be viewed from Alasdair MacIntyre's description of social practices. However, before accepting a general account of sports as MacIntyrean practices we must overcome two significant challenges. One objection to viewing sport as a practice is the insufficient justification of moral normativity and the other is MacIntyre's reliance on Aristotelian virtues. However, I shall argue that neither critique proves capable of rejecting a categorical description of sport as a social practice.

The second approach is the American pragmatism of Richard Rorty. The two major influences Rorty has had on moral conceptions of sport are an ethnocentric/anti-essentialist view of human nature and morality and the clear separation of the public and private sectors. The chapter will conclude by resurfacing one of the challenges presented to both views. Critics of each of the authors point to the potential for cultural relativism. I will conclude that this is a much more serious problem for Rorty. A Rortian view of sport reduces the activity to nothing more than a form in individual expression and thereby actually serves to undermine the community-oriented nature of sport as an activity that speaks to who we are as human beings. Ultimately, a Rortian view cannot see the intrinsic goods of sport qua sport but rather makes sport a means to some other end thus violating the internal consistency of the practice.

Therefore, between the two dominant philosophical views of sport I will suggest a MacIntyrean framework of social practices is a more accurate description of sport and provides a structural theory for the Christian account of sport presented throughout the rest of the book. However, Christianity has not always adopted a positive view of sport. In fact, Christian opinions on sport historically have fallen into one of three categories. The church has advocated variously (i) a view that sport is insignificant, (ii) the view that it is immoral, and/or (iii) a view that it is instrumental to other goods. Chapter 3 looks into these approaches to sport and offers critical analysis of the church's emphasis on each.

Though there are several biblical references to sport, these have been understood as mere analogies for the spiritual life and provided no substantive guidance for believers in the area of sport. In fact, some key figures in the early Church expressed extreme opposition to sport based on the idol worship, immoral behavior, and the anti-Christian mentality commonly associated with games and sport. Tertullian and Augustine were two of the more prominent Christian leaders to chastise those involved in sport with Augustine rejecting games as something which attracted his "attention away from some serious meditation."[3] For him, sport was at best irrelevant and at worst an obstacle to the higher calling of the church. The insignificant view and the immoral view are the two most frequently found in early Christianity.

With the exception of some prominent nineteenth-century Puritan leaders, the church slowly began to accept sport allowing a number of games to become common practice in theological circles. Rather than being a deterrent, sport became viewed as a tool for enabling spiritual growth. The physical activity associated with sport refreshed the soul and improved stamina for both Christian service and meditation. The door to this view was opened by Aquinas as he defended the need for physical and mental relaxation to rejuvenate both body and soul.

As a result, sport came to be seen primarily as an instrument in service of the spiritual life. The instrumental view was realized in full force during the mid nineteenth century when sport became a vehicle for drawing men back into the church. The Muscular Christianity movement was used as a tool to combat the perceived feminization of the church and though the movement itself was short-lived it fanned the flame of the new paradigm for a theological treatment of sport that still enjoys widespread support. Sport in the church has, as a result, often come to be seen as a resource for ministry. In other words, it is a means of evangelism, moral education and community development, and physical exercise.

This instrumental understanding of sport, while not necessarily misplaced, does not speak to any intrinsic value of sport. Here I will argue that whatever contribution theology has made to sport lacks complexity and depth. Certainly, there have been immoral practices associated with sport and sport often serves as an instrument to some other good but the value of sport reaches much further than this. Such a thin view of sport fails to recognize the created goodness of games which God intends for humans to enjoy, not as a means to "serious" work but as a fundamental source of enjoyment and human flourishing.

To arrive at this theologically informed view of sport it is important for Christians to take three key steps. We need to reconcile Christian ethics and sport, to remember the human essence of sport, and to recover the play element in sport. Each of these steps will be investigated through three sequential chapters.

Chapter 4 takes the first step by providing a theological analysis that seeks to develop a more robust theological framework from which to understand sport. This chapter will answer the three major challenges to Christian participation in sport in an effort to reconcile participation in sport with

3. Augustine, *Confessions of Saint Augustine*, X. 35, 241.

Christian practice. Despite the typically negative sentiment historically held by the church I will suggest that the purpose of sport complements and is harmonious with the Christian life. Even among its many pitfalls sport can be reconciled with Christian ethics. These three objections include problems in competition, adulterous or negligent views of the human body, and the morally corruptive influences prevalent in sport.

One serious problem for sport from a Christian vantage point is the apparent inescapable mind-set of putting one's self before all others. Can the attitude encouraged in sport of winning at the expense of others, gaining the upper hand and glorifying the strength of the human body be compatible with the Christian maxim of putting one's neighbor before oneself, not to mention the Christian virtues of meekness and humility?

Sport's tendency to elicit hyper-competitiveness often leads to a second challenge to Christian ethics and sport. The desire to "win at all costs" seems incompatible with the Christian tradition of putting others before oneself. The motivation for victory over others not only produces selfishness and pride but also typically results in one of two attitudes toward the body. Either athletes neglect proper respect for the dignity of their bodies or they idolize their bodies in a corrupted form of self worship.

The final major challenge facing the reconciliation of Christian ethics and sport is the negative influence many sports have on a Christian's moral behavior. The argument is often used that sport develops character but the statistics seem to suggest sport has the opposite effect. Violence, drugs, and scandals covering the sports headlines makes one question whether sport develops or corrupts Christian values.

I will argue that all three of these apparent conflicts have merit but many of the negative conclusions about sport's amplification of these sinful behaviors are based on faulty assumptions about sport. These corruptive influences are not indicative of sport as much as they are of the more innately corrupted individuals and institutions surrounding sport. Christian qualities can be expressed through participation in sport, though reconciling the two will certainly challenge Christians to reevaluate their involvement in some sports where our complacency in corruption is unbecoming of the values we strive to uphold.

A second step toward a theological account of sport calls us to remember that sport is most fundamentally a human activity, built upon human qualities. In chapter 5 I will argue that a Christian conception of sport is one based in creation. Sport is part of God's design for human flourishing. It is a gift to be enjoyed but unfortunately the prevalent view in the contemporary sports culture continually seeks to find ways of going beyond our physical limitations.

After critiquing the modern culture of sport for its "win at all costs" mentality I will suggest a new paradigm that more fully appreciates the humanness of sport. Recognizing our humanity is a central component in the development of a Christian ethic of sport. Instead of praising only the biggest, strongest and fastest we as Christians are challenged to recognize our physical limitations. My view rejects the idea that winning is the primary standard of excellence. Being the best is not always as important as doing one's best. It is the striving in sport, the effort of being human, that stands to be most depreciated in the current culture of competitive sport.

The human essence of sport is often best captured in the striving for excellence. I will use Special Olympics as a case in point. These athletes do not have the fastest times, the farthest throw, or the most technical form, especially when compared with professional athletes, but that does not mean their activity is less sporting. The mixture of effort, aspiration and talent provides the normative paradigm for sporting values.

The beauty of sport is that it demonstrates our mutually dependent human finitude and the possibility of astonishing physical accomplishments at the same time. Theology in sport calls us to recognize both dimensions. Sport stirs up admiration for both natural giftedness and human effort. The standards of excellence and the striving to achieve them surpass the sports culture's overemphasis on the outcome of one's effort.

The third step needed in a theologically informed approach to sport is to recover the play element in sport. In chapter 6 I identify play as the core component of sport. I will investigate the connection between play, games and sport. Tying this into the conclusions from previous chapters we can see the human essence of sport in the fact that play is an essential part of being human. There are instances where sport neglects the play element. My argument is that when this happens we are already headed down the path of taking sport too seriously. This usually occurs in the form of winning at all costs, a position we have already established as incompatible with Christian ethics. This is one reason why it is important for Christians to recover the spirit of play.

Engaging in sport without the spirit of play is a sign that we are taking the game too seriously but it also hints to the possibility that we do not take it seriously enough. This paradox is explained by the fact that play is a basic component of human flourishing. The pursuit of play is an intrinsically intelligible act that is characteristic of our humanness. It is what John Finnis calls a basic good. Play, therefore is intrinsically valuable and when we participate in sport without the element of play we are omitting a very significant portion of what God intended sport to be.

The topic of work is one which has received significant theological treatment, particularly from within the Protestant tradition. However, noticeably little attention is given to the topic of leisure. Chapter 7 will be the final chapter. There I will suggest the relationship of work and leisure carries great importance to the theory of sport I maintain. Thinking in this field by Catholic theologian Josef Pieper provides a helpful reorientation of our attitude toward the two activities.

Pieper claims that leisure is not merely a separate aspect of life but rather an all encompassing approach to life. The prevalent attitude of the Protestant work ethic has it backwards. Leisure, not work, is the basis of culture. To say that play is merely rest from and for work is to devalue the significance of play as a fundamental component of human flourishing. More importantly, the purpose of leisure is not a means of preparing for work but a form of worship. Play is an expression of gratitude to God who gives the gift of sport. Viewing leisure in terms of divine worship requires that we first follow the three steps outlined in the previous three chapters.

We must reconcile Christian ethics with sport by eliminating immoral sporting attitudes and activities. We must recognize sport as a deeply human activity that is given its meaning within the context of our physical limitations. We must recover the spirit of play in sport and see athletic activity neither as a trivial form of entertainment nor as a means to some external end but as an expression of who we are as human beings—an expression filled with grace, gratitude and a spirit of worship.

When we have arrived at this view of the theological purposes underlying sporting activity we find ourselves in a position to return to the concerns about doping in sport. From the attitude of grace, gratitude, and worship doping becomes incompatible with sport since the goals of sport (from a Christian worldview) and doping are fundamentally incommensurate. Sport intrinsically aims at a number of internal goods that are not advanced by employing enhancement technologies. This suggests that neither the sport itself nor the individual's moral or spiritual well-being stand to gain by sanctioning doping in sport. The only reason for its use is to advance a self-serving goal which undermines the basic good being sought by sporting practices.

This will by no means definitively clarify the blurred moral vision many sports ethicists concern themselves with in determining which substances should be allowed and which should be prohibited and why. My claim seeks to alleviate many of its problems by stepping back to ask what the purpose of sport is in the first place. What is or is not a natural behavior in sport is a secondary concern that can best be viewed in light of sport as a human expression of God's grace and our gratitude. From this starting point we will not only have dissolved many of the issues in doping but will have a clearer understanding of the more troubling issues underlying doping to gain a competitive advantage. More importantly, I hope to initiate a fruitful dialogue that will engage pastors, theologians, athletes, and fans from many theological traditions on the question of what it means for Christians to participate in sport well played.

1

The Landscape of Ethical
Arguments against Doping

What is Doping?

BARRY BONDS, ALEX RODRIGUEZ, Jose Canseco, Bill Romanowski, Marion Jones, Romario, Lance Armstrong. These names are just a few of the hundreds of professional and amateur athletes whose storied careers have been scandalously tainted by doping. Men and women who excelled in their respective sports are now brought low by the substances they believed would help them achieve their desired level of success. These doped athletes whose athletic feats made them celebrities and role models are excommunicated as accusations of doping destroy their reputation and report with a now crushed fan base. The dubious substances that ostensibly aided their rise to the top were also the cause of their downfall. In the usually glamorous world of sport, doping gives and doping takes away.

Why is this the case? What is it about these substances that cause the vast majority of the sports world to be so radically hostile to their use? Many answers have been given and, indeed, these answers form the basis of the prohibitive arguments against doping. They are often expressed in the form of just a few main ideas. Before we explore the validity of those it would be helpful to clarify what is meant by the use of doping in sport. Admittedly a vague term, I will use it in a broad sense to refer to any substances or method currently banned by the World Anti-Doping Agency (WADA).[1] Some of the

---

1. Throughout the book I will primarily use the terms "doping" or "performance enhancing substances" though other terms such as "biotechnology" may occasionally

more familiar types of performance enhancing substances include anabolic steroids, used in physically demanding sports, like body building, baseball, and football, as well as erythropoietin (EPO) usually associated with endurance sports such as cycling and distance running. Taking these substances, a practice commonly referred to as doping, produces physiological changes in the athlete to produce improved performance.[2] Other possible, albeit currently hypothetical, uses of biotechnology include genetic manipulation of embryos to enhance certain characteristics in that embryo such as the potential for size or speed with the purpose of creating a superior athlete.

For decades, scholars have been debating the morality of possible uses of biotechnology in the human body. Moral questions surrounding genetic screening, cloning, embryo selection, various forms of chemical enhancements, (i.e., pharmacological, sexual, cognitive, and so on) and many more possibilities have captured the thoughts of philosophers, theologians, doctors, lawyers and policymakers among others.

Technological progress has pushed a number of theologians and philosophers to consider the ethical ramifications of using these technologies in sport. Should athletes be allowed to use steroids? Is it acceptable for athletes to increase their stamina by injecting certain hormones? What counts for legitimate training methods and how do we distinguish them from illegitimate ones?

In recent years, many uses of medical and biotechnological enhancements have become generally acceptable in society. Examples range from highly technical procedures such as in vitro fertilization and gender reassignment surgery to simply taking a pill as in the cases of sexual performance enhancements like Viagra or eugeroic agents like Modafinil. While not without ethical concerns of their own these enhancements have a continually rising level of acceptance in Western culture.

Far from being limited to the realms of health restoration, reproduction, or productivity the use of biotechnology as a means of performance enhancement has become a highly discussed issue, particularly as it relates to the appropriateness of its use in sport. Taking a particular interest in these crossroads have been moral philosophers and policymakers. Books and

---

arise. I intend for any reference to enhancement to be used in a general sense as my purpose is to address doping as such more than it is to treat biotechnological or genetic versions of it in particular. In some instances I will turn to the phrase "biotechnological enhancements" to emphasize the point that these enhancements interact with the athlete's biological make-up in a way that purely technological enhancements, such as equipment or venue improvements, do not.

2. I will argue later in the following pages that it is not the performance one is attempting to improve by doping but rather the results.

journals have grown in popularity among academics.[3] Politicians are also spending an increasing amount of time investigating the legal parameters of doping in sport.[4] Sports media regularly report on enhancement scandals and keep fans up to date on new rules by providing regular commentary and expert panels.

Motivation for Victory

What is the motivation behind the painstaking preparation athletes put themselves through in order to be highly competitive? The love of the sport may be one factor but it is difficult to see how passion for the game requires the often extreme methods of training assumed by elite level athletes. Surely one can participate in the sport, assuming one is naturally talented enough, without such strenuous training. Perhaps the desire to do well compels the athlete but unfortunately experience has demonstrated that many athletes are not happy just to do their best. Certainly this may be true for some individualized sports such as mountain climbing where the climber "competes" independently of other climbers. But in most sports there is an interminable desire to win. Victory serves as sport's strongest motivation in the contemporary sports culture. It is the reason many athletes put their bodies through so many strenuous training programs. Winning has been the motivation that drives athletes to seek out any competitive advantage they can find. This is particularly true of athletes who make sport their profession. When athletes compete for a living they have an added pressure to perform well each and every time. An additional factor is insightfully noted by Carl Elliott,

> Professional athletes face a problem that some of us never have to think about. In many jobs people work their way up the career ladder, earning more money and more respect as they get older. But professional athletes often reach their peaks in their twenties, or even earlier. A thirty-year-old professional basketball player is a seasoned veteran, and a thirty-five-year-old is

3. For inquiries into the philosophy of sport see Weiss, *Sport: A Philosophic Inquiry.* There are a couple of important journals of interest: See *Journal of the Philosophy of Sport* and *Sport, Ethics and Philosophy.* Sociology and sport is also a burgeoning field. See, the *Sociology of Sport Journal.* For book length treatments see Elias and Dunning, *The Quest for Excitement: Sport and Leisure in the Civilizing Process*; and Giulianotti, *Sport: A Critical Sociology.*

4. See Senator Mitchell, "Report to the Commissioner of Baseball of an Independent Investigation into the Illegal Use of Steroids and Other Performance Enhancing Substances by Players in Major League Baseball," and House of Commons Science and Technology Committee, "Human Enhancement Technologies in Sport."

nearing the end of his career. Basketball players may get craftier as they get older, they may learn a few new tricks, but they are at the mercy of their physical skills. Many athletes simply flounder once they can no longer play competitively, squeezing out an unhappy existence at the margins of the sport.[5]

Athletes do not typically retire because they want to. Most often they are forced out by younger, stronger, faster athletes. The desire to play is still very much alive but the performance of the older athlete is reduced by the physical limitations of the relatively aged body. But as Elliott points out the life of the athlete is far from over. "When a doctor retires at age seventy, the arc of his career has run roughly parallel to the arc of his life. But when an athlete retires at age thirty-five, he can see a long future stretching out in front of him with no career to fill it."[6]

When the desire for victory is combined with the realization that an athlete's career is generally half as long as most other professions it becomes easy to see how athletes face the temptation to gain an edge whenever they can and however they can. Thomas Murray notes, "at the highest levels of competitive sports, where athletes strain to improve performances already at the limits of human ability, the temptation to use a drug that might provide an edge can be powerful."[7] We should note that this does not mean that athletes seeking performance enhancing substances for competitive advantages are necessarily of questionable moral character. There are other factors to be considered before moral judgments should be made. For now it is sufficient to say that athletes have traditionally used training and nutritional means to gain an advantage. But biotechnology is now presenting the athlete with a completely new way of gaining that edge. Genetic and other interventions may allow athletes to move beyond the realm of current physical limitations.

Anti-Doping Awareness

The Rise of Anti-Doping Programs

That present limitations of the human body may soon be greatly eclipsed because of technological enhancement has caused great concern for various governing bodies in sport. Out of this concern many organizations have risen seeking to defend sport from the invasion of biotechnology. Beyond doubt

5. Elliott, *Better Than Well*, 285.

6. Ibid., 285.

7. Murray, "The Coercive Power of Drugs in Sports," 24.

the most substantial work against performance enhancing drugs in sport has been done by the World Anti-Doping Agency (WADA). The 1998 Tour de France was an historic occasion in doping history. The French team *Festina* was disqualified when a soigneur was found in possession of large quantities of performance enhancing substances. Police raids thus ensued that resulted in protests from many cyclists in an event that nearly devastated the prestigious race. Of the 189 cyclists only ninety-three finished the race.

The International Olympic Committee (IOC) responded to this embarrassing incident by organizing a conference on the issue of drug use in sport. In February of 1999 the World Conference on Doping in Sport was held in Lausanne, Switzerland. The result of this meeting was the Lausanne Declaration on Doping in Sport, which called for action in six major areas relating to doping in sport. These ranged from education to proper sanctions to the need for international collaboration in the fight against doping. In November of the same year the World Anti-Doping Agency was established and was a functional entity by the Olympic Games in Sydney less than twelve months later.

WADA has since set out specific regulations on enhancement drugs in sport and at least once per year provides an updated, extensive list naming every banned substance deemed to give an unfair advantage in sport.[8] The purpose of WADA is "To protect the Athletes' fundamental right to participate in doping-free sport and thus to promote health, fairness and equality for Athletes worldwide; and to ensure harmonized, coordinated and effective anti-doping programs at the international and national level with regard to detection, deterrence and prevention of doping."[9]

To aid in the fight against doping in sport WADA has produced the World Anti-Doping Code, which has become the paradigmatic text for local anti-doping policies. In addition to the more than two hundred National Olympic Committees subscribing to the Code there are over one hundred government-funded anti-doping agencies in full agreement with WADA on the prohibition of doping in sport.

The Copenhagen Declaration on Anti-Doping in Sport resulted from another World Conference in March 2003. The resolution is comprised of nearly two hundred governments committed to fully endorsing and upholding the Code. These governments praise the work of WADA and collectively pledged economic resources amounting to half of WADA's annual budget.[10]

8. World Anti-Doping Agency, "2014 Prohibited List."
9. World Anti-Doping Agency, "World Anti-Doping Code," 13.
10. World Anti-Doping Agency, "Copenhagen Declaration."

Hundreds of other committees and organizations have accepted the position against doping as laid out in the Code. The Code currently consists of twenty-five articles divided into four parts. It is a detailed manuscript giving precise guidelines for doping control, education and research, roles and responsibilities, and acceptance and compliance issues.

> The Code is the fundamental and universal document upon which the World Anti-Doping Program in sport is based. The purpose of the Code is to advance the anti-doping effort through universal harmonization of core anti-doping elements. It is intended to be specific enough to achieve complete harmonization on issues where uniformity is required, yet general enough in other areas to permit flexibility on how agreed upon anti-doping principles are implemented.[11]

WADA has established five International Standards that help create solidarity in various sports organizations from around the world. These standards include the Prohibited List, testing, laboratories, therapeutic use exemptions and protection of privacy and personal information. Any organization wishing to be in compliance with WADA is required to abide by these standards. Several government sponsored organizations are eager to uphold WADA's principles. Two examples of this are found in the United Kingdom and the United States.

The United Kingdom Anti-Doping organization (UKAD) is "responsible for ensuring sports bodies in the UK comply with the World Anti-Doping Code, UK Anti-Doping is an intelligence led organisation that works with athletes and sports to develop and deliver education and information programmes."[12]

Another agency supporting WADA is the United States Anti-Doping Agency (USADA). USADA has been very active in producing literature pertaining to the use of enhancement substances in sports. *The Athlete's Handbook* was published to answer common questions and summarize policies and procedures relating to doping in sport. Among other things it presents a clear explanation to the obvious question of what constitutes a banned substance. They explain that substances are typically prohibited when they meet at least two of the following three criteria. "It has the potential to enhance or enhances sport performance. It represents an actual or potential health risk to the athlete. It violates the spirit of sport."[13]

---

11. World Anti-Doping Agency, "World Anti-Doping Code," 13.

12. United Kingdom Anti-Doping Organization, "About UK Anti–Doping."

13. United States Anti-Doping Agency, "USADA Athlete Handbook," 4.

The Code and various national anti-doping programs, such as UKAD and USADA, have set out the rationale behind prohibiting certain substances but it is up to specific sports organizations to implement their own methods of ensuring absolute compliance with the Code. Therefore, individual sports groups have created policies for testing procedures, disciplinary actions and processes for appeals. This seems to be the focus of official statements produced by governing sports bodies. Most simply presuppose the vices of doping in sport or briefly restate the arguments from the Code.

There are a few organizations that draw out further justification for prohibiting doping in their respective sport. One such example is the American National Football League (NFL). The NFL has adopted a policy that succinctly asserts the wrongness of doping and focuses predominantly on bureaucratic and logistical matters but they also offer an additional defense of substance prohibition. In briefly stating the league's disapproval of drugs in sport, specifically anabolic steroids and other similar substances, the NFL statement claims these substances have "no legitimate place in professional football."[14]

Three reasons are given for this. The first is actually a combination of two issues, namely cheating and coercion of other athletes. The second reason reflects concerns over the health risks associated with many performance enhancing substances. The third is an issue of the moral example the league expects players to set for younger athletes. A statement by the NFL Players Association says, "the use of Prohibited Substances by NFL players sends the wrong message to young people who may be tempted to use them. High school and college students are using these substances with increasing frequency, and NFL players should not by their own conduct suggest that such use is either acceptable or safe, whether in the context of sports or otherwise."[15]

A Response to the Anti-Doping Movement

There are numerous resources outlining the many reasons employed in the fight against doping.[16] While the reasons are many, one thing is clear; WADA has set a global precedent for the active elimination of biotechnological

14. National Football League, "Policy on Anabolic Steroids and Related Substances," 3.

15. Ibid., 3.

16. See Schneider and Butcher, "A Philosophical Overview of the Arguments on Banning Doping in Sport," 185–199; Simon, *Fair Play*, 72–86; Waddington and Smith, *An Introduction to Drugs in Sports*, 16–63.

enhancements in sport and has become the paradigm model for local organizations around the world. Yet, despite their large support base with so
many of the world's governments becoming involved in their cause there
is still a segment of the population who believe WADA is promoting the
wrong agenda. They believe enhancements could serve a valuable purpose
in sport whether it is through making a more efficient way of overcom-
ing various deficiencies in sport or by improving the performance to make
the event more aesthetically pleasing. They argue that prohibiting sports
enhancements rests on a set of faulty assumptions about the uses of biotechnology in sport.

In his book *Genetically Modified Athletes*, Andy Miah suggests that
enhancements in sport raise concerns in one of three categories of harm.[17]
Doping presents a level of harm to individuals, to society, and to the nature
of sport. I am not convinced that Miah has identified the best taxonomy for
the discussion. As we will see later, Miah believes that many of the moral
issues involved in athletic enhancement can be reduced to questions of
medical ethics. That is, the arguments are built upon a concern for health.
Cataloguing the issue in this manner he believes that several issues, including unfair competitive advantages, coercion, fan disappointment and disrespect for other athletes are among the problems that can be grouped into a
single category of harm to others.

Miah's structure helps clarify the discussion about who is being
harmed by enhancements and he offers three further subcategories that include harm to the user, the non-user and the spectator all as part of the first
type of harm. The problem with this model is that it tends to overlook the
validity of each argument in its own right by primarily focusing on the harm
that is to follow. Moreover, it presupposes that harm is the sole determining
factor in an actions moral worth. The cliché "no harm, no foul" holds true
for Miah's categorization. However, simply because no one is harmed by the
use of biotechnological enhancements in sport does not necessarily make
their use morally permissible.

Rather than attempt to categorize the arguments against enhancements I am interested in exploring the most commonly cited reasons for
prohibition. This approach has far more significant practical benefits since
it is these common arguments that tend to be more influential in matters of public sentiment and policy issues. Miah touches on this when
he claims that public opinion is relatively uninterested in sports doping.
"Spectators are, quite reasonably, not particularly concerned about athletes

---

17. Miah, *Genetically Modified Athletes*, 20.

gaining an extra hundredth of a second on their performance by using a banned substance."[18]

He then laments the fact that "it is often the case that many of the sophisticated arguments made within academic literature have had no place in informing anti-doping policy . . . it is still surprising to see the lack of appreciation for academic arguments that have endeavoured to reinforce anti-doping ideals."[19] If the public does not care and the academics are ignored then who is influencing the policy decisions? Miah attributes this to the agenda-propagating media. I believe he is misinformed about the public's neutral stance on enhancement. One only need look at recent doping scandals to see the outrage and disdain sports fans have for those who have tested positive for prohibited substances.

Miah's response would no doubt be to say that the athletic community is not genuinely indignant but instead have allowed themselves to be worked into a frenzy by media hype. Additionally, he would add, "even if this lobbying is sincere, it is more tied up with a social concern for drug use and harm deriving from it in general, than a concern for sporting values or performance enhancement."[20]

It is a mistake to think the public is indifferent unless they have been tricked into taking sides. Perhaps one of the reasons policy has neglected academic prose is because the voice of the masses is louder than the voice of the articulate. Even though they are arriving at the same conclusions the general public has a more vested interest in and influence over the display of sporting values than does the academy. In any case, several parallels exist in what has been written in academic journals and the language used by anti-doping policy makers. As we will see in this chapter there are several arguments to justify prohibiting enhancements in sport that are used in both academic circles and anti-doping policies.

Additionally, it is hardly contestable that different media outlets discreetly promote their respective agendas. Sports media is no exception though it is important to remember that it operates in an economic market that is fed by its audience. This means that the media is more likely to report on items of interest to the viewer. So it may be the case that the media is not indoctrinating previously uninterested spectators with an anti-doping agenda as much as they are acquiescing to an already interested and opinionated spectatorship.

18. Ibid., 17.
19. Ibid.
20. Ibid.

The purpose of this chapter is to sort through what I believe to be the most common and more persuasive moral arguments used in the case against doping for competitive benefits. As we have already stated, the three most often cited reasons include the belief that doping is a form of cheating, it promotes unjust coercion of other athletes, and it carries with it unacceptable health risks.[21] The purpose of the present chapter is to point out that these three arguments provide insights into very important issues in sport but fail to capture the bigger concerns arising from a theologically informed view of sport.

Doping as Cheating

Fairness in Sport

The first argument against doping very simply states that doping is cheating. There are those who will protest the use of performance enhancing drugs on the basis that they give an unfair advantage to the user in light of the rules governing a particular sport.[22] The idea of consensual rule abiding casts athletes in the light of a previously arranged contract. By participating in a sport an athlete submits himself or herself to the rules of that particular sport with the understanding that all other participants have agreed to the same regulations. This is what makes competition possible. An event governed by chaos will not determine who is the better athlete or the better team. All must compete under certain rules to exhibit their talents in a way

---

21. The President's Council on Bioethics helpfully identifies a fourth category. Doping also violates the dignity of human activity. In this chapter I am only going to explore the rationale of the first three arguments. The reason is that the rest of this work more fully accounts for the fourth category, specifically from a Christian theological perspective. See the President's Council on Bioethics, *Beyond Therapy*, 131–51.

22. It is important here to call attention to the uniqueness of each sport. Drugs used to gain an unfair advantage in one sport may not provide any benefit in another sport. Therefore, it is worth noting that universal prohibition against all substances that improve a specific performance might be difficult to justify on practical terms. For example, it seems superfluous to spend time and resources testing chess players for anabolic steroids because the competitive benefit of steroids is absent in the game of chess. On the other hand some substances such as alcohol and beta-blockers, which would impede performance in most sports, are prohibited from others such as archery for the competitive benefits derived from a slower heart rate and steadier hand. Prohibition applies where an explicit advantage is given to one individual or team over another by virtue of the agreed upon rules. WADA has divided the Prohibited List into three distinct sections. There are substances that are 1) prohibited at all times, 2) prohibited in competition, and 3) prohibited in particular sports. See, World Anti-Doping Agency, "The 2014 Prohibited List."

that will result in displaying the best athlete or team in the competition. Any other way is simply meaningless. When an athlete competes contrary to the predetermined rules he or she is breaking the contract tacitly agreed to before entering competition.

Some make the claim that at this point the athlete has ceased participating in that specific sport or at least has severely handicapped the opponent by cheating. For example, if a rugby team decided they would no longer observe the rule against forward passes then that team is given a clear advantage over their opponent who respects the official rule that allows only for the backward pass. It reasonably could be said that the forward passing team is playing its own version of rugby, (i.e., Rugby^n) instead of the official game that observes traditional rules. It is doubtful whether any traditional team would knowingly compete against such a team. Even in the event that they did compete any outcome would be essentially meaningless.

This argument is part of a position known as formalism, which states that a game is entirely defined by its rules.[23] From this perspective, when an athlete fails to uphold the rules of the game he or she, strictly speaking, ceases to play the sport. This line of reasoning is often extended to doping. An athlete who dopes is competing directly in opposition to the rules and therefore not technically playing the game. Robert Simon describes it this way, "Cheaters violate the rules by failing to make moves within the sport and therefore fail to play it . . . One can win the game only by playing it, and since cheaters do not play, cheaters can't win."[24] The fairness argument insists that introducing doped athletes to the sport illegitimates fair play and makes the results of the entire activity meaningless since athletes are not playing the same game.

Another strain of the fairness argument points to the implicit respect due to other athletes. The doping athlete, it is argued, is declaring himself or herself exempt from the rules that other competitors must abide by. The mutual respect for all participants in a shared venture for a common goal is a point that should not be overlooked. Sigmund Loland addresses this well when he suggests that sport gains its meaning within a social context where "as with any set of shared social norms, it is a more or less clear expression of human interests and goals."[25] The ethos of a sport is determined by a set of norms shared by these participants to achieve the goals specific to that sport. Loland presents a clear articulation of a sport-specific contract

23. A more complete discussion of formalism and rules in sport can be found in chapter six.

24. Simon, *Fair Play*, 46.

25. Loland, *Fair Play in Sport*, 9.

theory in which all participants have a mutual understanding of the structural goals involved in the sport. In this sense it is necessary that sport be built on a foundation of fair play in which all participants share an equal opportunity for victory.

Another principle of fair play is not unlike the golden rule. Do unto others as you would have them do unto you. Illegally taking performance enhancing substances not only breaks the mutual contract but also shows tremendous disrespect to the other athletes. Treating persons as a means to one's own selfish ambitions is unethical in all matters of life. Sport is no exception. Beyond the lack of respect for opponents breaking the rules to gain an illegitimate advantage shows a lack of moral virtue on behalf of the user. This behavior is also contrary to the spirit of a level playing field.

A Critique of Fairness in Sport

For those who wish to ban performance drugs from sport it is clear that the use of biotechnology does little to promote the idea of fair play since doping violates the rules. That breaking the rules is morally reprehensible is hardly contested. Many who favor the use of performance enhancing substances in sport agree that breaking the rules is wrong. Michael Lavin, a supporter of enhancements, contends that, "when athletes avail themselves of means that rules prohibit, they do act unfairly . . . But the present demand is for a compelling rationale for making the use of certain substances against the rules in the first place."[26] No contracts would be broken if the contracts allowed for their use. This would also eliminate the problem of disrespect since doping would become a legitimate form of enhancement. Doping would then be as acceptable as current training methods that are more traditional.

Significant carbohydrate intake by athletes is acceptable, even though it enhances their performance. Lavin and others are asking why the same type of consensus does not exist for performance enhancing drugs. If rules would allow for these more contemporary training methods there would be no reason to see doping as cheating. Lavin comments that most appeals to this justification for prohibiting doping are not really issues of fairness. Rather, "when people claim that using a particular drug is unfair, if they do not mean that its use is against the rules, they probably mean that it is either unnatural or secures players advantage at grave risk to themselves or, ultimately, coerces others into taking those same risks."[27]

26. Lavin, "Sports and Drugs," 266.
27. Ibid.

Lavin disperses the issue of fairness by redirecting it to one of the other major concerns we will address later in this chapter. But it is questionable whether or not we can so quickly marginalize fair play. The issue of fairness revolves around more than a set of rules. It is not sufficient to say that it would no longer be an issue of fairness if we made them legal since altering the rules would not guarantee fairness. Obviously, if they were legal it would no longer be considered cheating, but that does not mean athletic competition necessarily would be fair. Even most advocates do not endorse *all* forms of doping. It is difficult to conceive of a sport in which there are not at least some banned substances. Following the argument to its logical conclusion would result in allowing any type of biological agent for competitive purposes in the name of fairness. Such a policy no doubt would be unsafe and unwise.

One side of the argument says doping will make athletes more equal while the other side says that doping actually degrades the level playing field on which all athletes compete. But it is legitimate to ask both sides, to what extent is the playing field level already? Inequality among athletes is unavoidable. Some athletes naturally have more talent than others.

Doping advocates claim it is precisely the notion of fair play that makes the use of performance enhancing substances so appealing. Biotechnology does not undermine the spirit of fair play but rather enhances it.

Currently, people are at the mercy of the genetic lottery. Many aspiring athletes have a passion for their sport but their physical abilities limit their success. It is suggested that doping may allow those athletes to perform at the elite level by eliminating the performance gap between average and elite athletes. Tamburrini contends doping will give everyone an equal opportunity to achieve success in professional sports. "Genetic technology makes it possible to reduce current gaps in skills and inherited traits between individuals."[28]

Presumably, the best athletes will become not those who are most gifted but those who are most dedicated. Doping would level the playing field by "allowing the winners to become those who *do* the best rather than those who *are* the best."[29] I would point to two problematic areas in Tamburrini's assertion that fairness is best served by allowing doping.

First, the natural unfairness is part of what makes sport so competitive and exciting. There is a modest sense of wonder at the performance of those who excel at physical activities. If everyone were able to achieve these feats it would remove much of the awesomeness of sport by tarnishing key characteristics of the game. A highly motivating factor in sports is the

28. Tamburrini, "After Doping, What?" 261.
29. The President's Council on Bioethics, *Beyond Therapy*, 132; italics original.

realization that one's opponent is superior. Ambitious athletes who know they will be competing against more talented people than themselves are motivated to train harder thus improving the overall quality of the sport. One of the beautiful aspects of sport is the satisfaction that comes from defeating someone felt to be better than oneself. This means an inferior athlete performed better than a superior opponent on a particular occasion. There is a real sense of accomplishment in defying the odds and achieving victory over a bigger, stronger, and faster opponent. This could not be experienced if all competitors begin with the same ability. There would be no "Cinderella story" to inspire and captivate the hearts of countless fans.

A second difficulty involves two mistaken assumptions about the effect doping might have on fairness in sport. (i) Doping advocates seem to assume that doping will create identically talented athletes. To believe doping will allow the average athlete to compete on par with elite level athletes fails to account for the possibility of elite athletes doping as well. Doping may raise the performance of average athletes but elite athletes will keep pace in the improvements brought about by their own doping. This negates the whole concept of creating an equal playing field.

But a further point can be made to show that doping fails to be the equalizer advocates claim it to be. (ii) It is unrealistic to think that the same quality of enhancements will be available to everyone. Undoubtedly, the most effective substances will be available to those in better financial situations. By the time the enhancements are inexpensive and accessible enough for everyone to buy them the cycle will perpetuate itself all over again with new, more powerful methods only within reach of the wealthy. Furthermore, a purely equal playing field brought about by doping is highly improbable since the motivation to gain an edge over others would still exist. This would result in new forms of cheating merely shifting the focus from biotechnology to other methods of unfair competitive tactics.

What then are we to make of the issue of fairness in sport? It is clear that biotechnology is unlikely to create a state of athletic equality. It has also been suggested that the rules against enhancements beg the question of why such rules exist in the first place. The conclusion I wish to put forward is that the current debate over fairness points us to some important issues in sport. It helps clarify a point of agreement within the argument, namely that both sides are calling for fairness to be at the core of athletic activity. The disagreements are in the details of how that is best achieved. As a result, a detailed rationale of the fairness topic is a requirement of any ruling for or against enhancements in sport but is insufficient on its own to establish regulations.

Doping as a Form of Coercion

Ambiguity in the Coercion Argument

Introducing biotechnology into sports creates a second area of concern. This common argument goes as follows. If athletes were permitted to use performance enhancing substances then other athletes who otherwise would be morally opposed to their use would be put in a terrible dilemma. They either can do something against their own moral conscience, or they can refuse to take these substances and so fail to achieve the level of competition appropriate to their talents. The general use of coercion in the doping debate includes a less than accurate definition of coercion. This section intends to clarify what is meant by coercion as well as how it specifically relates to doping in sport.

Critics are quick to point out that coercion can be a very subjective and, therefore confusing, term. They rightly suggest the common usage of "coercion" in the doping discourse often means nothing more than placing someone in a position where he or she must make a difficult decision. Doping advocates point out the fact that athletes who wish to remain competitive are *coerced* all the time. The athlete who trains six days a week is coerced by another athlete who trains seven days a week. If the first athlete wants to have the same opportunities as the second athlete he or she will be required to train an equal amount of time and equally as hard.

When defined by these standards there seems to be little wrong with coercion. As Thomas Murray states, "there is, then, an *inherent coerciveness* present in these situations: when some choose to do what gives them a competitive edge, others will be pressed to do likewise, or resign themselves to either accepting a competitive disadvantage or leaving the endeavor entirely."[30]

The problem of coercion is not limited to co-competitors. Coaches and trainers demand athletes do more extensive and harder work than they are comfortable with. That is what is required to stay on top of their respective sport. Robert Simon points out the reality of elite level competition. "No one is coerced into world class competition . . . If they find the cost excessive, they may withdraw."[31]

Nevertheless, if doping were legalized those who wish to remain clean may be coerced by more than their own desire to remain competitive. For example, assume that a clean athlete is competitive enough to stay at the highest levels of competition. In spite of his or her superior performance, the owners of the organization for which he or she competes may require

30. Murray, "The Coercive Power of Drugs in Sport," 27.
31. Simon, *Fair Play*, 78.

the use of performance enhancers to make the athlete's performance even better. If the athlete refuses he or she may be threatened with dismissal from the team. Do the owners have a right to put this burden on the athlete just as a boss in any other place of employment may demand certain job requirements from an employee?

However, this begs the question of the athletes' suitability for elite competition if they are not willing to do what is required of that level of sport. In order not to get ahead of ourselves we can set aside for the moment issues of fairness and health risks and look specifically at whether or not the coercion argument carries enough merit on its own account to justify prohibiting biotechnology. Many have made the claim that it does not. In part this is because the argument has made coercion synonymous with pressure. In this context coercion has come to mean the obligations one does not like having imposed upon oneself by the activity. This understanding of coercion is evident in other areas not related to sport and even in areas that are not necessarily competitive. Musicians, dancers, lawyers, students, and the like all have pressure from inside and outside sources to be the best in their field. Robert Simon remarks, "the problem with such claims is that all competitive pressure becomes 'coercive.' As a result, the term 'coercion' is deprived of any moral force because virtually no competitive behavior is left over that would not be coercive."[32]

There is something instinctive in humanity that drives a person to be not only the best but the best that he or she can be. Add to this the fact that spectators demand to see increasingly difficult accomplishments. Not only do fans love to see their team win they love to see records broken. This type of atmosphere compels athletes to seek out progressively more strenuous training methods. Does this mean the fans are guilty of coercion as well? Take a non-sport example. Students must study hard to be among the top of their class. If they want to get into the best universities to get the best jobs they must study harder than if businesses did not place so much emphasis on education and academic performance. Can blame rightly be placed on the potential employers or the teacher for this requirement? In teasing out the argument Simon continues, "Isn't it more plausible to say that although there are pressures on athletes to achieve peak physical condition, these amount to coercion no more than the pressures on law or medical students to study hard? Rather, the athletes (or the students) have *reasons* to try hard to achieve success; the pressures are self-imposed."[33]

32. Ibid., 76.
33. Ibid., 75; italics original.

The motives certainly vary depending on the athlete but as Simon points out those who reject the coercion argument often do so by claiming athletes willingly submit themselves to such rigorous training so they can be among the best. Yet, as Simon again points out "if we use 'coercion' that broadly, it becomes unclear who, if anybody, is left free."[34]

A More Specific Understanding of Coercion

Such an ambiguous definition of coercion fails on several accounts. This type of argument not only defines coercion too broadly, it effectively neutralizes coercion altogether by placing the source of the pressure within oneself. In this case, no coercion is present since the pressures are internal. The coercion problem arises when one's motivations are forced upon another. It is in this sense that the anti-doping argument objects to coercion, not the broader definition promoted by doping advocates. It could be argued that other forms of employment typically do not require employees to alter their bodies. Coercing employees to do *something* is very different from coercing them to do something *to their bodies*. It is a difficult proposition to accept that club management has the right to force the athlete to impose physical changes to his or her body.

If they are willing to do what is necessary to remain the best, do certain other individuals have the right to force athletes to risk bodily harm? The primary example of this is the increasing expectation of athletes to compete injured. First-rate athletes are often required to play in spite of an injury. Insufficient treatment of a sports related injury may result in long term health effects.[35] What is being questioned here is not the voluntary participation in professional sports but whether coaches or other athletes should be able to coerce a player into significantly risking his or her post-career wellbeing. This still does not escape the charge that athletes voluntarily submit themselves to the pressures of elite sports and the requirements that come along with competing at that level.

Norman Fost makes an important observation about coercion when he says, "athletes confronting the choice of whether to use steroids face an

---

34. Ibid. A further point of my own reflection is worth noting about the schooling analogy. To be sure, competitive pressures exist among legal, medical, or any other kind of student to finish at the top of the class to improve their post–schooling career prospects. But this is often an indirect competition whereas sport is an explicit and immediate competitive structure. In a race there can be only one winner but there often are many good jobs to be had post–education. Therefore, the analogy is not as strong as its advocates would suggest.

35. Lumpkin, et al., *Sports Ethics*, 147.

opportunity to be better than they are, admittedly at some risk, but with no loss of property, health, or basic rights if they refuse."[36] He goes on to add, "the worst consequence is that they might fail to gain some extraordinary honor, such as a gold medal or a financial reward. Great opportunities are typically accompanied by extraordinary demands and risks."[37]

In Fost's view, the accusation of coercion requires the athlete be placed in a position where he or she "will be worse off by failing to act in the suggested way."[38] Since he does not believe this is the case he argues that we can dismiss the coercion argument. Defining coercion in this way, however, does little to help clarify whether or not coercion is an acceptable justification for prohibiting doping in sport. His criterion is too ambivalent. Who and what determines the standards for "worse off" and how is one to arrive at that conclusion given the number of possible scenarios in which an athlete is pressured to do something without which he or she would be none the better? An athlete potentially would be worse off, in a competitive sense, for failing to take the illegal substance. So too would the athlete be worse off by failing to train properly. His definition does not address these types of distinctions.

Fost also believes the clean athlete's loss is limited to competition since, as he states above, the worst that can happen in refusing to take steroids is that the athlete does not win. This response to the coercion problem neglects the point being made that the fate of athletes who refuse enhancements would be more than a simple experience of not winning. It would be the loss of the ability to compete at all in the higher levels of athletic competition.

Coercion and the Freedom of the Athlete

In addition to this point, permitting doping in sport places the freedom of the individual athlete above the sport one participates in. It is suggested that the collective interest in sport by society is being subjected to the autonomy of the athlete.[39]

Nevertheless, autonomy is not a self-sustaining supreme rule. This has been well noted by Beauchamp and Childress who are accredited with

36. Fost, "Banning Drugs in Sport: A Skeptical View," 7.

37. Ibid., 7.

38. Ibid.

39. For a more detailed discussion of the tension between an athlete's private privileges and public responsibilities, see my treatment of Richard Rorty's influence on the philosophy of sport in chapter 2.

establishing autonomy as one of the four principles that have saturated many medical ethics policies in the United States. "Morality generally demands that we not override individuals' rights to maximize social consequences."[40] In this context that would mean it would be wrong to prohibit athletes from subjecting their own bodies to the effects of doping simply because it might negatively affect the sale of tickets. "But if we can more effectively protect almost everyone's interests by overriding some property rights or autonomy rights, this course of action might not be wrong merely because it contravenes conventional morality and pursues the goal of social utility."[41] That is, if doping jeopardizes the wellbeing of society (by, say, undermining the social values within sport) it becomes morally problematic.

Superseding autonomy, then, may be acceptable when it serves the greater good. Many governments and sports organizational authorities have adopted this principle and uphold strict standards and policies against doping.[42] Governments have found it in the public's best interest to intervene in certain athletic training methods. The important issue here is that governing bodies are only intervening in very specific circumstances.

This can be attributed to the fact that there are right ways and wrong ways to control an outcome. To be sure, there are other ways of controlling substance use without condoning it. The fact that some will use performance enhancing substances regardless of the rules is not a justifiable reason to allow everyone to use them. The medical side effects on the few using them illegally certainly would be inconsequential compared to the side effects on everyone using them legally, even with appropriate medical supervision.

Rather than beginning with the pressures imposed I would suggest the real concern in the coercion argument should be the moral nature of the activity one is being pressured to do. The employee seeking a promotion justifiably may be pressured by superiors to complete menial tasks but being sexually coerced to receive the promotion rightly ignites moral outrage. The pressure to advance, in the business and sports world alike, is unavoidable. The question of coercive doping in sport is more about the morality of the underlying pressure than it is about either the act of pressuring or what the athlete might gain or lose as a result of those actions.

Yet the coercion argument continues to focus on the more trivial issue of being pressured to stay competitive. So long as the dominant motivation in sport is to win the pressures for a competitive advantage will not subside. The coercion argument against doping is more powerful and instructive

40. Beauchamp and Childress, *Principles of Biomedical Ethics*, 349.

41. Ibid.

42. World Anti-Doping Agency, "Anti-Doping Community."

than it may first appear but it only offers a superficial response that is unable to address the root problem. Coercion will continue to be a problem until the sports culture recognizes an authority in sport other than winning.

Doping and Unacceptable Health Risks

The primary objection to the use of biotechnology and other physically invasive substances in sport involves the health risks doping presents to the user. Currently, the long-term effects of many substances are unknown while the effects of some, such as anabolic agents, have been well documented. Doping in its various forms can lead to tumors, disorders, and diseases. Still, advocates point to three key problems with the health risk argument. They include the autonomy of the athlete, the preference for regulation instead of prohibition, and the arbitrary nature of limiting risk in sport.

Individual Autonomy and Acceptable Health Risks

The fact that scientific research confirms substantial health risks associated with the use of many doping substances presents a compelling case for the prohibition of doping in sport. Doping advocates, however, point to the ambiguity of *substantial*. What objective criteria can be used to determine an acceptable level of risk? More directly, can an athlete be denied the liberty of choosing what training methods he or she can use if the athlete is fully informed of the risks associated with that particular method and consents to its use? Critics of prohibition claim that banning performance enhancing substances due to potential harm is a violation of the athlete's rights. The right to self-governance is fundamentally important in the debate over an athlete's personal decision to use or not to use performance enhancing drugs.

The current bioethical debate seems to render the concern for the athlete's health somewhat irrelevant so long as the athlete consents to the enhancement. As discussed in the previous section the athlete's rights as an individual may trump the paternalistic rules set forth by bureaucratic boards supervising the sport when the future wellbeing of the athlete is at stake. Indeed, team officials' primary concern should be the wellbeing of the athletes. Even if coercion was no longer a concern what is to be done in the cases where athletes autonomously pursue means of doping?

The freedom of the athlete to undertake certain risks presents a significant problem to those favoring prohibition. Part of the reason for this is the quick dismissal of concerns over the health risks associated with performance enhancing drug use. Everyone takes risks as they are an ines-capable part of life. Actions ought not necessarily be precluded or banned because they present a risk. Julian Savulescu writes, "Many of [humanity's] greatest achievements have occurred in the face of very significant risk . . . Life is about living rationally with risk, not avoiding it."[43] Great achieve-ments are not the only human endeavors that involve risk. Certain forms of recreation as well as everyday decisions also pose potential health risks.

Overwhelming medical research suggests that smoking presents a major health risk resulting in lung cancer, heart disease and hundreds of thousands of deaths each year but smoking is an individual liberty protected by societal ideas of human rights.[44] Proponents of enhancement say that doping ought to be a similar liberty and given certain conditions should be acted upon by any athlete who desires it. It is a violation of the athlete's rights for anyone else to forbid that athlete from taking what risks he or she deems necessary.

The majority of experts currently believe that most forms of biotech-nological substances present a risk too great to the athlete and therefore cur-rently should be banned. This is the primary reason why these substances are prohibited. However, critics will again suggest that banning some risks while allowing others is arbitrary. They argue that preference is to be given to the athlete's right as an autonomous being to be responsible for the risks he or she assumes.

Regulating Enhancement Substances and the Removal of Health Risks

Doping advocates will also suggest that the risk to an athlete's health can be significantly decreased by allowing research and monitored use of doping substances. The argument states that given adequate funding research could reduce the risks associated with banned substances. It is therefore suggested that regulation is better than prohibition since banning these substances will force those athletes still willing to use them to go underground. If they were permitted under proper medical supervision the health risks would dramati-cally decrease. This argument works on the assumption that athletes are going to find ways to use performance enhancing substances regardless of the rules. The governing authorities in sport have an obligation to protect these athletes as much as possible. Since athletes will use banned substances anyway the

43. Savulescu, "Compulsory Genetic Testing," 146.
44. Center for Disease Control, "Health Effects of Cigarette Smoking."

best option for athletic governing bodies is to offer medical assistance. It is believed that this will give some element of control over the risks.

Yet this argument is not conclusive enough to lift the ban of enhancement substances. Some contend on the other side that allowing them at all sends a message of acceptance. This is obviously the position taken by the National Football League, which condemns illegal substances in part to deter young athletes from taking banned substances. It fears that sending the message of acceptance means substance abuse will become a much larger issue among young athletes. The implication of such an approach would be that it becomes ethically permissible to allow an action believed to be morally wrong in order to control that action's result.

It is suggested by Angela Schneider that dissuading athletes from doping because of the health risks may instigate thought about some other deep issues with doping in sport. "The process of discouragement itself may be worth it if it could act as an educational tool that would get athletes thinking about some of the underlying issues and principles at stake."[45]

Arbitrarily Limiting Health Risks

Furthering the argument for the freedom of the athlete there is another aspect of athlete safety to be considered. Some argue that biotechnology presents no more of a risk than does boxing or any other physically violent sport. "Chronic traumatic brain injury occurs in approximately 20 per cent of professional boxers."[46] Facts like this one lend support to the idea that there are other dangers in sport in addition to gene doping. Repetitive hits to the head, it is argued, must be at least as dangerous as taking steroid pills. Why is one celebrated as a legitimate sport and the other condemned for being too dangerous? This argument does not, however, recognize the distinction between the uncertain risks associated with the particular sport and the intentional self-inflicted harm of performance enhancing substances. The President's Council on Bioethics distinguished the types of risk in the following way: "The hazards intrinsic to the game are generally unavoidable, while those associated with taking the drugs are utterly unnecessary."[47] There are risks associated with certain sports that cannot be avoided without drastically changing the nature of the sport. Boxing would cease to be boxing if the athletes were not permitted to hit each other with great force.

---

45. Schneider, "Genetic Enhancement of Athletic Performance," 36.

46. Savulescu, "Compulsory Genetic Testing," 136.

47. The President's Council on Bioethics, *Beyond Therapy*, 138.

Unfortunately, the President's Council, led by Leon Kass, failed to demonstrate the practicality of their conclusion. Kass does not explain why among two risks one is accepted as essential to the sport and the other rejected as an unnecessary health threat. If the level of risk is comparatively equal why should they share different fates? Either both should be allowed under the principles of freedom or both should be banned in the name of public safety.

Another way in which the account given by the Council is problematic involves the way in which they use what is necessary in sport to define what should or should not be permissible. For example, is one to conclude from the Council's report that since drugs should be banned because they are unnecessary, that the boxers' shoes should be banned as well since they are not required to compete?

Neither drugs nor shoes are required of athletic competition but the argument presented by the Council assumes a clear distinction between the two. Performance enhancing substances should be banned not because they are unnecessary but because they are superfluous. Shoes add traction that will help prevent the athletes from slipping and falling down. Doping does not restore minor flaws in the game but seeks to add external dimensions to the competition. In this sense they do not contribute anything of value to the sport itself and as such are unnecessary.

This idea is discussed further in the next chapter where I will introduce Alasdair MacIntyre's concept of a practice that distinguishes internal from external goods of an activity. This framework provides a helpful distinction within the argument presented by the council. It may be the case that equipment, such as shoes, is necessary in that they enable an athlete to achieve the internal goods of a practice. Doping, on the other hand, is unable to contribute any essential elements to the achievement of internal goods and is restricted to the acquisition of external goods alone.

A further defense of this idea is needed and will be explored more thoroughly in subsequent chapters. Doing so now would digress from this argument's main point that the health risks of doping can and should be minimized through actively researching and regulating substances that are currently prohibited. Presently, the objection by the pro-doping crowd remains strong enough to call our attention to the often arbitrary standards set for acceptable health risks in sporting activity. If this group's optimism becomes reality and the potential harms of doping are eventually eliminated, or at least significantly reduced, there remains little justification for their prohibition from a health-related perspective.

Health as the Final Barrier to Acceptance

In fact, this point is the biggest difficulty facing those who would prohibit doping based on the unacceptable health risks. Doping advocates ask what happens if (or when) scientific research provides convincing evidence that there are minimal long term risks. This is a considerable challenge to the prohibitionists since it would require them to justify prohibiting biotechnological enhancements on other grounds. As a result, the idea that doping should be banned because it subjects athletes to unnecessary harmful side effects is in itself inadequate justification for its exclusion from sports. As long as these substances remain detrimental to the health of the athlete they are rightly banned. Once that concern is alleviated the argument loses all credibility.

This has led some to restrict the argument to the realm of medical ethics. Andy Miah states, "sport ethics is already subservient to medical ethics to the extent that, what is ethically acceptable in sport relating to drug enhancement and doping is contingent upon what is ethically acceptable in medicine. Indeed, the policy statements concerning gene doping precisely reflect the ethical norm in medicine presently."[48]

Miah believes the conditions for enhancement in sport should be determined by the same standards that are used in medicine. All concerns are ultimately reducible to a concern for health. He claims, "it seems that both a concern for coercion and a concern for social harms only have moral weight when they are also a concern for health."[49] Miah believes the strength of these arguments resides in the areas where they overlap with health risks. As a result, if the concern for health is alleviated all reasons against doping collapse. He argues, "there is currently no unobjectionable argument against many forms of doping and, collectively, such arguments also lack persuasiveness, if—and only if—the basis for rejection relies solely upon some ethical component of *sport*. This caveat is necessary, since there are many reasons why it is sufficient to reject doping on the basis of a concern for health alone."[50]

This is not to say that Miah ignores ethical concerns in sport that do not involve health. He rightly points out that the use of some equipment may raise ethical concerns without jeopardizing the health of the athlete. Instead he is questioning, "whether *sports ethics* offers anything more meaningful about the ethics of genetic modification in sport, beyond the *medical ethical* concern for

---

48. Miah, "Gene Doping," 48.

49. Miah, *Genetically Modified Athletes*, 31.

50. Ibid., 13; italics original.

health."[51] Miah believes this to be a key question in the enhancement debate. However, I would contend that it is the wrong kind of question. His attempt to marginalize sports ethics in favor of medical ethics lacks effectiveness for two reasons. First, his conclusion that the other concerns are reducible to a concern for health is problematic. For example, the weight of the coercion argument does not necessarily involve health. Even if the health risks were minimal an athlete could be unjustly coerced into doping if he or she believed doping to be, for instance, a violation of sport's nature.

Secondly, it is doubtful the concern for harm will ever be fully eliminated. Even if some forms become less risky, new, more dangerous forms of doping are sure to follow. We should be careful about how much significance we hang on the alleviation of health risks. Miah is generally cautious to use phrases like "many forms of doping" rather than general blanket statements. Some forms will predictably become less risky as biotechnology advances. Presumably these are the enhancements he has in mind and when they no longer carry the same risks he argues they should be allowed. He does not favor removing the limitations on all forms of enhancement.

The argument for the athlete's safety is very important and remains one of the fundamental concerns in the bioethics of sport, chiefly because the probability of long term health risks is high. The President's Council, when taking into account the unknown effects of biotechnology, suggest this maxim be considered, "No biological agent powerful enough to achieve major changes in body or mind is likely to be entirely safe or without side effects."[52]

But again, the argument claims that when scientific research progresses enough the side effects will be known and depending on the result of this knowledge athletes may medically be cleared to undertake the risks of certain types of genetic intervention at their own discretion. The current risks associated are clearly unacceptable when weighed against the outcomes but the likelihood of these risks diminishing, given certain parameters, suggests that if performance enhancing substances are to be banned permanently from sport the source of that justification will have to be found elsewhere.

The third reason I believe Miah's position is incorrect is because he rejects the idea of an essential nature of sport. This topic will be covered in detail in the following chapter. Briefly, he discards the idea "that doping challenges some alleged essence of sport."[53] Articulating this essence is a problem according to Miah. The challenge facing an argument for a nature of sport, he says, "is to present an explanation of precisely what this essence

51. Ibid.; italics original.
52. The President's Council on Bioethics, *Beyond Therapy*, 137.
53. Miah, *Genetically Modified Athletes*, 26.

or nature entails, but also to provide some way of negotiating conflicting views on this essence."[54] In the next chapter I will lay a foundation for addressing both of his concerns through identifying sport in the notion of social practices as described by Alasdair MacIntyre.

Natural and Unnatural Forms of Doping

So far this chapter has sought to discuss the ethical issues involved in doping. I have argued that none of the three arguments presented against it is sufficient justification for prohibiting biotechnology from being used in athletic competition. However, each does suggest deeper concerns about the moral underpinnings of how to engage others and ourselves in social activities like sport.

The questions surrounding these three primary arguments have led to well reasoned commentary on the ethical implications of biotechnology in sport. They each contribute some clarifying points about morally acceptable behavior in sport. For instance, the argument from coercion points to a deeper problem, which shows that the moral issue is not simply about forcing someone to do something they do not want to do. It is not necessarily coercion at the heart of the issue as much as it is the moral nature of the activity being "forced" onto someone.

The arguments presented above remind us of the importance of fairness, justice and mutual respect for others in our engagement of social activities. They also challenge us to treat our bodies with dignity and to have the courage to refuse substances that may lead us to material gain at the cost of our health. However, these arguments only scratch the surface of a much larger concern. They ask important questions but fail to address the core of the issue, which involves the purpose of sport.

A fourth major argument in the discussion begins to address this topic. It is suggested that doping violates the nature of sport as a human activity. It degrades the integrity of the game. As the argument says, doping is an unnatural activity forced into the purity of sport.[55] This line of thinking often quickly turns to questions of what is natural and unnatural in sport.

54. Ibid., 26–27.

55. Commonly found in this line of argumentation is the concept of sport's essence. Clearly, the multitude of sports played around the world express different goals, tend to promote various social values, and have their own unique "essence," as it were. However, in the same way that I am treating the idea of sport, as noted in chapter one, I will here refer to sport in its most common and generalized sense. I do not wish to single out any specific sport or the qualities that are commonly exhibited therein though I do recognize that unique sports often display a unique set of skills, attitudes,

One way of looking at this has been to point to a distinction between therapeutic enhancements and non-therapeutic enhancements. More commonly referred to as the therapy/enhancement distinction this argument suggests that doping is rightly prohibited because it is an unnatural method of gaining a competitive advantage. A good deal has been written about the alleged distinction between therapy and enhancement.[56]

I maintain, however, that looking at methods of performance improvement through the lens of a natural/unnatural distinction is unhelpful in the doping debate. It is too ambiguous to contribute anything meaningful to the discussion. What is meant by natural and on what moral or conceptual grounds can that be distinguished from unnatural? To amplify this, let us consider the two kinds of answers to this questions that are typically made. (i) Some argue there are differences between biotechnological enhancements and the equipment used in sport where the former are unnatural to the game while the latter are natural. Then (ii) there is the more difficult distinction to justify that separates doping from the nutritional benefits of certain diets and vitamins.

Enhanced Equipment

One response that defends a notion of the natural suggests that there is a clear distinction between our equipment and performance enhancing substances. The President's Council on Bioethics addresses this line of reasoning.

> Unlike training or drugs that change the agent directly, the equipment that boosts our performance does so indirectly, yet it does so quite openly and in plain sight. We can see how the springier running shoes, the lighter tennis racket, and the bigger baseball glove enable their users to go faster, hit harder, and reach the formerly unreachable - yet without apparently changing them in their persons or native powers.[57]

The Council goes on to question to what extent this holds true. In many ways we are shaped by the equipment we use. We take the use of technology for granted and eventually become seemingly dependent upon the gadgets

---

and sentiments that give it a distinctive "essence." Instead, I will refer to sport and its essence in a general sense. See chapter two for my rejection of the idea that sport lacks any kind of fundamental essence.

56. See Parens, *Enhancing Human Traits*; Resnik, "The Moral Significance of the Therapy–Enhancement Distinction in Human Genetics."

57. The President's Council on Bioethics, *Beyond Therapy*, 124.

and tools we use so frequently. In some sense we allow our equipment to change who we are. Yet these changes are not irreversible or indistinguishable from the changes resulting from biotechnology. "We can still separate in our mind those means of altering or improving performance that work by giving us tools to perform in new ways, and those interventions that work by changing us directly."[58]

One may also question to what extent this distinction is helpful in determining the permissibility of enhancements in sport. The fact that it is equipment rather than the body that is enhanced does not as such make an enhancement acceptable for use. For instance, a bat is required to play the game of baseball but not all bats are acceptable. In professional baseball several types of bats are illegal including ones made of aluminum and corked bats. There are multiple reasons for this, not the least of which is the advantage given to the batter over the pitcher. These bats allow a player to hit the ball much harder and farther than the legal wooden bats. This results in a serious risk to infielders as well as reduces the skill and power necessary to hit home runs. That is why there are strong objections to their use by Major League Baseball and by fans.

The issue is not over corked bats and illegal equipment. What is being called into question by doping advocates is the consistency of those who readily accept some forms of equipment improvements but wholly reject improving the athlete at the biological level on the grounds of naturalness. For example, improved golf clubs are acceptable enhancements to the game of golf. Thanks to technological progress golfers today use titanium and graphite clubs that are much more advanced allowing for greater accuracy and distance than the clubs from previous generations.

This, among other equipment improvements, has changed the way the game of golf is played. Likewise, fiberglass poles for pole vaulting award greater marks for the athlete than many performance enhancing substances would. New poles that are stronger and more flexible have made it easier for average vaulters to scale heights previously unattainable even by the best. Yet these equipment enhancements are accepted while doping is not. Those in favor of doping in sport wonder why similar changes at the biological level are not equally embraced. How would doping fail to improve the game where non-biological enhancements succeed?

Some may respond that the winner will be the one whose body reacts best to the substance rather than the best athlete per se. If this is true then the natural integrity of the sport has been violated. But how, advocates may ask, is equipment any different? In one case the winner is supposedly the

58. Ibid., 126.

body with the best reaction. In the other it is about the athlete with the best equipment. In neither case does the victory necessarily go to the most talented athlete. More to the point, in neither case does a natural/unnatural distinction bring clarity to the murky waters of sports enhancements.

Some rightly suggest that enhancements at the biological level alter the fundamental composition of the athlete's body while the equipment remains distinct from the athlete. "Despite the fuzziness at the boundary, it still makes sense to distinguish our tools and equipment from our practice or training, as well as from the more direct biotechnical interventions aimed at improving our native bodily capacities."[59] This is particularly relevant in sport since the equipment is only used during the game. The athlete's body is involved in all activities of life while the equipment stays on the playing field. Even so, this point of clarification speaks more to the status of the receiver of the enhancement than it does to natural and unnatural distinctions within the receiver. Calling one natural and the other unnatural is unhelpful since the issue involves two different targets of enhancement, namely our tools and our bodies.

While the intuition of many may suggest a clear cut distinction at the practical level between improvements to our equipment and improvements to our selves the articulation of that clarity from a naturalness argument remains elusive for yet another reason. Advances in technology often contribute to the development of our bodies through training equipment, dietary supplements, and advanced scientific knowledge of the human body. These technologies are used, albeit in a less direct way, to improve the human body. Therefore, trying to draw a distinction between our tools and our bodies proves less helpful than one's intuition might initially suggest.

Nutritional and Training Enhancements

The more difficult distinction is between the nutritional benefit derived from eating certain foods or taking vitamins on the one hand and the athletic benefit of taking performance enhancing substances on the other. We can add to this the performance benefits derived from traditional training methods as opposed to doping. Athletes are among the toughest evaluators of the body, spending hours upon hours in intense physical training on a daily basis. The fact that athletes put their bodies through strenuous training programs is no surprise. Likewise, it does not come as a shock that such practices are not modern developments.

59. Ibid., 127.

Obviously, science has altered the techniques used to gain a competitive edge but athletes have always realized the importance of training and nutrition. One of the earliest accounts of this is credited to Dromeus of Stymphalos. Athletes in ancient Greece consumed diets consisting of fresh cheese and figs. Dromeus (480 BC) was an outstanding athlete recording twelve victories in the Ancient Games. At the time the Games were located in four separate geographical areas. He reportedly won several times at each location and became a legendary athlete. His dominance may be in part due to his unique diet. Some historians credit him with being the first to have "thought of eating meat as part of his training diet."[60]

It is difficult to say if his impressive stretch of victories is the result of purely superior athletic ability or whether they can be attributed to his atypical diet but it is hard to ignore the connection between his dominance in the long foot race and a diet different from the other athletes. Subsequently, there was a shift in the diet of all athletes to one that included a heavy dose of meat.[61]

Modern athletes have the nutritional knowledge available to be very precise not only in what they eat, but also in how much they eat. To put their bodies through the physical training necessary to compete at the highest levels athletes have to eat far more than their bodies require. The International Olympic Committee commented, "In our laboratory, women say that they have to force themselves to eat far beyond their appetites to consume the amount of food that compensates their dietary energy intake for their exercise energy expenditure."[62] One way athletes have responded to this problem is through sports drinks. Rather than eat foods high in fiber, they turn to high energy drinks that provide essential nutrients absent from water.[63] Athletes have discovered the advantage of rejuvenating energy quicker through drinking liquids high in electrolytes.

It is quite obvious that these practices go beyond a fitness trend. Meticulous food consumption is necessary to compete at elite levels because of the resulting improvement in physical performance. Athletes make it a priority to follow scientific guidelines for food consumption that will allow them to achieve optimal physical performance. For example, carbohydrates account for approximately 60 to 70 percent of an athlete's energy intake but in order for the body to maximize the effectiveness of the carbohydrates

---

60. Grivetti and Applegate, "From Olympia to Atlanta," 862.

61. Ibid.

62. Maughan et al., *Food, Nutrition and Sports Performance*, 4.

63. Maughan and Murray, *Sports Drinks*, 5.

they will need to consume them in the right amount and at the right time.[64] This requires a stringent schedule carried out to perfection.

In addition to carrying out such a schedule some athletes need to be conscious of their weight. Activities such as boxing and martial arts carry distinct advantages to heavier athletes. Thus weight classes are formed to keep the sport fair. To compete in their desired class athletes must take into account all factors influencing the target of reaching a highly specific weight. Athletes wanting to participate in a specific weight class often will continue to train as usual but will reduce food intake resulting in a loss of energy. "Many athletes, especially female athletes and those who participate in endurance and aesthetic sports and sports with weight classes, are chronically energy deficient. This energy deficiency impairs performance, growth and health."[65]

On the other hand, athletes participating in sports that display power see advantages to increasing body mass and alter their diet accordingly. Protein has been an important part of the athlete's diet since Dromeus revealed his secret to the Greek athletes. The extent to which protein gives athletes an advantage remains controversial but there is some evidence to suggest that consuming large amounts of protein leads to increased lean body mass.[66]

It was reported that Milo, a superior wrestler in the Games who won five successive Olympiads from 532 to 516 BC, consumed twenty pounds of meat, twenty pounds of bread and eighteen pints of wine a day.[67] While this amount is questionable it does establish the athlete's obsession with nutrition in antiquity. Even now scientific knowledge about the specific role of certain foods in athletic performance is still in its infancy. Sports nutritionists have only discovered particular details within the past fifty years and it is certainly reasonable to suspect that further knowledge about the performance benefits from certain foods will only further the thorough dieting habits of athletes.[68]

---

64. Maughan et al., *Food, Nutrition and Sports Performance*, 26.

65. Ibid., 18.

66. Ibid., 111.

67. Grandjean, "Diets of Elite Athletes," 874. This is the Milo whom Aristotle discusses in Nicomachean Ethics in relation to his idea of the mean always being equidistant from two extremes while at the same time being relative to each individual. "For if ten pounds [of food], for instance, are a lot for someone to eat, and two pounds a little, it does not follow that the trainer will prescribe six, since this might also be either a little or a lot for the person who is to take it—for Milo a little, but for the beginner in gymnastics a lot." See Aristotle, *Nicomachean Ethics* 1106b 2–5, 24.

68. Ibid., 876.

Similar emphasis is placed on training. Training is the practical means of adapting the athlete to certain demands of a specific sport.[69] In ancient Greece the importance of an athlete's training was not limited to the athlete himself. Socio-political concerns were subject to the training needs of men preparing for the Games. Truces were called when times of war overlapped with the Olympiads. Athletes were required to begin training ten months prior to the games and it has been suggested that these truces were effective the entire training period.[70]

Historical references aside, the important point here is the extent to which athletes have always subjected their bodies to painstaking exercises for the purpose of competing well. Athletes train for hours every day for months on end for the purpose of competing in a particular or series of sporting events. Often times, such as in sprinting, the event one spends months and years preparing for what, from start to finish, lasts only a matter of seconds.

Many question whether there are moral guidelines for how much and what types of substances athletes may consume to provide the energy they need. The problem is establishing ways to distinguish what athletes legally can put in their bodies from what they cannot. Why are carbohydrates an acceptable form of dietary training while performance enhancements are not? Robert Simon explains that, "until we can say why the advantages provided by steroids are illegitimate and the advantages provided by other conditions are legitimate, the charge of unfairness must be dismissed for lack of support."[71]

Laura Morgan also points out that the arguments for a clear distinction between natural and unnatural methods of enhancement fail on multiple levels. "The trouble is that the existing arguments for banning certain performance-enhancing drugs do not provide adequate justification for the positions they recommend. These arguments are often inconsistent or vague, or fail to engage the important issues."[72] This is a fact that Morgan laments. "So even though I agree with their conclusions, I cannot endorse them on the basis of the justifications offered thus far."[73] The irony in Morgan's concern is that her discussion of the issue is also vague, inconsistent and fails to engage the distinction presently sought. She begins her article by

69. Dick, *Sports Training Principles*, 148.

70. Messiniesi, *History of the Olympic Games*, 24–25. The modern Olympics, however, have not been as conducive to truces. The Games of 1916 (Berlin), 1940 (Tokyo) and 1944 (London) were cancelled due to the two World Wars.

71. Simon, *Fair Play*, 79–80.

72. Morgan, "Enhancing Performance in Sports," 182.

73. Ibid.

pointing out the insufficiency of notions of harm to prohibit performance drugs but her conclusions do not address the nutritional distinction and ultimately rely in part on a notion of harm. She says, "ethical competition ought not require an athlete to incur greater health risks from an activity that is not an intrinsic feature of the game itself."[74]

One attempt to answer this question has been presented in *Beyond Therapy* by the President's Council on Bioethics. It makes an assertion based on human experience that there is a difference between, "Changes that result from our putting our bodies to work and those that result from having our bodies 'worked on' by others or altered directly."[75] This means the foods one ingests have a reaction on the cells in the body that result in improved performance. Genetic intervention alters the athlete at the fundamental level of human biology. The result may be the same but means are entirely different.

In this sense the distinction between endogenous and exogenous products seems irrelevant. What matters is the type of method involved and the reasons for choosing that method. There appears to be little to no distinction in terms of the results produced but critiquing the means of performance enhancement reveals distinctions in the motivations behind certain types of enhancement. Even if this is the case, claiming one to be natural and the other unnatural fails to provide credible justification for accepting one and prohibiting the other. It also fails to recognize the difficulty in regulating motivations.

More importantly, it assumes the motivations are different between the two types of performance improvements. Whether an athlete takes banned substances or maintains a supercharged diet the motives are likely to be the same. The athlete is making one or the other part of his or her training regiment to perform at the peak (or beyond?) of his or her limitations and to gain the best competitive advantage allowable. We can see then that while a clear distinction exists between doping and equipment the lines between nutrition and doping are considerably more blurred.

That conclusions concerning why one is natural and the other is unnatural are difficult to uphold gives us enough reason to discount the argument as a powerful force for prohibiting biotechnology in sport. Moreover, as Savulescu points out, some currently banned substances are quite natural. "Drugs such as erythropoietin (EPO) and growth hormone are natural chemicals in the body. As technology advances, drugs have become harder to detect because they mimic natural processes."[76] If these are natural sub-

---

74. Ibid., 187.

75. The President's Council on Bioethics, *Beyond Therapy*, 129.

76. Savulescu, "Why We Should Allow Performance Enhancing Drugs in Sport,"

stances in the body it seems strange to prohibit them on the grounds that they are unnatural to sport.

Developing policies from the argument of naturalness also shows weakness in trying to clarify substance use for therapeutic and non-therapeutic purposes. For example, in 2007 Rodney Harrison was suspended by the National Football League for four games after testing positive for Human Growth Hormone (HGH), a substance banned by the league. "Harrison said that his actions stemmed from his desire to 'accelerate the healing process' from his various injuries the past two seasons."[77]

That same year Yankees pitcher Andy Pettitte admitted to taking HGH to recover from an elbow injury. Pettitte went on the record as saying, "In 2002 I was injured. I had heard that human growth hormone could promote faster healing for my elbow."[78] Two questions arise about these cases. One is to ask why Harrison was suspended but not Pettitte. The reason for this is because HGH did not become banned from professional baseball until 2005, whereas it was already prohibited from the NFL. Pettitte was the target of public scrutiny and was named in *The Mitchell Report* in which a federal investigation led by Senate Majority Leader George Mitchell named Pettitte one of eighty-five baseball players connected to performance enhancing drugs.

A second question is to ask whether the use of HGH in each of these cases was therapy or enhancement. If the substance was taken to restore health then it would be reasonable to consider it therapy. But taking the substance still violates the rules clearly defined in the Prohibited List legislated by WADA. They are not blind to this problem as one of their International Standards is concerned with precisely this issue. "In such a case," says WADA, "a Therapeutic Use Exemption (TUE) may, under strict conditions, provide an athlete with the authorization to take the needed medicine, all the while competing in sport, with no resulting doping offence." Therapeutic Use Exemptions are granted on rare occasion through a strictly regulated and monitored process that is determined by the athlete fulfilling four criteria.

> 1. The athlete would experience a significant impairment to health if the Prohibited Substance or Prohibited Method were to be withheld in the course of treating an acute or chronic medical condition.

666.

77. Pasquarelli, "Pats' Harrison Suspended for Violating NFL's Drug Policy."

78. Associated Press, "Pettitte Admits Using HGH to Recover from an Elbow Injury in 2002."

2. The therapeutic use of the Prohibited Substance or Prohibited Method would produce no additional enhancement of performance other than that which might be anticipated by a return to a state of normal health following the treatment of a legitimate medical condition. The use of any Prohibited Substance or Prohibited Method to increase "low normal" levels of any endogenous hormone is not considered an acceptable therapeutic intervention.

3. There is no reasonable therapeutic alternative to the use of the otherwise Prohibited Substance or Prohibited Method.

4. The necessity for the use of the otherwise Prohibited Substance or Prohibited Method cannot be a consequence, wholly or in part, of prior non-therapeutic use of any substance from the Prohibited List.[79]

Only after meeting all four criteria may an athlete apply for a TUE. The current system has articulated a reasonable solution to the therapy/enhancement problem in sports doping. The issue is far from settled, however, since proponents of enhancement would point out that TUEs are approved by the governing authorities who support a strong anti-doping agenda. Perhaps governing bodies will be stricter in their rulings than they need to be since, as we saw in the fairness argument, the rules against enhancement provide no justifiable reasons for their illegitimacy in the first place. Doping proponents would argue that an exemption system does not tell us why enhancements stand in need of approval in the first place, and that therefore a distinction between therapy and enhancement is not helpful in any normative sense, but merely serves to facilitate exceptions to the rules.

Unsympathetic to these arguments the prohibitionists maintain there is a clear sense in which we can label doping as unnatural to the purposes of sport. The reason, they say, enhancements violate the nature of sport is because the nature of the activity is premised on our humanity. Doping is believed to adulterate the purely human essence of sport. By adding to our biology we are taking away from our humanity. Savulescu believes this view of sport is mistaken. It is what he calls a "test of biological potential" and "the old naturalistic Athenian vision of sport."[80] He agrees that sport is about our humanity but takes the premise to a different conclusion. He argues for a creative approach to sport that is marked by human courage, determination, wisdom and creativity.

79. World Anti-Doping Agency, "Therapeutic Use Exemptions Guidelines," 6.

80. Savulescu, "Why We Should Allow Performance Enhancing Drugs in Sport," 666.

It is this judgment that competitors exercise when they choose diet, training, and whether to take drugs. We can choose what kind of competitor to be, not just through training, but through biological manipulation. Human sport is different from animal sport because it is creative. Far from being against the spirit of sport, biological manipulation embodies the human spirit—the capacity to improve ourselves on the basis of reason and judgment. When we exercise our reason, we do what only humans do.[81]

Contrary to Savulescu's argument, the ability to make decisions about enhancing our biology is not a suitable reason for doing so. Just because we can be creative or courageous does not mean all actions of those sorts are automatically justifiable in sport. It is true enough that sport is about our humanity. In chapter six I present the challenge to recognize the human essence of sport but to do so in a way that does not diminish the realization of our state of mutual dependency. Almost paradoxically, we also need to be careful when choosing actions, in the name of human creativity, that might inadvertently place restrictions on our humanness.

The President's Council on Bioethics notes this caution when they state, "though we might be using rational and scientific means to remedy the mysterious inequality or unchosen limits of our native gifts, we would in fact make the individual's agency *less* humanly or experientially intelligible to himself."[82] The idea in this quote points the debate in a constructive direction, which begins with the premise that the display of sport is primarily about being human. Yet how are we to settle which view of sport is most human? Does Savulescu's view that promotes our creativity and decision making give us freedom to more fully express our humanity through enhancements in sport or does his proposal have the reverse effect and in a sense reduce the human beings we might otherwise be?

This brings us back to the question asked at the beginning of this chapter. What is it that brings about hostility toward doping? While there is credibility in regards to the way we value ideals like fairness or physical health, my contention is that doping threatens something more fundamental. Doping is an attempt to circumvent a basic expression of our humanness. As we will see through the rest of this work a Christian view of sport will rely upon certain theological underpinnings that inform our understanding of the purposes and values inherent in sport. A theological account fundamentally alters the types of questions being asked in this debate. As we have

81. Ibid., 667.
82. President's Council on Bioethics, *Beyond Therapy*, 128; italics original.

surveyed the landscape of ethical arguments against doping it has become clear that the standard approach is a failing project. Rather than trying to strengthen arguments like these we need to develop a more holistic account of sport that will inform the way we think about why sport matters. If sport didn't matter, why would we care about cheating? If sport had no value, why wouldn't we just walk away when feeling coerced? If sport is entirely meaningless, why would we accept any level of physical health risks?

Throughout the rest of this book I hope to initiate a conversation about an alternative approach. The reason we have an uneasy feeling about doping in sport is not *just* because it is cheating or risky. More astutely, we sense the increasing athletic accomplishments come at the expense of our human identity. Exploring this approach from a theological perspective, we are able to offer a distinct understanding of how sport fits within the Christian narrative. Rather than attempting to answer the question "What is wrong with doping?" I want to take a step back and suggest that we must first articulate a view of sport's *telos* within God's redemptive work before we can address what we mean by "wrong."

The pragmatic nature of the current ethical debate points to a lack of meaningful conversation about why we participate in sport. Media sources report on doping among athletes in a way that strikingly resembles the celebrity gossip columns. Public opinion is being informed by a shallow rationale for why these practices are unwelcome in the sports world. When these arguments are examined more closely a persuasive case can be made that in themselves they are not sufficient to justify the prohibitive status they claim. For example, prohibiting doping *on the basis of* its health risks becomes a problematic position to hold when technological advances minimize those risks. Some might be tempted here to suggest that even though these arguments individually do not justify prohibition, perhaps together they build a stronger case.

Yet, there is something in this idea that does not seem correct either. Several leaky buckets stacked together still lose water. Moreover, even if we concede these major arguments we still might feel uneasy about allowing doping. I am suggesting the reason for this is because, in sport, we express who we are as human beings on a much deeper level than these arguments attempt to address. Thus, these sorts of arguments in themselves will always remain unsettling to us since they never really get to the nature of sport's purpose. In sport, we find something elementary to who we are as human beings that goes beyond the typical depth of these types of arguments.

This is not to say that fairness, coercion, health, and the like are unimportant. Rather, it is to shift our focus from these secondary concerns to exploring the question of why sport exists and to what ends, if any, it leads us as human beings. Does sport have anything to say about who we are or how we are to be? Is it an expression of, or contribution to, our understanding of what it means to be human? After exploring these questions we will be in a stronger position to see how fairness, coercion, and health fit into a thicker understanding of sport. To begin answering these questions we will explore three competing philosophical frameworks that will assist us in developing theological reflections on sport.

A Philosophical Framework for Sport

Introduction

IN THE FIELD OF sport and philosophy there are three conceptual frameworks that rise above the rest. In this chapter I will discuss each of these and ultimately will arrive at the conclusion that the final option is the best of the three for articulating a view of sport that is consistent with the theological account given in the following chapters. Each of these views attempts to justify the ways in which we determine social values. I will briefly address the least influential of the three first by discussing an objective view as it is presented by Randolph Feezell's use of Thomas Nagel.

Most of the discussion will then focus on the two views that have been most influential in the literature on philosophy and sport. The philosophies of Alasdair MacIntyre and Richard Rorty respectively have informed much of the dialogue in this field. For this reason I will analyze both theories to see in what ways they may or may not be helpful in the theological project of the following chapters. I will conclude that MacIntyre is more helpful than Rorty in this respect and will use MacIntyre's framework of practices and tradition to elucidate the theological grounding for developing a Christian view of sport.

The current ethical debate, as I argued, is in many ways unfruitful since it fails to appreciate the deeper significance of sport. Debates about the uses of biotechnology lack the depth needed to include conversations about the value inherent in sport itself. This point elicits two fundamental questions. One asks what it is that we value in sport. The other seeks justification for the ways sport fits into certain value systems. It asks how we are to bring together conflicting views about those values into a mutually agreeable theory that provides a more constructive exchange of ideas.

Is sport only valuable to those who enjoy it or does sport have some sort of universal value? If the value in sport is subjective then how are we to handle contradictory opinions? The first section of this chapter will look at an attempt to understand the value of sport, which draws on Thomas Nagel's *The View from Nowhere*.[1] Attempts have been made to develop a view in which values are determined without the added component of one's tradition.

I will argue that a criticism of this subjective/objective dichotomy reveals that the best approach is one that accounts for sport as an inter-personal communitarian activity where participants are in direct relation to other participants.

One theory that takes a community based approach comes from the work of Richard Rorty. Two prominent strains of his thought have been influential in the philosophy of sport. First, Rorty's ethnocentric position sees human beings and their social activities as contingent. Denying a transcendental essence or nature frees the individual to pursue his or her own perfection through self re-creation. For the athlete this means removing as many restrictions as possible, giving the freedom to express personal values. As we saw in the previous chapter, autonomy plays a pivotal role in the discussion of enhancements in sport, particularly when addressing the coercive effects of doping. But Rortian influence reaches beyond simple appeals to autonomy and suggests that everything is a series of contingencies with no fundamental essence or authority. This means there is no real standard for moral judgment of other narratives.

A second element in a Rortian interpretation of sport is closely connected to the first. Rorty's pragmatic philosophy often focused on the tension between society's public and private spheres. He endorsed a political liberalism that enlisted the public realm in the service of the individual member. Here again there is heavy emphasis on individual autonomy. One prominent Rortian sports philosopher, Terrence Roberts, suggests that since we are without essence the goal of the athlete should be to create and recreate himself or herself. On his view, giving the athlete such freedom reduces the corruptive powers that currently govern sports organizations. My criticism of Rortian views of sport, including Roberts' is that such a theory will have an opposite effect from that which they intend. I will argue that making the public realm subservient to the private subjects the goals and purposes of a social activity, like sport, to individual preferences.

1. Nagel, *The View from Nowhere*.

An alternative approach that also begins in community is that of Alasdair MacIntyre. His account of social practices has received much attention in the philosophy of sport. I will describe and critique his notion of a practice and explore reasons why sports may or may not be properly understood as practices in MacIntyre's sense.

Included in this analysis are three major objections to MacIntyre's account of practices. One frequent criticism finds MacIntyre guilty of arbitrarily ascribing goodness to practice and claims that there may be practices that are intrinsically evil. An example of this would be torture. MacIntyre himself addresses this objection and quickly dismisses it.

A second criticism is taken up by Graham McFee. He argues that MacIntyre's theory lacks normative value and therefore does not address how practices from different cultures are to be measured against each other. Contrary to his objections I will show that this is precisely the issue practices are intended to address. Within the context of MacIntyre's broader theory, practices are a method of housing diverse notions of the virtues. I will argue that it is the community aspect that gives practices their strength and that we fail to understand what MacIntyre means by a practice if we neglect the unique social composition of the activity and its internal authority.

A third challenge confronting MacIntyre's account is one posed by John Gibson. Gibson suggests that MacIntyre is mistaken to defend an either/or theory of morality in which we are confronted with either a neo-Aristotelian account of the virtues or a Nietzschean form of nihilism. Gibson praises the idea of sports as practices but rejects the idea that they must be encompassed in the Aristotelian virtues. Instead, he retains the structure of practices but replaces the content with what he labels a "misunderstood" Nietzschean view that is not the moral wasteland MacIntyre describes. Gibson's quasi-practice view must be rejected since it mistakenly removes the virtues from practices. Answering these challenges will show MacIntyre's theory to be a suitable moral framework for sport.

The chapter will conclude by pointing to a philosophical problem faced by both MacIntyrean and Rortian views of sport. Both theories are community dependent and therefore have been accused of being a form of cultural relativism. However, the arguments presented in this chapter will show that MacIntyre's theory more closely identifies with the present task of gaining a theological understanding of sport. Yet MacIntyre has been criticized by other Christians for his questionable separation of philosophy and theology. I will suggest these critics are right and move to a more theologically informed basis for developing a Christian view of sport.

Objective and Subjective Perspectives on Sport

The View from Nowhere

In a thesis like this one where two subjects have a relatively rare encounter it is important to clearly explain the reasoning for addressing the matters presented. Undoubtedly there will be philosophers and theologians who read this who do not particularly care about sport. Similarly, there will be sport enthusiasts who may not be well versed in philosophical or theological inquiries. Some may wonder why so much attention is given here to the existing philosophy of sport literature. First, one does not have to care about sport to take an interest in my larger argument. One could replace sport with other art forms such as music or dance. Many of the broader arguments I will make throughout this thesis could equally be applied to these areas. Secondly, sport provides many interesting possibilities in philosophy partly because it transcends every culture and value system in the world. As such it is worth asking how and why we are to value sport, as well as what we are to do if opposing worldviews collide when they meet in the arena? Does sport have objective value or is it a matter of personal interest?

Randolph Feezell describes these two distinct ways of thinking morally about sport. Deriving his theories from Thomas Nagel's *The View from Nowhere*, Feezell contrasts the subjective view with the objective view of sport. Briefly, the subjective view is how one views the world from a personal perspective while an objective view attempts to remove all influence of personal experience. For instance, from a coach's subjective view nothing, or virtually nothing, may be more important than winning the next game. From another subjective view, an individual who has no interest in the game may find the outcome of the match irrelevant. The latter is said to have a more objective view because personal interests have been removed from the situation. However, we must be careful not to confuse objectivity with apathy. Just because someone is not interested in something does not mean they have a purely objective view.

Instead, objectivity attempts to gain a non-personal view of the world. "The claim" Nagel says, "is that there are reasons for action, that we have to discover them instead of deriving them from our preexisting motives—and that in this way we can acquire new motives superior to the old."[2] Nagel's project is to show that there is often an irreconcilable difference between the subjective and objective views. Having a vast number of subjective views creates difficulties in comparative measurement among the things each individual considers valuable. This creates a situation that has a need for an

2. Ibid., 139.

objective view that does not take into consideration personal experiences. Nagel uses his own life as an example of this dichotomy. "From far enough outside my birth seems accidental, my life pointless, and my death insignificant, but from inside my never having been born seems nearly unimaginable, my life monstrously important, and my death catastrophic."[3]

To explain the subjective in terms of sport Feezell gives the example of the parent of a substitute player on a high school basketball team. The young person does not get to play as much as desired and is frustrated. The parent may also be frustrated (the subjective view) but should be reminded of the objectivity of the sport and "judge relative abilities more accurately, where judgment is less tainted by subjective concerns."[4]

When viewed up close by those who participate there is no question about sport having value. In fact, for many fans and athletes it is among the highest of values. The philosophy of footballer Bill Shankly is frequently adopted by those who watch and play sports. The famed player/manager often said that "football is not a matter of life and death. It's much more important than that."[5] Still, there are often occasions that put sport into perspective. Very few would place sport at the top of their value list. Any number of events may occur that will cause a person to, "step back and compare sport to other parts of your life, you see your involvement in relation to other things that seem to matter, and sport loses."[6]

To some, taking an extreme objective approach may suggest that sport has no value at all. As Nagel points out, "The pursuit of objectivity with respect to value runs the risk of leaving value behind altogether. We may reach a standpoint so removed from the perspective of human life that all we can do is observe."[7] The outcome of a sporting event then may appear arbitrary at best and seems absurd given its relationship to "ordinary life." The need arises then for an appreciation of both vantage points. This paradoxical view is rooted in the notion that we need the objective "view from nowhere" to monitor our subjective views while at the same time allowing value to be determined subjectively. This "double consciousness", as Feezell calls it, allows both to exist by attempting to find "ways of regarding sporting activities that produce as much harmony as possible between the perspectives."[8]

3. Ibid., 209.
4. Feezell, "Sport and the View from Nowhere," 2.
5. Zirin, Bad Sports, 173.
6. Feezell, "Sport and the View from Nowhere," 6.
7. Nagel, The View from Nowhere, 209.
8. Ibid., 10.

Feezell believes this is achieved through the concept of irony. "Irony is a way to regard sports participation, including the pursuit of athletic excellence and the desire for victory, *as if* it really matters, while at the same time recognizing that it is relatively trivial in the larger scheme of things."[9] Where I disagree with Feezell is on his practical application of the dichotomy he derives from Nagel that positions us to view sport "as if it really matters."

Objectivity presents a troubling dilemma for philosophy. Nagel opines that "the human duality of perspectives is too deep for us reasonably to hope to overcome it. A fully agent-neutral morality is not a plausible human goal."[10] However, Nagel still maintains some level of objective detachment from our acculturated perspective. How are we to make sense of our value judgments of the activity of sport if those judgments are being pulled in two very opposite directions? Feezell bridges the gap by way of what he calls the "athletic ironist" whose engagement with sport is "modified by objective detachment and whose detachment is mediated by immediate engagement."[11] This is what Feezell means when he says the athlete may participate in sport "*as if* it really matters." She may engage in sport with all her might and be deeply committed to the activity while at the same time keeping in mind that "it is just a game."

It is important to note that Feezell is not calling for a middle ground approach where these value judgments are balanced on a sliding scale between subjective and objective. If this were so then his emphasis on irony would lose its strength. Feezell attaches importance to both ends of the spectrum. A middle ground approach is not possible. Instead what we must face is the paradox of accepting the tension of both extremes. We must look at sport, Feezell contends, from both perspectives simultaneously, not from somewhere in between.

Critique of a Purely Objective View

Such an approach is not compelling for the primary reason that to say we are to act "as if" it really matters is to say, in effect, that it does not matter at all in any meaningful sense. In this case we only pretend that it has value to justify our participation in it. Which is to say that our pretending actually is nothing more than subjectively aiming at objectivity. As a result sport truly is an absurd activity unless it is explained within a subjective framework. As William Morgan points out objectivism does not shed any

9. Ibid., 11; italics original.

10. Ibid., 185.

11. Feezell, "Sport and the View from Nowhere," 11.

light on our ethical conceptions of sport. "Social practices like sports cannot be made ethical sense of, either by clambering inside our subjective selves and endorsing whatever preference rankings they harbor or, contrarily, by clambering outside of ourselves in search of some perspectiveless, objective vantage point."[12]

According to Morgan, what is needed is an alternative approach. After explaining why the Feezell approach "gets us nowhere" Morgan outlines an interpersonal perspective that "combines critical reflection with an appreciation of the cultural and historical situatedness of sports."[13]

The subjective view is not helpful because it does not provide a rational basis for our moral understanding of sport. Relying on our own subjectivities makes it easy to see why we might participate in sport. We participate in activities that we enjoy and therefore some form of subjective value is evident. However, the bigger problem Morgan draws our attention to is that because these attitudes are so extremely subjective they are often directly at odds with the values internal to the sport. "What all this means is that for far too many contemporary practitioners, sports matter because of the instrumental payoff they provide, the usual suspects include money and fame, not the intrinsic requirements of skill and excellence they pose."[14]

It is precisely these intrinsic qualities that give sport its moral value. From the subjective viewpoint these goods are supplanted by the participants' own appetites, rendering the sport void of independent meaning and value. In doing so the value of sport becomes inseparable from the external benefits derived. Sport becomes a means to the individual's own desires rather than a good in and of itself.

On the objective end of the scale Morgan is equally critical. He points out that Nagel and Feezell try to distinguish degrees of objectivity, albeit in slightly different ways. Nagel says "it is true that with nothing to go on but a conception of the world from nowhere, one would have no way of telling whether anything had value. But an objective view has more to go on, for its data include the appearance of value to individuals with particular perspectives, including oneself."[15]

Morgan suggests such a distinction fails to account for the difference between *recognizing* moral value and *justifying* moral value. Ultimately, Morgan contends, extreme objectivity and relative objectivity arrive at

12. Morgan, "Why the 'View from Nowhere' Gets Us Nowhere in Our Moral Considerations of Sports," 51.

13. Ibid.

14. Ibid., 57.

15. Nagel, *The View from Nowhere*, 147.

the same conclusion that sports are found "without exception, to be irrational, trivial, morally insignificant practices."[16] The problem as Morgan sees it is that both Nagel and Feezell are subscribing to a flawed form of moral universalism.

Morgan sees potential for common ground with Feezell in what they call "objective reengagement." Feezell says that "sport is an arena within which it is possible to develop and display the excellence of good moral character, and the development of good character can be endorsed by an objective viewpoint."[17] This character development comes by way of certain attitudes reflected in sports, namely irony, humility, playful competitiveness and sportsmanship.

For this common ground between the two thinkers to flourish Morgan claims Feezell will need to see "the wisdom of abandoning his unswerving commitment to Nagel's moral universalism and of anchoring moral reflection instead in a more situated and historically informed point of view."[18] If Feezell will leave behind the subjective/objective dichotomy Morgan believes both individuals can contribute to moral reflection of sport through an intersubjective approach.

"In the case of sports" Morgan argues, "the best account is one that provides the most perspicacious answer to the following key question: What forms of life and standards of excellence best exemplify the practice of sports?"[19] Rather than being tied to Nagel's particular version of moral universalism Morgan believes "objective reengagement" is best suited for a position that takes into account other members of the community in non-instrumental ways.

The objectivity challenge Feezell faced—of being able to recognize moral value but not being able to justify it—is thus solved through seeing sports, or any other human activity, as morally justifiable through an interpersonal approach that is rooted in community. We will return to see Morgan's ethnocentric position more fully later. At the moment it is important to note that by briefly looking at subjective and objective value claims on sport we have uncovered the significance this debate has in our understanding of sport, namely the extent to which sport contributes to both individual and corporate expressions of human flourishing.

Richard Rorty and Alasdair MacIntyre both advocate an interpretation of value that sites community as the normative standard for truth. However,

16. Morgan, "Why the View from Nowhere Gets Us Nowhere," 61.

17. Feezell, "Sport and the View from Nowhere," 12.

18. Morgan, "Why the View from Nowhere Gets Us Nowhere," 61.

19. Ibid., 64.

they offer vastly different accounts for the way in which community is normative. Rorty maintains that objective truth, truth "out there", is a myth. He calls for an ethnocentric theory that discards notions of mind-independent truth. Rorty advocates a highly individualized morality that hinges upon a societal distinction of public and private realms *and* rejects any essential nature or sport that would be violated by biotechnological enhancement.

MacIntyre also relies upon communities but in a very different sense. He offers a complex theory of rationality in which a society's tradition, being based in the virtues, is narrated and expressed through a highly specific system of social practices. For MacIntyre, as we will see, communities discover objective meaning through these commensurable practices.

Rorty's and MacIntyre's are certainly not the only interpretations of sport. The reason for applying their views to this debate lies not in any of their respective idiosyncrasies but rather in the ease with which their positions are applicable to moral interpretations of sport. Additionally, their work has made significant contributions to philosophy of sport discussions resulting in the formulation of the two most dominant frameworks in the field. Let us begin with a Rortian interpretation of sport.

Rortian Interpretations of Sport

Ethnocentricity and Objective Moral Truth

Rorty has contributed significantly to philosophical and political conversations about morality. Drawing considerably on the thought of Nietzsche, Heidegger and Dewey he has articulated his own version of American pragmatism that has numerous implications for the development of moral systems within society.

One aspect of Rorty's thought that is directly involved, indeed at the core of, the debate over enhancement technology in sport is his ethnocentric conception of truth, morality and human nature. Rorty calls into question many of the assumptions of traditional philosophy exposing what he sees as epistemological and metaphysical problems. His post-analytic approach seeks to provide a philosophical framework that is void of any metaphysical claims.[20] Therefore, he rejects any notion of a human nature or essence as well as any concept of a *summum bonum*. What we are left with is a system

---

20. Jason Boffetti distinguishes the early Rorty from the late claiming that the later Rorty seeks to "unify public and private under a metaphysical notion." Those referred to in this paper who interact with Rorty do so with the earlier Rorty and for obvious reasons I will do the same. See Boffetti, "How Richard Rorty Found Religion."

of morality that is determined by mind-dependent language. "Truth cannot be out there—cannot exist independently of the human mind—because sentences cannot so exist, or be out there."[21]

Rorty says that a rational objective truth that is outside of any particular perspective is impossible since any claim to that truth is created by acculturated language. Influenced by Wittgenstein, Rorty emphasizes the necessity of language in making truth claims. Each individual has his or her own vocabulary that is based on nothing more than the contingencies of that individual's life. There is no ahistorical view from nowhere with which to compare our own perspective as Nagel tries to do. The conclusion of such a claim is simple. "To accept the claim that there is no standpoint outside the particular historically conditioned and temporary vocabulary we are presently using from which to judge this vocabulary is to give up on the idea that there can be reasons for using languages as well as reasons within languages for believing statements."[22]

One initial reaction to this statement may be to accuse him of relativism. This pure form of moral relativism, it may be argued, is incoherent. If there is no reason for believing any statement to be true then each individual may create his or her own moral truth. If each athlete could create his or her own rules the only possible result would be utter chaos.

What Rorty suggests is to keep morality "just insofar as we can cease to think of morality as the voice of the divine part of ourselves and instead think of it as the voice of ourselves as members of a community, speakers of a common language."[23] This means that truth, either objective or subjective, is an irrelevant concept. Instead, we are left with a community of individuals who share a common understanding of the types of things they do or do not do. Ethnocentricity, Rorty argues, enables us to move beyond the fallacies of philosophical realism. It creates a common ground that allows us to engage in meaningful conversations with one another.

> To be ethnocentric is to divide the human race into the people to whom one must justify one's beliefs and the others. The first group—one's ethnos—comprises those who share enough of one's beliefs to make fruitful conversation possible. In this sense, everybody is ethnocentric when engaged in actual debate, no matter how much realist rhetoric about objectivity he produces in his study.[24]

21. Rorty, *Contingency, Irony, and Solidarity*, 5.
22. Ibid., 48.
23. Ibid., 59.
24. Rorty, *Objectivity, Relativism, and Truth*, 30.

In this sense then, Rorty believes he is only guilty of favoring his own community, not of relativism. The goal for Rorty is the perpetual expansion of interesting ideas within a given community. He rejects any objective view, like the ones presented earlier in this chapter, in part because "no description of how things are from a God's-eye point of view, no skyhook provided by some contemporary or yet-to-be-developed science, is going to free us from the contingency of having been acculturated as we were."[25] The ability to step "outside of our minds" and view reality from an objective perspective is, again, impossible. Correlating to this is Rorty's anti-metaphysical claim that neither humans, nor their activities, have any nature or essence outside themselves towards which to aim. People do not share a common nature and are nothing more than "what has been socialized into them—their ability to use language, and thereby to exchange beliefs and desires with other people."[26]

What this means for sport is, as Terence Roberts contends, that "both sporting selves and sporting practices [are to be seen] as centreless, reweaving webs of contingent beliefs."[27] Roberts' assertion that sport lacks an ahistorical nature is echoed in the contemporary debate over athletic enhancement. The debate is formulated, as Andy Miah noted in an earlier chapter, around medical ethical principles of genetic intervention and more or less ignores the case sport provides for "a discussion about genetics specifically within a complex social context."[28] In other words, the ethics of genetically modifying athletes is primarily a debate over acceptable health risks. There is no essence of sport to be violated by biotechnological enhancement.

On Rorty's view, therefore, we are not representing or mirroring some objective truth about sport. No overarching moral law exists to prohibit the introduction of enhancements into sport. What exists is a common language between members of a community who agree upon the types of actions they will or will not do. Rorty identifies this as a problem of metaphysics for traditional philosophy. The problem is "that nobody feels clear about what would count as a satisfactory argument within it [metaphysics]."[29]

This is the other reason why Rorty has such a difficult time accepting Nagel's paradoxical approach to objectivity and subjectivity. As a result of the fact that we are unable to escape our own acculturation we have no basis upon which to verify an objective perspective. We are unable to say with any certainty what constitutes good or ideal sporting activity. Only within

25. Ibid., 13.

26. Rorty, *Contingency, Irony, and Solidarity*, 177.

27. Roberts, "Private Autonomy and Public Morality in Sporting Practices," 243.

28. Miah, *Genetically Modified Athletes*, 6.

29. Rorty, *Philosophy and the Mirror of Nature*, 335.

a shared vocabulary does sport have any value and that value is determined by the agreement of the community. Rorty maintains that there is no ideal that we are to replicate or represent, (i.e., an ideal form of a specific sport) but rather the closest we will come to objectivity is an agreement among a particular ethnos.[30] In this way we can account for communities holding very different cultural values about a very similar sporting practice.

The Public and Private Realms

In addition to his role in helping to deny a natural essence to both sport and sporting persons Rorty's other influential contribution to moral reflections on sport has been his insistence on a sharp separation of the public and private realms of society. His view is one in which his political system precedes and gives life to proper philosophic inquiry.[31] A liberal society, says Rorty, is the best candidate for ensuring that an individual's particular vocabulary is allowed to flourish. This political idea is the driving force of Rortian liberalism. Individuals ought to have as much freedom as they need to pursue their own interests and desires. "A liberal society" Rorty suggests, "is one which is content to call 'true' (or 'right' or 'just') whatever the outcome of undistorted communication happens to be, whatever view wins in a free and open encounter."[32] Rorty's politics of the free exchange of ideas is compatible with the communicative reason theory developed by Jürgen Habermas.[33] Within a free democracy individuals are able to interact with and adopt other vocabularies as one sees fit.

Such a liberal democracy is, for Rorty, the apex of human political achievement. "J.S. Mill's suggestion that governments devote themselves to optimizing the balance between leaving people's private lives alone and preventing suffering seems to me pretty much the last word."[34] Here we see clearly the divide Rorty makes between the public and private realms. The public exists to facilitate the growth and expansion of the private. This Rortian divide has specific implications for conceptions of sport and to express these I will draw upon a dialogue between Terence Roberts and William

30. Ibid., 337.

31. See Rorty, *Objectivity, Relativism and Truth*, 175–96.

32. Rorty, *Contingency, Irony, and Solidarity*, 67.

33. Rorty agrees with the political ramifications but rejects Habermas' attempt to maintain a form of universal validation through the rationality of communication. See Habermas, *The Philosophical Discourse of Modernity*, esp. 296–35; and *Theory of Communicative Action*: Vol. 1, *Reason and the Rationality of Society*. For Rorty's critique of this aspect of Habermas see Rorty's, *Contingency, Irony, and Solidarity*, 61–69.

34. Rorty, *Contingency, Irony, and Solidarity*, 63.

Morgan. Roberts defends Rorty's distinction as an appropriate method for addressing contemporary problems in sport.

> It suggests that if the private sphere of sport can be expanded and protected, while at the same time limiting the public sphere, there will be more freedom, space and opportunity for creativity, invention and self-definition; and appropriate to any practice of which a principal portion is private and therefore publicly irrelevant, sport will seem more like other ultimate pursuits such as art and religion and less like politics, business and economics.[35]

Roberts argues that this Rortian interpretation will allow us to shed the essentialist view that has dominated the philosophy of sport since its coming of age and re-describe sport as having a public and a private dimension, "each of which needs to be protected from the universalizing tendencies of the other."[36] This claim presents a couple of problems for Roberts.

First, what he portrays as a balance of spheres is heavily biased toward one side. He explains that the private needs protection from the public when governing bodies enforce rules that are too comprehensive to allow adequate freedom of individual athletes. On the other hand, the public needs protection from the private when "an individual's or group's idiosyncratic pursuit of private perfection in a sporting practice is imposed on others."[37] His explanation of how one might infringe upon the other clearly favors the private.

Secondly, Roberts explicitly calls for a reduction of the public's role in wanting to re-create sport in such a way that the "aesthetic, creative dimension is highlighted while the public and moral is diminished."[38] What Rorty and Roberts want is to reduce any notion of external moral norms. To diminish the moral aspect of sport is to reduce sporting activities to exercises in private perfection. The moral code of the activity is nothing more than what those who are current members say it should be.

This is a public, as William Morgan points out, "that is completely in the throes of the private, that exists primarily to serve the individual preferences and goals of private life."[39] This, of course, is not a problem for Rorty or Roberts. Within a privately dominated society we are free to create and re-create ourselves as Nietzsche foretold. While it is undeniable that the private dimension is important to sporting practices the extent to which they are more private than public is rightly contested by Morgan. Roberts' idea of balance

35. Roberts, "Private Autonomy and Public Morality in Sporting Practices," 243.

36. Ibid., 242.

37. Ibid.

38. Ibid., 248.

39. Morgan, "Are Sports More So Private or Public Practices?," 19.

between public and private ultimately is one that advocates a re-description that places sport firmly in the realm of private pursuits of self-creation.

Morgan is unconvinced and suggests that "following Roberts's Rortian precepts will prove to be the undoing of sports rather than their redemption, that when all is said and done it will undermine rather than rescue their aesthetic charm and moral salience."[40] In order to see how an overemphasis on the private might actually corrupt the practice of sport we need to draw attention to a distinction concerning two types of public sphere.

Rorty's view implies we necessarily live in one of two worlds. Either we are engaged in private pursuits that concern only ourselves (private) or we are fulfilling our sociopolitical duty to others (public). Contrary to this as Morgan points out, "the better part of our lives are, in fact, lived in neither of these spaces, but rather in the large and relatively uncoerced space of what is commonly known and referred to as civil society and in the social patchwork of associations that fill it up."[41] Morgan's argument relies upon this distinction between the public as a political realm and a realm composed of associations in the sense of a hybrid category just described.

What this means, for Morgan, is that Roberts has confused the public aim of sport as a political venture toward justice when it is, in fact, a public community aimed at realizing "ends rooted in shared conceptions of the good."[42] Morgan distinguishes between political communities and associational communities by a Rawlsian distinction between good and right. "The social glue," Morgan explains, "that holds members of associations together is the (common) good, while the social glue that holds members of political communities together is the right (justice)."[43] Roberts neglects this distinction and thereby misses the point of sport as a community aimed at a specific set of ends based on a common good.

Instead Roberts is preoccupied with defending the private autonomy of athletes to re-create themselves since this is where he sees "great promise as a powerful redescription that can help to overcome some of the blindness, frivolity, and cruelty of conventional sporting truths."[44] Mirroring the work of Rorty he champions the metaphor of a strong poet as "one who makes things new."[45]

---

40. Ibid., 23.
41. Ibid.
42. Ibid., 24.
43. Ibid., 25.
44. Roberts, "Sport and Strong Poetry," 105.
45. Rorty, *Contingency, Irony, and Solidarity*, 13.

As we have seen, Rorty and Roberts believe humans to be centre-less selves or webs of contingent beliefs. In Roberts' view such a position is the only way to reverse the immoral landscape of contemporary elite sports. However, such a position will have the opposite effect. As Morgan points out, the Rortian strong poet-athlete is not concerned with "talent per se, doing things that no one else has done as well, but a certain eccentric flair, doing things that no one has ever done or even thought about doing. When all is said and done, then, the only way to be a strong poet-athlete in sports is to subvert the purpose of sports."[46]

Since neither sport nor athlete has an essential nature both are free to be remade in a whimsical fashion. Morgan concludes, "strong poet-athletes put the resources of sports to use to reinvent themselves not to reshape existing sport practices or invent new ones."[47]

Sports as MacIntyrean Practices

Alasdair MacIntyre has noted three major approaches in the history of Western moral thought that have contributed to the current moral climate. The highly influential historian of philosophy describes a neo-Aristotelian view of the virtues, the Enlightenment project, and finally a Nietzschean framework.

MacIntyre has described the current state of moral thought in the Western world as being a time "after virtue". It is a time in which moral thought has become disordered. Morality may be compared with a puzzle scattered about and only certain pieces can be found resulting in a fragmented moral picture. The biggest cause of this disarray was the removal of morality's telos. The Enlightenment project was comprised of attempts to discover an alternative rational, universal account of justifying morality.

MacIntyre argues however that the Enlightenment project was destined to fail and that as a result we are left with two alternatives. Either we accept a Nietzschean framework that seeks to distinguish individuals from their past by enabling them to "create themselves" or we must return to an account of the virtues. Those who adopt his theory typically follow MacIntyre's own outline and with good reason. He lays bare both options and confronts the challenges of each concluding that a neo-Aristotelian conception of the virtues is superior to Nietzsche's framework. However, the virtues are not without their own difficulties, namely the challenges of identifying and justifying competing lists of virtues.

46. Morgan, "Rortian Interpretations of Sport," 27.
47. Ibid., 28.

To begin with, virtue theory revolves around the agent rather than moral rules or consequences. As such it relies heavily on the close relationship between the agent and the community to which he or she belongs. It is easy to see the parallels with sport since it is a highly social activity. But how are we to measure one society's conception of the good of sport versus another? A sport in one region of the world may have significantly different meaning (not to mention rules) than that same sport in another part of the world. What criteria are we to use to arrive at a common conception of the good of sport? Is it possible to identify a universal sense of value and meaning in sport?

Defining Practices

One of the difficulties with a virtue theory of ethics, the theory MacIntyre himself holds, is the seemingly innumerable accounts of what qualifies as a virtue. Several lists of what constitutes a virtue have been given. MacIntyre informatively describes several such accounts from a Homeric account emphasizing social roles to Aristotle's and Aquinas' teleological accounts to Benjamin Franklin's utility of the virtues.[48] How are we to make sense of the virtues given the number of positions regarding the nature of virtue? As MacIntyre summarizes, "they offer us different and incompatible lists of the virtues; they give a different rank order of importance to different virtues; and they have different and incompatible theories of the virtues."[49] As a result we might conclude that there is no core concept of virtue to unite these competing theories.

In response MacIntyre develops his notion of a practice. What MacIntyre means by practice is this.

> By a "practice" I am going to mean any coherent and complex form of socially established cooperative human activity through which goods internal to that form of activity are realized in the course of trying to achieve those standards of excellence which are appropriate to, and partially definitive of, that form of activity, with the result that human powers to achieve excellence and human conceptions of the ends and goods involved, are systematically extended.[50]

48. MacIntyre, *After Virtue*, 121–203.
49. Ibid., 181.
50. Ibid., 187.

Central to this definition is the concept of internal goods. One important sense in which these goods are internal is that they can only be achieved as a result of the practice. They are unique to a given practice's ends. Moreover, internal goods are only recognizable by those who are participants in the practice surrounding the goods in question. For instance, money and fame are often goods associated with sports. However, they are not internal goods since they can be attained through other means and their attainment is of a material nature. One need not be an athlete to gain wealth and fame as these are goods achievable through other activities as well. It is also the case that one may heartily engage in sport for an entire lifetime and never reap the rewards of money or social status.

As an example of internal goods consider the practice of American football. Learning to execute a well thrown pass is an internal good. There are many parallels between the internal goods of a practice and the skills needed to achieve a practice's standards of excellence. MacIntyre goes on to explain by way of example. Imagine he wants to teach a young child how to play chess (for our purposes, any sport may be substituted for chess). He bribes the child, who is not particularly interested in chess, into playing once a week by offering candy every time he or she plays. MacIntyre further tempts the child by offering double the amount of candy if the child wins. So long as it is the candy that motivates the child to play he or she is driven externally. Candy is not part of chess itself. It is an external good.

MacIntyre points out that so long as the child is motivated solely by external goods he or she has no reason not to cheat in order to win the game and gain the candy. He defines these external goods as "contingently attached . . . by the accidents of social circumstance -in the case of the imaginary child candy, in the case of real adults such goods as prestige, status and money."[51]

More importantly, the understanding of a practice requires knowing that external goods are "never to be had *only* by engaging in some particular kind of practice."[52] The child may gain the external goods, (i.e., the candy) in any number of other ways. He or she may have to play in order to get candy from MacIntyre but typically does not have to play chess to get candy from another source.

MacIntyre believes that eventually the child will come to appreciate the game of chess in its own right. In realizing the goods of chess itself, it is hoped, the child will no longer be motivated solely by candy but will begin to enjoy the goods internal to chess. As another example, someone may take up swimming because of its health benefits but over time develops a love

51. Ibid., 188.
52. Ibid.

for the sport. He or she will then continue to swim, not because it is healthy but because they enjoy it for its own sake. It is often the external goods that draw us to a particular practice but equally so it is the internal goods that keep us there.

Contrary to the external goods that may be gained through other means the internal goods are only realizable through that particular practice. MacIntyre notes that there are "goods internal to the practice of chess which cannot be had in any way but by playing chess or some other game of that specific kind."[53] It follows from this, as MacIntyre notes that since these goods are only attainable as a result of participating in a specific practice only those who have experienced that practice are in a position to judge its internal goods.

A practice is defined, at least in part, by the standards of excellence appropriate to that practice. These are the technical skills related to the activity. The internal goods are realized by trying to achieve the techniques necessary for that type of practice. Not only do they partially define the practice, they become the motivation behind participating. William Morgan points out that the excellences of a practice "furnish a reason for taking up a practice such as soccer that makes the realization of the particular physical and strategic skills it calls for, and the practical judgment, competitive mettle, and challenges it requires, if not the whole, then certainly the main point of its practice."[54]

A key component of a practice as it applies to sport is the relationship between achieving the standards of excellence and obedience to rules. "To enter into a practice is to accept the authority of those standards and the inadequacy of my own performance as judged by them."[55] Each sport has a history by which to judge the standards of excellence within that sport. To involve oneself in a specific practice requires one to submit to the authority of that historically situated practice.

In this sense sport is normative for all participants. The rules and historical setting of a sport, established through tradition and honored by those who are more experienced in the practice, serve as instructors to the practice's newcomers by helping to shape the way they participate in the practice. Obviously, coaching would be an excellent example of this. Inexperienced participants are taught the standards of the practice by those who are in a better position to judge the goods of that practice. "In the realm of practices" MacIntyre says, "the authority of both goods and standards

53. Ibid.
54. Morgan, *Leftist Theories of Sport*, 132.
55. MacIntyre, *After Virtue*, 190.

operates in such a way as to rule out all subjectivist and emotivist analyses of judgment."[56] It is illogical to think of a sport in which all the participants create their own rules. Such an activity would be utterly meaningless.

Similarly, it is very important to note that a practice is not the activity of one individual. Those who engage in a practice, whether it is a sport or some other type of activity, are yielding to the authority of the community surrounding that practice and allowing himself or herself to become part of that community.

Communal Aspect of Practices

At this point in the discussion most sports ethicists skip straight to MacIntyre's treatment of the three virtues required of any practice.[57] In doing so they neglect a highly important feature of practices to which MacIntyre is attuned. My understanding of MacIntyre on this point is that there is much more to being part of a particular practice's community than merely beginning to participate. "It belongs to the concept of a practice as I have outlined it . . . that its goods can only be achieved by subordinating ourselves within the practice in our relationship to other practitioners."[58] He goes on to state,

> We have to learn to recognize what is due to whom; we have to be prepared to take whatever self-endangering risks are demanded along the way; and we have to listen carefully to what we are told about our own inadequacies and to reply with the same carefulness for the facts. In other words we have to accept as necessary components of any practice with internal goods and standards of excellence the virtues of justice, courage and honesty.[59]

These three virtues comprise the core of all practices since without them practices are essentially meaningless. "For not to accept these . . . so far bars us from achieving the standards of excellence or the goods internal to the practice that it renders the practice pointless except as a device for achieving external goods."[60]

56. Ibid.

57. Feezell might be considered one of the few exceptions to this. He states that "Certain things immediately follow from this" and outlines MacIntyre's thoughts but he does not satisfactorily emphasize the point I believe MacIntyre wishes to make. See Feezell, *Sport, Play & Ethical Reflection*, 128.

58. MacIntyre, *After Virtue*, 191.

59. Ibid.

60. Ibid.

One does not become a member of the baseball community because one suddenly decides to take up baseball. The language MacIntyre uses throughout, particularly the idea of learning and striving for the internal goods implies a progression toward a bond with that community rather than an instantaneous assimilation. In fact, he goes on to describe it in this way. "Every practice requires a certain kind of relationship between those who participate in it."[61] It is on the basis of this interpersonal relationship that these three virtues of justice, courage and honesty are required since they are foundational to any healthy relationship.

We can summarize MacIntyre's thought here by saying that the virtues enable us to achieve the goods internal to a practice while the virtues are acquired, at least in part, through developing relationships inside the community of a given practice. This does not mean, however, that one must be an expert in all matters pertaining to a particular practice before becoming part of that community. Instead it suggests that what is required is an attitude reflective of the desire for the goods internal to the practice and recognition of our dependence upon others to achieve the standards of excellence specific to that practice. One does not need to be a professional athlete to be part of the baseball community but simply show a willingness to be a part of the game and join others in the pursuit of the goods appropriate to baseball.

Becoming part of a community, we have noted, requires accepting the history and traditions of that community. Every practice has a narrative that informs all who are involved. This is critical to MacIntyre's account of a practice. "To enter into a practice is to enter into a relationship not only with its contemporary practitioners, but also with those who have preceded us in the practice, particularly those whose achievements extended the reach of the practice to its present point."[62]

This idea of tradition is captured well by Michael Mandelbaum as he recounts the significance of baseball in American culture. Having its genesis in the late eighteenth and early nineteenth centuries baseball today serves as a reminder of the past more so than any other American sport. The lack of a time clock and consequent leisurely pace stands in contrast to the highly efficient, materialistic and machine-like nature of Western society today.[63] "Baseball returns the spectator, for a few hours, to an earlier, simpler, happier time. It offers a brief sojourn in a lost paradise, a sip from the fountain

61. Ibid., 191.

62. Ibid., 194.

63. I am not saying that baseball avoids the problems of materialism and mechanistic efficiency. If anything, baseball is a game of statistics and precision, making it at times a very mechanical sport. However, it is less rigid and precise in terms of time, being one of the few major sports without a game clock.

of youth."[64] He goes on to describe baseball as a "time machine, transporting spectators back into the past" and defines this as "the heart of its status in American culture."[65]

Not only does baseball return the spectator to earlier times, it also invokes memories of some of the sport's greatest players who are responsible for changing aspects of the game forever. George Herman Ruth is one of the greatest examples of someone who revolutionized the game. With debts to Whitehead's famous statement about Plato and European philosophy Mandelbaum suggests "the modern history of the game of baseball consists in some ways of a series of footnotes to Babe Ruth."[66] Ruth shifted the emphasis in baseball from the defense to the offence with his uniquely successful way of swinging the bat.

During his day the batter gripped higher on the bat in an attempt to gain better control over where the ball would be hit to. The ability to place the ball away from the fielders allowed the batter to make it safely to the base. Ruth chose to hold the bat at its base and swing as forcefully as he could in order to hit the ball as far as possible. When he retired he had more than five times the number of career home runs (714) than did the previous record holder. Even though it is no longer the record, is still seen by many as a point of reference by which to compare contemporary professional baseball players. Ruth altered the game of baseball by popularizing the home run and "the new emphasis on it made the game more dramatic and exciting."[67]

For MacIntyre then, it is "the achievement, and *a fortiori* the authority, of a tradition that I then confront and from which I have to learn."[68] At this point MacIntyre introduces what he calls institutions. He is careful to distinguish institutions from practices by pointing out that where practices are concerned with the goods internal to an activity institutions are "characteristically and necessarily concerned with" external goods.[69] This must be the case since practices are focused on internal goods, immaterial goods that can only be gained through participating in the practice. External goods such as money, power and status are awarded to the practitioners by the institutions that govern and sustain the practices.

---

64. Mandelbaum, *The Meaning of Sports*, 52.

65. Ibid., 53.

66. Ibid., 68. Alfred North Whitehead stated that "the safest general characterization of the European philosophical tradition is that it consists of a series of footnotes to Plato." See Whitehead's, *Process and Reality*, 39.

67. Mandelbaum, *The Meaning of Sports*, 69.

68. MacIntyre, *After Virtue*, 194.

69. Ibid., 194.

Despite their distinct differences practices and institutions "characteristically form a single causal order in which the ideals and the creativity of
the practice are always vulnerable to the acquisitiveness of the institution,
in which the cooperative care for common goods of the practice is always
vulnerable to the competiveness of the institution."[70] This is why the virtues
are of such importance to practices, for without them they "could not resist
the corrupting power of institutions."[71]

It is for this distinction that many sports ethicists rely most heavily on
MacIntyre. Much has been written about the commercialization of sport
and the internal/external goods distinction. Many philosophers lament the
current state of sports and find MacIntyre's institutions a fitting agent of
blame. Feezell comments, "in the context of sports little needs to be said to
interpret this point [sc. institutions corrupting power]. MacIntyre's distinction . . . provides an enlightening way to view this much-talked about and
much criticized phenomenon."[72]

By way of example we can see that golf is a practice while the Professional Golfers' Association is an institution that governs and facilitates the
external goods of golf. The external goods cannot be gained by way of the
practice itself. Playing golf will not result in goods like prize money. Those
types of goods are gained only through the institutions. Similarly, institutions are unable to provide the internal goods that are only to be found
in the practice.

It is also worth noting that external goods are, in fact, goods and should
not be discounted merely because they are not internal goods. Simply because they are external to the practice does not mean they lack moral value,
though often it is the case that the influence of the external goods corrupts
the pursuit of internal goods. This corrupting power is kept at bay by the
three specific virtues mentioned above that are required of every practice.

It seems as though sports clearly are practices. William Morgan agrees
when he states that sports are "associations founded on common, substantive conceptions of the good that inform the collective aims, values, and
standards of judgment of their members, of the practice communities
formed in their name."[73] At first glance there is little to suggest otherwise.
In fact, as was just demonstrated, sports make for some of the most illustra-
tive examples when defining practices. It does not follow, however, that just
because certain examples help clarify what is meant by a practice that all

70. Ibid.
71. Ibid.
72. Feezell, *Sport, Play and Ethical Reflection*, 132.
73. Morgan, "Are Sports More So Private or Public Practices?," 24.

sports are, in fact, practices. Not surprisingly, the thesis MacIntyre proposes in *After Virtue* is not without criticism.[74] Two critics working directly in the philosophy of sport have challenged the unqualified acceptance of sports as practices. The first criticism wholly rejects applying MacIntyre's notion of practices to sports on the grounds of normativity. Graham McFee suggests that there must be some justification for following the rules of a particular sport. He disagrees with those who would attempt to use practices as this justification because, in his view, the concept of a practice lacks normative value. The second objection sees promise for the structure of MacIntyrean practices but rejects MacIntyre's insistence on using an Aristotelian theory of the virtues. Instead, John Gibson argues, those virtues can be replaced with a Nietzschean system of value. Let us first turn to McFee's reasons for why he believes sports are not practices.

The Normative Justification Critique of MacIntyrean Practices

As MacIntyre has explained, being involved in a practice requires submitting to the authority of the tradition and rules of that practice. In this sense sport is a normative activity in that its rules or principles tell the participant how he or she ought to act in specific situations. Graham McFee disputes the claim that the use of MacIntyre's practices provides a normative element to the rules of sport.

He begins making his argument by outlining two opposing theories of the ethos of sport. One account is descriptive while the other is a normative account of ethos. A purely descriptive account has a significant risk of relativism since there is no way of judging competing rules in the same sport. Different communities may have different understandings of the rules and a descriptive account can only tell us what *is* happening rather than what *should* happen. Siding with William Morgan on this point McFee says that when "faced with the general question of how it is possible for rules to have application, a descriptive answer will not do."[75] There must be a prescriptive element behind the rules of sport that compels athletes to obey those rules.

Morgan attempts to provide this element in his normative conception of sport's ethos, which "appeals to some idealization of the way a sport's rules

74. Many of the objections to MacIntyre's framework digress too far from the present task of determining the applicability of practices to sports and will not be mentioned further here. For detailed discussions on problems with MacIntyre's theory more generally see Horton, *After MacIntyre*; Knight, *The MacIntyre Reader*; Lutz, *Tradition in the Ethics of Alasdair MacIntyre*; Murphy et al., eds., *Virtues & Practices in the Christian Tradition*; D'Andrea, *Tradition, Rationality, and Virtue*.

75. McFee, "Normativity, Justification, and (MacIntyrean) Practices," 18.

have developed conceptions of 'what should happen' for us."[76] This theory relies heavily on the community's agreement of how the sport ought to be played and how the rules ought to be enforced and what sporting behavior can rightly be called moral or immoral. A theory like this relies heavily on the social aspect of the activity not unlike MacIntyre's account of practices. Indeed, that is where Morgan goes in his account of sport, describing sport in the context of moral social practices.

However, McFee identifies three reasons why MacIntyre's account of practices is ill-suited for sports. He argues that MacIntyre's theory assumes normativity without justification, is descriptive in nature, and is trapped by a communitarian view of normativity. The first two criticisms touch on the same ideas and for our purposes will be taken together.

Simply because there are internal goods and standards of excellence does not mean practices necessarily provide justification for behaving in a certain manner. If Morgan, who is sympathetic to a MacIntyrean interpretation of sport, is correct in classifying sports as practices he must make sense of how it is we understand internal goods as authoritative. That is, what standards determine our adherence to the rules of the practice and why are the internal excellences necessarily morally good?

McFee cites the frequently invoked example of torture. It seems to fit the qualifications of a practice. It has internal excellences and may be sought as an end in itself. If we are to deny that torture is a practice then "the account becomes stipulative toward positive excellences."[77] The accusation of evil practices is anticipated by MacIntyre when he writes that there may be practices that are evil though he is "far from convinced that there are" and does not "believe that either torture or sadomasochistic sexuality answer to the description of a practice."[78]

In fact, MacIntyre acknowledges that given their broad description, practices sometimes lead to evil acts. But McFee is undeterred since in his view such an account returns to a description of the activity and does not provide any normative justification for action.[79] These reasons are enough for McFee to dismiss the idea of sports as MacIntyrean practices, but he also adds a third critique of practices.

Should sport pass the scrutiny of McFee's first two points, an idea he finds very unlikely, it still must account for the merely communal basis of its normativity. Recall MacIntyre's claim that only those inside the practice

76. Ibid., 19.

77. Ibid., 20.

78. MacIntyre, *After Virtue*, 200.

79. McFee, "Normativity, Justification and (MacIntyrean) Practices," 20.

are able to judge that practice. Since the practice is rooted in the community's tradition is seems as though the judgment of that practice is a circular process. Members of the practice's community are to be judged by that same community. McFee believes the only way to avoid this dilemma is to ground the normativity of MacIntyrean practices in the logic of the rules. One follows the rules of a practice because that is what one must do to be a part of that practice's community. More to the point, his criticism suggests moral judgments are completely self-contained in the practice and determined by the constituents of the practice.

His conclusion on the normativity of practices is that it "cannot really get us beyond the descriptive conception of ethos; moreover, it is unsatisfactory applied to normativity in general."[80] Identifying sports as practices is nothing more than describing certain properties of sport. Those properties are descriptive elements of sport and are incapable of providing justification for any normative component.

He proposes a Wittgensteinian conception of normativity based in the idea of "customs" though McFee similarly rejects equating sports with customs. Interestingly, the argument used against MacIntyre that his theory "does not explain normativity but simply assumes it" is the same justification McFee uses for customs when he says "normativity rests on customs, but this, again, does not explain the origin of that normativity—and does not seek to."[81]

This apparent contradiction does not go unnoticed. McFee recognizes this objection and states the need for further work on the topic. He is still able to maintain his argument that MacIntyre's theory is largely uncritical due to the exclusivity of the communal nature of practices. We may concede the point that many practice communities have an elitist attitude. Only those who have a relatively significant role inside the community are able to shape the future of the sport (or any other practice for that matter) but it is difficult to understand how Wittgensteinian customs are much different.

More will be said in a moment about the normative justification of sporting activity. Pending a fuller discussion of this point, let us grant that such normativity is justified whether it is in the language of practices, traditions or habituated customs. MacIntyre is correct that the only way one will achieve the internal goods of the activity is by actually participating in the activity. McFee also seems correct in questioning how those activities may be judged if they are restricted to members of that particular community. We will return to this apparent conflict in the conclusion to this chapter.

80. Ibid., 22.
81. Ibid., 26.

As we will see, this is a problem for both MacIntyre and Rorty though, I will argue, it is more troublesome for the latter. Before developing a Rortian interpretation of sport I want to explore a second criticism of MacIntyre. John Gibson offers an idiosyncratic approach that modifies MacIntyre's theory to avoid what he perceives as internal problems and attempts to blend components of MacIntyre, Rorty, and Nietzsche into a moral criticism of contemporary sport.

Invoking Nietzsche

MacIntyre's notion of social practices is set within his larger task of identifying and explaining the current chaos in moral theory. In *After Virtue*, MacIntyre historically traces the downfall of traditional morality as a result of emotivism and the Enlightenment project. As a result of these destructive ideologies MacIntyre concludes that we have but two options.

In arguing for a theory of moral virtue MacIntyre stresses the importance of returning to an Aristotelian framework that takes into account the telos of humanity. For MacIntyre, ethics presupposes a telos in that "the whole point of ethics—both as a theoretical and a practical discipline—is to enable man to pass from his present state to his true end."[82]

Belief in a human telos eroded as the Enlightenment period gained prominence. Both Aristotelian and theological moral philosophy was replaced by forms of subjectivism, most notably, emotivism. The dominant moral framework of the Middle Ages now lacked credibility in the minds of moral philosophers. In an attempt to discover a system of moral rules that applied equally to all rational persons, tradition and community gave way to individualism and emphasis was placed on personal values and claims of feelings.[83] This project ultimately failed and caused the crisis MacIntyre claims exists in contemporary moral philosophy.

John Gibson concurs with MacIntyre in his historical sketching of moral thought from the ancient Greeks through the Enlightenment. "The moral vacuum left by the failure of the Enlightenment to produce a rational basis for values led to the application of scientific method to human relationships

---

82. MacIntyre, *After Virtue*, 54.

83. Moore, *Principia Ethica* and Stevenson, *Ethics and Language* were two major works in this movement. Moore was foundational to the emotivist position while Stevenson articulated it better than any other, summarizing emotivism by saying the statement "This is good" essentially means "Hurrah for this."

. . . In the absence of a substantiated moral framework, trying to be good for its own sake has given way to trying to look good for one's own sake."[84]

Several moral theories arose out of the Enlightenment. Two of the dominant theories in contemporary Western morality, Kantian and utilitarian ethics, arose during this period. But one stands out to MacIntyre above the rest. If we will not return to Aristotle we are left with only one alternative. MacIntyre chooses Nietzsche not only because he was one of the Enlightenment's most unsympathetic critics but because he most accurately represents contemporary philosophy's answer to post-Enlightenment morality. "In five swift, witty and cogent paragraphs he disposes of both what I have called the Enlightenment project to discover rational foundations for an objective morality and of the confidence of the everyday moral agent in post-Enlightenment culture that his moral practice and utterance are in good order."[85]

The importance of Nietzsche is clear. Since rational justifications of objective morality fail it must be that "belief in the tenets of morality needs to be explained in terms of a set of rationalizations that conceal the fundamentally non-rational phenomena of the will."[86]

This is the contrast MacIntyre points out. Either Nietzsche is right and morality is ultimately based on the non-rational will or something like Aristotelianism is right and we were wrong to ever go against it in the first place.[87] Gibson seems to have no quarrel with the moral contrast MacIntyre articulates. In fact, Gibson also accepts the notion of practices and believes they give a well suited description of sport as a human activity.

Where he dissents from MacIntyre is on which path to follow. For MacIntyre, it is clear that Aristotelianism, or something like it, must be recovered. Gibson believes Nietzsche is often misunderstood by philosophers like MacIntyre and a Nietzschean world is not as dreadful as initially suggested. Gibson argues in favor of keeping MacIntyre's concept of social practices because they provide an excellent framework for tackling many of the moral problems in modern sports.

However, he finds MacIntyre's reliance upon Aristotle problematic and proposes to replace Aristotelianism with a Nietzschean form of moral value. In his rejection of MacIntyre's Aristotelianism Gibson offers little

84. Gibson, *Performance versus Results*, 24.

85. MacIntyre, *After Virtue*, 113.

86. Ibid., 117.

87. There are those who suggest that Aristotle and Nietzsche are not as opposite as MacIntyre believes them to be. Swanton points to several similarities and gives a virtue theorist interpretation of Nietzsche. See Swanton, "Can Nietzsche Be Both an Existentialist and a Virtue Ethicist?"

more than a few paragraphs. His relatively brief critique of MacIntyre's reliance on the virtues is far from sufficient. He simply highlights the three major problems MacIntyre himself identifies with the Aristotelian view and claims MacIntyre is unable to distance himself from the problems inherent in Aristotle, namely, the denial of the tragic, the ahistorical essence of the virtues and the metaphysical biology of humanity. Beyond pointing out the challenges MacIntyre himself addresses there is little substantive criticism in Gibson's work. Perhaps the most astute judgment is that of MacIntyre's ambiguous description of telos. "It is not clear that in his desire to be open ended, MacIntyre has sufficiently delineated what does and does not count as a possible telos of human life."[88]

Gibson argues that Aristotle's ahistorical orientation, a major challenge MacIntyre seeks to overcome, is required of Aristotle's theory. Gibson clearly states that without this ahistorical dimension the theory makes no sense. As an example he cites justice as the central virtue for Aristotle with justice being what each member of that society getting what he deserves. He says the "internalization of the framework of society made the imposition of an outside order redundant to the ancients."[89] Aristotelian virtues are based upon the class and role of a citizen within society. Removing the structure of the *polis* is to make the virtues unintelligible since they are the traits required to achieve one's purpose within that society.

Laying aside the fact that this crude analysis is a gross oversimplification of Aristotle it also neglects the significance of MacIntyre's claim to restore Aristotelian virtue *or something like it*. Replicating Aristotle's own ideas is not what MacIntyre is trying to do. That is precisely why he addresses these problems in Aristotle. He rightly wants to keep Aristotle's moral framework while rejecting certain aspects of his theory. In itself this is not a solution to the problem. It begs the question of whether or not he succeeds in sufficiently distancing himself from Aristotle's problems. To answer that question we now turn to the most crucial of the three challenges.

Gibson argues that, "without offering a rational vindication of Aristotle's cosmic order and claims about the truth of human nature, MacIntyre cannot make a rational case for the Aristotelian tradition."[90] Two of the three difficulties in Aristotle's theory of virtue come to the foreground here with one finding its source in the other. Aristotle's view of the *polis* is presupposed by his metaphysical biology. Without his biological view it is impossible for Aristotle's theory to know the telos of human beings, (i.e., citizens of the

---

88. Gibson, *Performance versus Results,* 81.

89. Ibid.

90. Ibid., 80.

polis). The cosmic order is determined by the truth about human nature. Gibson and MacIntyre are correct to question Aristotle's metaphysical biology on issues such as slavery. Both, most notably MacIntyre, are quick to dismiss Aristotle on this point.

We need not draw the conclusion, however, that this entails a complete dismissal of *something like* an Aristotelian account of human nature. Virtue theory requires a human essence, something by which we can say that this is good or bad behavior, that this is ideal or not ideal for what a human being ought to be. Herein lays the importance of the telos. This is what MacIntyre is referring to when he identifies the categories of "human-nature-as-it-happens-to-be" and "human-nature-as-it-could-be-if-it-realized-its-*telos*" with the virtues being what enables us to move from the former to the later.[91] To disallow human biology is inconsistent with the teleological ethical theory MacIntyre is defending.

These metaphysical insights are necessary to give an account of morality from the virtues. But metaphysics is not enough. It is undeniable that biology plays a significant role in human nature. We are comprised of biological material. How is it possible, then, to give an ethical account of the good human life that does not factor in our biological nature? The answer must surely be that such an account is not possible. In a later work MacIntyre acknowledges this error and concludes, "No account of the goods, rules and virtues that are definitive of our moral life can be adequate that does not explain—or at least point us towards an explanation—how that form of life is possible for beings who are biologically constituted as we are, by providing us with an account of our development towards and into that form of life."[92]

This does not mean MacIntyre now accepts Aristotle's view whole heartedly. There are aspects he rightly still rejects but his rational account of morality must include our biological nature since it is here that we realize our vulnerability as dependent, rational animals.

Gibson relies upon Nietzsche to dispel the need for virtue, and thus a human nature, in any neo-Aristotelian sense. So how is he able to retain the framework of practices without the support of Aristotelian virtues? Nietzsche rejected science as the method for human expression. For him, art was the true form of knowledge. Gibson suggests that "the Nietzschean view of art as the true medium for understanding human existence calls for the athlete to be viewed as a performing artist, and, as such, can link a

---

91. MacIntyre, *After Virtue*, 53.

92 MacIntyre, *Dependent Rational Animals*, x.

Nietzschean individual into MacIntyre's framework of practice . . . without recourse to Aristotle."[93]

To do this he outlines two competing interpretations of Nietzsche as they apply to sport. He argues that there is a vulgar and tender reading of Nietzsche in relation to his concept of the *Übermensch*. Gibson believes MacIntyre only explores the vulgar Nietzscheanism. This interpretation sees the Nietzschean world as one in which extreme individualism and selfishness reign and where morality is nothing more than violent acts of strength by the powerful against the weak. In this case the mentality of athletes will be one where "victory in the contest is excellence, and excellence through the exercise of animal power can open many doors to power in society as a whole."[94]

This vulgar interpretation of Nietzsche attributed to MacIntyre is a brutal sporting world with no sense of moral value. There is no sportsmanship, no loyalty, and no respect. It is only about individual athletes gaining an advantage over the competition to advance their own self-interests. Contrast the vulgar Nietzscheanism with what Gibson calls the tender interpretation. According to him, this view represents more accurately what Nietzsche envisioned the Übermensch being. Gibson points out that a proper understanding of the "will-to-power" and subsequent Übermensch is power over self, not others. The result is an individual who is a "creative athlete, making his own values and transcending the arbitrary limitations of society."[95]

What Gibson describes is a Nietzschean who is able to overcome himself, to define himself in spite of the corruptive powers of institutions. Where MacIntyre sought external help in the virtues to resist corruption Gibson argues that the athlete must look inside his or her own being. With nothing upon which to base moral decisions, save oneself, the athlete must choose to overcome "arbitrary values imposed from without to create and define himself in his own terms."[96]

Three points need to be made in response to Gibson's support of the Nietzschean athlete. First, the vulgar and tender distinction does not work, particularly in attributing MacIntyre's interpretation to the vulgar side. A vulgar Nietzscheanism is something of a straw man setting up a worst-case scenario that is easily defeated by Gibson's preferred view of the tender Nietzscheanism. Gibson makes such a distinction to save elements in Nietzsche he finds favorable.

93. Gibson, *Performance versus Results*, 93.
94. Ibid., 94.
95. Ibid., 93.
96. Ibid., 96.

However, the result of tender Nietzscheanism may be equally as horrifying as the vulgar reading. The second point to make here is that Gibson's view does not alleviate the problems he sees as most pressing in contemporary sports. Working within the MacIntyrean practice scheme Gibson identifies the biggest problems in sport as the all-consuming desire to win and the overbearing emphasis on external goods such as money.

It is a bit naive to expect these problems to be conquered by encouraging Nietzschean athletes to overcome the "arbitrary values" of sporting institutions. How they are to overcome these values Gibson does not say. Presumably they would do so by rejecting the temptation to focus solely on winning and external goods. Relying on the self to withstand the magnitude of corruption Gibson describes is indeed a task for someone more than human. This might even be labeled the telos of humanity for Nietzsche since "man is something that must be overcome."[97] The revaluation of values is the goal of the Übermensch in order to create a new code of morality that is based upon the rudimentary principle of human action, the will to power. Even more basic than life itself, the will to power is the motivation in human behavior. "Every living thing does everything it can not to preserve itself but to become *more* (italics in original)."[98]

Gibson does not explain how this self-realized morality will protect the practices he seeks to apply it to from the institutions he fears. Nor is there a clear understanding of why these arbitrary values present a problem for Gibson's virtue-less theory of social practices. What remains to be seen here is a justification for the claim that the problems in sport are the result of arbitrary values and how Nietzscheanism, even a tender interpretation, is able to ward off the corruption rather than fall deeper into it.

The third response to Gibson's application of Nietzsche to practices is similar to the first in that he inaccurately ascribes the vulgar interpretation to MacIntyre's reading of Nietzsche. Nietzsche's ideas as portrayed by MacIntyre have neither a vulgar nor tender reading since such a distinction is unfounded. What MacIntyre describes is the logical outcome of the Nietzschean views Gibson himself endorses as a tender interpretation. If a rational account of morality can be justified then Nietzsche's entire project is pointless. Yet Gibson insists such an account cannot be given, at least not by MacIntyre so long as he relies on Aristotelian virtue.

Gibson builds his case for invoking Nietzsche around the notion that he is able to separate MacIntyrean practices from Aristotelian virtues. To do this he attempts to show how postmodern thinkers like Jürgen Habermas

97. Nietzsche, *Thus Spoke Zarathustra*, 23.
98. Nietzsche, *The Will to Power*, aphorism 688.

and Richard Rorty are not only addressing the same issue as MacIntyre but from within the same post-Enlightenment tradition and do so successfully without the virtues.

For the reasons listed above Gibson's approach to social practices as a separation of "good MacIntyre" from "bad MacIntyre," (i.e., practices from virtues) is wholly insufficient. If his attempt to discard the "bad MacIntyre" and fill in the pieces with Nietzsche's self-creating athlete fails, can Gibson fall back on his prior claim that Rorty (and to some extent Habermas) is ringing the same philosophical bell as MacIntyre? "The key point of agreement between the three contemporary philosophers," says Gibson, "is that we must acknowledge the contingency of our starting points, or traditions, of our temporal nature. MacIntyre agrees with Habermas that we cannot judge an act without knowing the agent's intentions and values, which are themselves contingent on traditions."[99]

Gibson points to a couple of significant common views in an effort to show how MacIntyre's framework can be kept while rejecting his dependence on Aristotle. "All three contemporary philosophers support the democratization of life and as such are all part of the Enlightenment tradition."[100] It seems curious to try and identify MacIntyre as part of a tradition he wholeheartedly rejects and with someone, namely Rorty, who holds to such a contrary philosophical outlook. Nevertheless, Gibson sees similarities between them.

> MacIntyre's concept of the narrative unity of a single life is mirrored in Rorty's work by his belief that all of our achievements are part of the unfolding of our lives, and purely temporal. To Rorty the purpose of our conversation is to keep the conversation going. It is something worthwhile in itself, a practice through which we can gain internal goods. To Habermas the goal of rational thought is to expand its realm through communicative action. For Habermas and Rorty this is a kind of telos, but for MacIntyre this is not enough. MacIntyre wants an underwriter: Aristotle.[101]

In response I will propose that Gibson's attempt to coalesce the philosophical framework's of Rorty and MacIntyre inaccurately represents certain fundamental components of their respective views. In the first instance, the two thinkers offer incommensurate epistemological accounts of truth. Secondly, as a result of this the two are embarking on entirely different

99. Gibson, *Performance versus Results*, 89.
100. Ibid.
101. Ibid.

projects. MacIntyre's, as we have seen, is to point out the failure of the En-lightenment project and call for the return of teleology to our morality as in the traditions of Aristotle and Aquinas. Rorty on the other hand believes, as we will see, that there is no telos.

Gibson's effort to integrate Rorty's and MacIntyre's methodologies is unfounded. MacIntyre's framework of practices carries with it latent assump-tions about human nature that are inextricably connected to conceptions of virtue and telos. Rorty and MacIntyre certainly share a number of ideas as Gibson has demonstrated above. However, he has failed to appreciate the fundamental discord between them. Paul Roth after seeking some synthesis between Rorty and MacIntyre has concluded that their disagreements are "not rationally decidable. Each side rests on a particular understanding of human history, and yet neither side is in a position either to establish its own case or definitively to refute its opposition."[102] Roth further summarizes that theirs is a "debate which centres on opposed conceptions of human nature, of human development, and of the good for human beings."[103]

Gibson has neglected the thickness of MacIntyre's view in erroneously reducing it to a continuation of Enlightenment rationality by finding com-mon ground with postmodern thinkers in abstract notions and then adding Aristotle. MacIntyre does not seek to supplement his post-Enlightenment philosophy with Aristotle but rather calls for a return to a pre-Enlighten-ment, teleological morality that is *something like* Aristotle. As a consequence it is incoherent to accept MacIntyre's notion of a practice and reject virtue. What remains then is a conception of sport that is developed around either MacIntyrean practices or Rortian/Nietzschean activities of self-creation, but cannot be developed around both simultaneously. Since we have already explored the MacIntyrean option let us now develop Rorty's views and see how they might apply to moral interpretations of sport.

MacIntyre or Rorty?

Rorty and MacIntyre both face the challenge of making moral judgments on other communities. However, this is only a problem from an objectivist perspective, which as we have seen fails to provide any normative value. Instead we are left with competing subjective viewpoints and what we call ethics takes up the task of sorting through each one to determine, as best as possible, the most accurate one. Taking an example from sport we can present the dilemma of commensurability of enhancement technology use.

102. Roth, "Politics and Epistemology," 189.
103. Ibid.

How will international sporting competitions work if one country allows enhancement technologies while the other does not? Do we need a world-wide prohibition or acceptance of doping? The current bans enforced by the International Olympic Committee and other international sport governing bodies explicitly affirm that sporting practices have a nature that would be violated by the use of enhancement technologies. Removing these prohibitions would result in a dramatic increase in the variety of sporting practices as each specific community would be free to pursue athletic enhancement at their own discretion. How would MacIntyre and Rorty each respond?

Inter-Communal Moral Criticism

My conclusion is that MacIntyre is in a better position to address the concern over inter-communal justification than is Rorty. Both individuals rightly stress the importance of community in formulating a system of morals, but it is MacIntyre who is able to offer something more. The MacIntyrean account of rationality I have presented here is grounded in a theory of virtue that is made sense of by a tradition-bound emphasis on the intrinsic goods of practices and the virtues required to achieve the standards of excellence. MacIntyre famously prefaced his theory by saying every moral philosophy presupposes a sociology. "For every moral philosophy offers explicitly or implicitly at least a partial conceptual analysis of the relationship of an agent to his or her reasons, motives, intentions and actions, and in so doing generally presupposes some claim that these concepts are embodied or at least can be in the real social world."[104]

Presupposing some element of truth in the justification of our community's actions also presupposes that truth, in some form, transcends our community. For MacIntyre, this transcendence is expressed through participation in practices. These practices house specific intrinsic goods that are valued by the community. This means that there are common elements of sport that transcend particular communities. The commensurability of a framework of social practices provides for inter-community dialogue and critique. Recall that, as was said in previous chapters, while particular sports have unique elements that distinguish them from other sports there remains a general sense in which an essence of sport is evident.

The intrinsic goods of sport partially constitute sport's ontological nature, a notion Rorty would wholly reject since we are to give up

104. MacIntyre, *After Virtue*, 23.

"attempts to ground some element of our practices on something external to these practices."[105]

Rorty, in attempting to remove an essence of sport, is bound by his ethnocentrism to withhold any moral judgment on the sporting practices of other communities. If there is no external nature to sport then we have no right to tell others to play the sport the way that we do, (i.e., with or without enhancements). Instead of morally criticizing others we ought to be engaged in philosophic communication with them to expand solidarity. But such a position entirely eliminates the need for any moral reflection. Moral theory has been reduced to a countless number of contingent vocabularies rather than representing or mirroring some external, objective moral truth.

Rorty would favor such an outcome since there is no ontological necessity requiring a sport to be practiced precisely as it is today. The sports being played now exist as they do because we have made them that way not because we are mirroring some Platonic form of sport. Sporting persons ought to be free to re-create themselves and their practice as they desire so long as all members of the community are in agreement on the changes made to the practice. The only conceivable way to arrive at this universal agreement is to separate sports into "enhanced" and "clean" categories but this is an undesirable situation since one or the other would surely dissipate and return us to the present discussion.

Rorty's view, like MacIntyre's, is faced with the challenge of inter-community moral critique, though I suggest it is a much more serious difficulty for Rorty. It was pointed out by McFee earlier in the chapter that normative authority of a practice is suspect for MacIntyre since only those who engage in the practice are in a position to experience its unique internal goods and thereby be judges of the skills required to participate. As a result, MacIntyre's account of practices, McFee suggested, is ill-suited to speak to the moral dimension of sport. It offers nothing more than a descriptive account of a particular activity and because judgments are restricted to the practice itself, they lack normative force. Such a criticism may be brought against Rorty's ethnocentric position as well but to a much stronger degree.

MacIntyre is able to address this issue by speaking about practices in terms of the virtues needed to achieve the standards of excellence for *any* practice. By framing the discussion around an account of virtue MacIntyre enables very different practices to engage one another with some level of commensurability. Most notably, MacIntyre points to the three virtues of justice, courage and honesty as indispensable components of every practice. Since the virtues transcend sport to encompass other social practices there is a common basis upon which to construct moral dialogue and answer McFee's criticism of community exclusive normativity.

Rorty is not afforded the same luxury even though he too encourages inter-community conversation. His approach is that of an agnostic amoralist.[106] By that I mean simply that Rorty, in his attempt to discredit truth as something objective or "out there" has succeeded only in claiming that truth cannot be empirically verified. As a result we have no non-circular method of testing our own theories and are therefore stuck with nothing more than our own *ethnos*. There remains no justification for moral pronouncements on the *ethnos* of another that is anything more than a comparison with our own.

Such a position is what Mary Midgley has labeled moral isolationism. She identifies the ultimate downfall of this view in that those who hold it are not only unable to judge the actions of others but are wholly unable to make moral pronouncements upon even themselves. "When we judge something to be bad or good, better or worse than something else, we are taking it as an example to aim at or avoid. Without opinions of this sort, we would have no framework of comparison for our own policy, no chance of profiting by other people's insights or mistakes. In this vacuum, we could form no judgments on our own actions."[107]

Rorty would have no quarrel with Midgley on this point. Midgley is contesting the position that we cannot make moral judgments against a culture we do not understand. We can, however, know enough about foreign cultures to offer blame as well as praise by contextually identifying their actions relative to the standards of our own.[108] Seeking to understand others is an idea Rorty is very comfortable with as is the suggestion that we have to understand others in our own terms. Rorty would call this our contingent vocabularies meeting in the free exchange of ideas. So while a Rortian interpretation does call for inter-community dialogue it does not offer an answer to the charge of amoralism. The anti-essentialist position suggests that such engagement over issues in sport is not, indeed cannot be, of a moral nature. A Rortian interpretation of sport sees the question of enhancements as one of preferences.

106. See Frisina, *The Unity of Knowledge and Action* for an account that denies Rorty was an amoral Nietzschean. See esp. chapters 2, 7 and 8.

107. Midgley, *Heart and Mind*, 72.

108. Ibid., 73.

Universal Sporting Practices

As we saw in the previous chapter, one could plausibly argue that every sport is affected by advances in technology. As an example we could look to the sport of golf to see its evolution due in large part to the latest technology that continues to produce better clubs, better golf balls, and so forth. The golf community agreed to alter the sport for the better by allowing their use. Biotechnology, a Rortian would argue, should be afforded the same opportunity. It is a matter of the sport's progression rather than a moral issue.

An essentialist vantage point would surely be rejected by a Rortian interpretation and welcomed by a MacIntyrean position. William Morgan, however, who has drawn on both thinkers to develop his moral theory of sport, attempts to bridge the gap by offering a mild form of Rortianism. Like Rorty, Morgan rejects an ahistorical representationalism and believes there are "no vantage points beyond the existing world that provide a privileged view of sport or of any other social practice."[109] Since there is no view from nowhere we necessarily operate from an ethnocentric perspective, a claim MacIntyre would find little to disagree with. But Morgan is not content with the implications of what he calls vulgar ethnocentrism.[110] The vulgar reading is similar to Midgley's moral isolationism in that it lacks the ability for any moral reflection. Morgan advocates an inter-subjective approach he calls reflective ethnocentrism.

> What distinguishes these two variants is that the former [vulgar] appeals to the prima facie, taken-for-granted, precritical conventions of a culture that are internalized as its dominant beliefs, whereas the latter [reflective] appeals to the deep, reflectively secured, critical norms of a culture (such as the present belief in equality and fairness) that form a background repository of beliefs that can be tapped to criticize its dominant beliefs.[111]

With this then we have come full circle back to the issue of the relationship between objective and subjective perspectives of sport. A primary facet of Morgan's alternative to vulgar ethnocentrism is that "while the rationality of sport is immanent to its social practice it is not immanent to

---

109. Morgan, *Leftist Theories of Sport*, 183.

110. Morgan undergoes scrutiny for this distinction from more committed Rortians like Terence Roberts. For an exchange on different Rortian ethnocentric positions see Roberts, "Sporting Practice Protection and Vulgar Ethnocentricity"; and Morgan, "Ethnocentrism and the Social Criticism of Sports," 83–102.

111. Morgan, *Leftist Theories of Sport*, 190.

the social systems and institutional networks in which it is situated."[112] That is, sports are not relativistic trivialities because they are not bound by the social systems in which they are practiced. Nor does he believe their value is universally applicable since there is no transcendent quality or essence. "When we prick the rational core of a practice like sport, we find not something natural, pure, inviolate, or necessary—not an essence—but something social, impure, and contingent."[113] Despite the contingency of the activity sport maintains its sense of normativity through what Morgan refers to as the gratuitous logic of sport. That is to say,

> The logic of sport binds us to formal criteria of inefficiency with respect to the means we are allowed to use to attain its ends, and normative criteria of virtuous action with respect to the just, honest, and temperate ways we are to conduct ourselves in its practice.[114]

Morgan seems correct on some level about his inter-subjective, reflective ethnocentrism but goes astray in denying sport an essence. Simon Eassom articulates a similar view but one that offers a slightly stronger emphasis on the objective dimension. He suggests, "its distinctive logic enjoys a universal standing that bubbles away beneath the surface of the socially constructed, historically located, and culturally differentiated ways in which sport is manifested throughout the world (and throughout history)."[115]

Eassom points to a couple of problems with Morgan's reliance upon a Rortian anti-foundationalist view of sport. First, Morgan denies a natural essence to sport but has not given an historical account of sport's gratuitous logic. Sport's contingent status suggests that the gratuitous logic of sport was invented. If sports are cultural universals, (i.e., the logic of sporting practices is found in every culture in the world and as such provides a common ground for moral dialogue) as Morgan believes, are other cultures able to keep *their* logic when adopting *our* sports? Such a question scarcely makes sense given that without the logic as it is the activity ceases to be the same sport. But the same or similar sports practiced around the world seem to intuitively share the same logic.

Eassom points out a major problem with a Rortian approach to sport. "Morgan wants to use the cultural universalism of sport as a bridge between different societies, but wants to do so, like Rorty, without admitting to sport

112. Ibid., 216.

113. Ibid.

114. Ibid., 227.

115. Eassom, "Sport, Solidarity, and the Expanding Circle," 92.

being in any way a product of what 'we' are as human beings."[116] But is such a venture possible? My conclusion is that Morgan's (and by extension Roberts's and Rorty's) theory fails to capture the moral significance of sport in part because it denies our human nature.

A better approach is one that embraces an essential human nature and its relationship to human activities. "The internal logic reflects a fairly open instinct within us for play that becomes structured by a rationality tied up with our very nature as beings with altruistic tendencies: tendencies that need careful nurturing and development to enable our existence as social animals."[117] Eassom continues, "the internal logic of game-playing is as reflective of our humanness as is morality, language, rationality, child-rearing, laughter, love, hatred, or any other of our capacities."[118]

A Theological Narrative

A view of sport that entirely rejects an intrinsic nature will ultimately yield to a Rortian/Nietzschean framework of radical individualism that utilizes social practices as means to self re-creation. This pursuit of private perfection comes at the expense of both the traditions and internal goods of sporting practices. Additionally, it undermines the commitment to mutual submission within community valued by the Christian tradition. MacIntyre's theory of social practices, virtues and community enables us to appreciate the significance of our humanness in relation to the intrinsic goods of certain human activities, namely sport. The essence of sport is linked directly to our human nature in that it is "a peculiarly human orientation towards the world that is as much a product of our constitution as is language."[119]

Rorty sees sport, not as a moral activity but merely an exercise in private, individual expression. With a MacIntyrean approach we can begin to see sport as a social practice that is connected to a theological tradition. Rorty's rejection of social constructs having a moral nature or essence means there is nothing intrinsically valuable about sport. Therefore it will not necessarily be corrupted by improper uses of biotechnology. A Rortian approach to sport emphasizes individualism in a system of dialectics.

MacIntyre's account is similarly sympathetic to moral dialogue between traditions though he does much more to emphasize the primacy of the community and individuals submitting to its internal authority. Community

116. Ibid., 93.
117. Ibid., 94.
118. Ibid.
119. Ibid., 93.

informs our moral understanding of the activity and in this sense is normative for all who seek to be a part of its practices. In a lot of respects the differences between Rorty and MacIntyre on the role of community are subtle but in this instance they are profound. Rorty seeks to place the desires of the individual at the core of community whereas MacIntyre's focal point is on the virtues required to achieve a practice's standards of excellence.

In applying the MacIntyrean framework to the issue of biotechnology in sport we can say in the first instance that the authority of the practice governs the rules and values contained therein. However, this does not escape the criticism of question begging explored in the previous chapter. Why does the practice have rules against enhancements in the first place? If this is how MacIntyre's practices are to be utilized in sport then surely McFee is right that practices are merely descriptive accounts of particular human activities.

Fortunately, much more can be said on behalf of MacIntyrean practices. As we saw earlier in this chapter, MacIntyre provides a normative element in practices through the role of the moral virtues. The rules against certain behavior are descriptive in the sense that they relay the values held by the community but there is a very clear and strong underlying normative force for the rules in achieving, through the virtues, the standards of excellence.

Practices also avoid question begging over the rules against enhancements in sport on the basis of the transcendent nature of virtues. Proponents of sports enhancements often use the argument to suggest a biased agenda by the governing powers of the practice. For example, in an *Intelligence Squared US* debate journalist Radley Balko argued in favor of accepting performance enhancing drugs in competitive sport. "I'd suggest it's about paternalism and it's about control. We have a full-blown moral panic on our hands here, and it's over a set of substances that, for whatever reason, has attracted the ire of the people who have made it their job to tell us what is and isn't good for us."[120]

However, arguments like this one do not speak against the nature of sport as a practice but rather reaffirm it. The paternalism Balko is referring to involves the institutions surrounding sport. As MacIntyre is careful to point out, the virtues of the practice act as safeguards against the corruptive influences of the institutions. So it becomes necessary to distinguish between the authority of the practice and the authority of the institution.

As a result, when MacIntyre states that participants are to be in submission to the authority of the practice he does not necessarily mean the institutional authority but the authority of the practice's excellence that

120. Intelligence Squared, "We Should Accept Performance-Enhancing Drugs in Competitive Sports."

can only be achieved through the virtues. Ultimately then, submitting to a practice means to be in conformity with the moral virtues, particularly justice, courage and honesty. This gets us closer to a Christian account of sport but there is more work to be done. MacIntyre has been criticized for not completing the relationship between virtue and tradition. These critics, most notably John Milbank and Stanley Hauerwas, have praised MacIntyre's rejection of Enlightenment philosophy but are skeptical of his proposed solution.[121] MacIntyre advocates a return to an Aristotelian version of the virtues, something Milbank and Hauerwas cannot accept since the Greek virtues are built upon "a fundamentally heroic image that has no telos other than conflict."[122] Instead, they propose we develop an understanding of virtue from our own tradition of Christianity. Virtue will look different to the Christian than it does to the pagan.

The objective view discussed at the onset of this chapter cannot make such a claim. Its task is to identify a common account of virtue recognized without the bias of a particular narrative. However, as we have seen in this chapter the objectivity view is a failed attempt to universalize values in a framework void of subjective experience. Rorty is right to suggest a community based foundation to values but goes too far in two major respects; namely by placing too much emphasis on individualism within one's own community, (i.e., it is more about the self than the tradition one comes from), and by dividing values, particularly moral values, into public and private spheres.

MacIntyre also begins with a community approach but rather than celebrating the individual, he balances the two by both allowing the individual to flourish and submitting the individual to the authority of the tradition. It is this third philosophical framework that most closely identifies with the present task of gaining a theological understanding of sport. Of the three views discussed here MacIntyre best provides a suitable foundation for viewing sport in light of Christian revelation but as we have said Christians must push his theory further by reorienting our understanding of virtue in a way that is consistent with Christian claims.

A Christian theological tradition that is based in the Scriptures submits the individual to the authority of the community that is founded upon one person, Jesus Christ; believing that he is the Son of God and "all things were created through him and for him."[123] Therefore, every aspect

---

121. Milbank, *Theology and Social Theory*; and Hauerwas and Pinches, *Christians among the Virtues*.

122. Hauerwas and Pinches, *Christians among the Virtues*, 63.

123. Col 1:16.

of the lives of His followers rightly falls under His authority. Paul writes concerning Jesus,

> He is the head of the body, the church. He is the beginning, the firstborn from the dead, that in everything he might be preeminent. For in him all the fullness of God was pleased to dwell, and through him to reconcile to himself all things, whether on earth or in heaven, making peace by the blood of his cross.[124]

Becoming a member of this community called Christianity involves recognizing Christ's glory as superior to one's own. In accepting this claim, Christians place themselves firmly in the grasp of a theological narrative that gives complete jurisdiction to Jesus of Nazareth. As a result, the convictions of those operating within a Christian narrative ought to have an understanding of all activities, including sport, which is unique from other communities.

124. Col 1:18–20.

---- 3 ----

Three Views of Sport
Adopted by the Church

A Critical Assessment

Introduction

IN THE PREVIOUS CHAPTER it was established that value systems must necessarily include a subjective viewpoint. We are now ready to explore the
value placed on sport from within a particular tradition. Not surprisingly,
the Christian tradition itself has seen a variety of positions and continues to
develop its views on sport. In exploring some of these traditional views we
will be in a position to see that the common attitudes toward sport adopted
by Christians throughout history have not typically corresponded to the
account of social practices defended in the previous chapter. In fact, I will
argue that the Church has, perhaps unknowingly, more frequently viewed
sport from a Rortian view than from that of MacIntyre.

There is no doubt that a large percentage of Christians feel perfectly
at home in the sports world. Over the last century the church has focused
much of its energy and resources in the realm of sport. Several Christian
ministries have risen up in the last half century, including one of the largest Christian ministries in any context, the Fellowship of Christian Athletes
(FCA), which has seen significant growth since its beginning in 1954. Today, the sports-oriented ministry can be found on more college campuses in
the United States than the next three campus ministries combined.[1]

---

1. Fellowship of Christian Athletes, "Beginner's Guide to FCA."

Local churches are rapidly building sports complexes for their congregations. Several Christian universities in the United States and elsewhere carry undergraduate degrees and some even offer graduate degrees in sports ministry.[2] It is not uncommon to hear sermons from pastors that are full of sports analogies or to see worship services cancelled or rescheduled on account of a major sporting event such as the Super Bowl. There is even a sports devotional Bible filled with daily messages "designed to drive home the lessons of Scripture with inspiring stories from all corners of the world of sports."[3]

Yet only in the last couple of hundred years have Christians become so openly fixated on sport. Historically the church has had a slightly negligent attitude toward them. The sparse references to sport in historical Christian literature are often found in the more general topic of leisure or games. While lacking systematic qualities and theological clarity these references provide enough details to trace the progression of ideas in relation to sport and leisure. As we will see, different historical periods and theological influences have offered diverse opinions on the role of sport. Many doctrines of the Christian faith have been interpreted differently throughout history. Still, one observation that makes sport unique is that for a topic with notably insufficient theological reflection it has been approached with such opposing viewpoints. In other words, for an issue apparently unworthy of the church's intellectual attention it has produced some very strong and polarizing views.

This sundry history includes the view that sport is sinful on one extreme and the view that sport is the purpose of life on the other extreme.[4] The objective here is to show that these assorted views offer an interesting and informative starting point for how Christians might inform their present assumptions about sport, its significance for the Christian life, and what values should govern our participation in it.

While a chronological progression of these views may be discernible, I am going to propose my own categorical account that offers a more synthetic way to see how Christians have historically understood sport and leisure. There are three prominent views I wish to address. They are what I will call the insignificant view, the idleness view, and the instrumental view. All three

2. Malone University in Canton, Ohio, currently offers a Master's degree in Christian Leadership in Sports Ministry.

3. Branon, *Sports Devotional Bible*.

4. A detailed historical account of the relationship between sport and religion is beyond the scope of this work. See Hoffman, *Good Game*; and Baker, *Playing with God*. Higgs presents a thorough history that is distinctly American in his book, *God in the Stadium*.

are apparent in different periods of church history and an outline of the major tenets of these views will serve us well in identifying a contextual basis for a theology of sport that is closely aligned with the concept of play developed in a later chapter. In developing these historical elements in this manner I hope to avoid the criticism of Christian sports fans offered by Robert Johnston that "rather than ground their discussion in biblical reflection and careful observation of play itself, Christians have most often been content to allow Western culture to shape their understanding of the human at play."[5]

Sporting Imagery in the Writings of Paul

Any Christian who is a sport enthusiast will be able to quickly point to a handful of verses in the Bible that make references to sport. The most common of these is penned by the apostle Paul in 1 Corinthians 9:24–27.

> Do you not know that in a race all the runners compete, but only one receives the prize? So run that you may obtain it. Every athlete exercises self-control in all things. They do it to receive a perishable wreath, but we an imperishable. So I do not run aimlessly; I do not box as one beating the air. But I discipline my body and keep it under control, lest after preaching to others I myself should be disqualified.[6]

The parallels between sport and the Christian life are evident in this passage and it is at once clear why he chose athletics as his metaphor. The ideas of training practices, discipline, and goal-oriented attitudes used by athletes are easily applied to Christian devotion. It also was a metaphor that his audience certainly would be familiar with since Corinth had been the host city of the Isthmian Games for more than five hundred years by the time Paul wrote these words.

Yet it was not only the Corinthians to whom Paul would use athletic metaphors. A number of other New Testament passages exist that refer to athletics in some fashion, most of which come from Paul. This has caused some speculation about Paul's experience with the Greek games, as Stuart Weir points out. "Because of Paul's insights into sporting matters and his use of sporting jargon, some writers have speculated as to whether he might have received some sport coaching, participated in the games or at least been a spectator at them."[7]

5. Johnston, *The Christian at Play*, 83.

6. 1 Cor 9:24–27.

7. Weir, *What the Book Says about Sport*, 17.

One such suggestion comes from historian Harold Harris. He puts forward the possibility that Paul was "a devotee" of the games and therefore they "escaped condemnation by the Church."[8] He points out that many early Christian leaders followed Paul's lead and took advantage of the sporting language as illustrations for the Christian life. However, such speculation is unlikely when one more closely inspects Paul's language and the historical context in which he was writing. The games were such an integral part of ancient Greek society that sporting language would have been common coinage. Victor Pfitzner, in his important work on the ancient Greek *agôn* tradition, says,

> The Pauline metaphors from the sphere of the games are so general in their lack of concrete details that it is not hard to imagine that any Hellenistic Jew could have either written or understood them without himself having gained a first hand knowledge of the games from a bench in the stadium.[9]

This idea becomes more plausible when one thinks about the sporting language used today in non-athletic contexts. One can understand the phrase "par for the course" to mean "average" without having a working knowledge of the way in which golf is scored. Being "in a pickle" or a "sticky wicket" are phrases from baseball and cricket, respectively, commonly understood to mean someone is in a rather difficult situation. A great many other sporting phrases have been adapted to common language thus taking them away from their original sporting context. In fact, more than two thousand sports metaphors have been documented.[10]

Pfitzner suggests that Paul may have been in a similar situation. "We may accept this verdict if it is limited to the adoption of an image and terminology that had become popularized in Paul's day, but not if it also extends to the adoption of its content and application as well."[11]

The appearance of athletic imagery in Paul's writings is not enough evidence to imply Paul's participation in or even approval of the Greek games. In fact, Paul certainly would have opposed many of the practices associated with athletic contests. Shirl Hoffman concurs: "the pagan religious ceremonies that were an integral part of the contests, and the sharp contrasts between the ethos of the competitions and Paul's exhortation to

8. Harris, *Sport in Greece and Rome*, 227.

9. Pfitzner, *Paul and the Agon Motif*, 187.

10. Palmatier and Ray, *Dictionary of Sports Idioms*.

11. Ibid., 188.

the spiritual life, make it quite likely that he shared the largely negative views of influential church leaders who followed in his wake."[12]

Indeed, the church leaders over the next several centuries were adamantly opposed to athletic contests. One reason may be traced to the point at which Paul terminates the sporting metaphor. He separates athletes from Christians by using a "they/we" contrast. The athletes (they) compete for a perishable crown. The Christians (we) "compete" for an imperishable. This led to an apathetic attitude towards sport that turned critical under monastic influence.

Sport as Insignificant

The passion many present-day Christians share for sports is profound. However, Christianity has had relatively little to say about sport throughout history. This may come as a surprise to us in twenty-first century Western society. Sport and leisure have become staples of both modern society and the church. It is reasonable then to assume that such an important activity in the lives of millions of people would also be an important issue in Christian thought. Yet, sport has not always held the overwhelming status it now enjoys and perhaps as a result has not always been an obvious target for significant theological reflection.

Two points are worth noting about this view. First, the idea that sport is theologically insignificant seems to be an underlying attitude expressed in the other two views. Therefore the ideas typically overlap and to state them here as well would be redundant. Secondly, I mention the attitude of sport's insignificance if for nothing else than to point out an area where the church can concentrate more serious theological thought. It is unfortunate that the church has neglected an issue so important in society.

Augustine is one of the earliest to adopt an apathetic stance. He lists his brief complaint against sport in *the Confessions* when he says,

> I no longer go to the Games to see a dog coursing a hare; but if I happen to be going through the country and see this sport going on, it may attract my attention away from some serious meditation—not so much as to make me turn my horse's body out of the way, but enough to alter the inclination of my mind. And unless you showed me my infirmity and quickly admonished me either by some thought connected with the sight itself to rise

---

12. Hoffman, *Good Game*, 44.

up toward you, or else to pay no attention to the thing at all and
to pass by, I should stand there empty-headed like a stock.[13]

For Augustine, the problem with sport lies in the distraction it creates
from the more important work to be done by the Christian, namely "serious
meditation." He stopped attending the games in order to focus on obtaining
what Paul described as an "imperishable wreath." His view suggests that
sport lacks any soteriological or sanctifying qualities and is therefore not
significant enough to merit even the briefest of thoughts. It is a distraction
from the loftier demands of the Christian faith.

It is reasonable to assume that if the early church thought sport had
any theological significance they would have written about it. Instead, the
overwhelming themes of pagan worship and immoral behavior preoccupied any discussion of games. In the minds of the early church leaders these
prevailing themes were so entrenched in public sports that they could not
separate the idolatry from the games. As a result, they threw out the baby
with the bath water, denying any attention to the intrinsic value of sport.

The consensus in this view is that sport lacks any sort of eternal value
and therefore is not worth Christians paying it any attention. There is an implicit denial that sport has a fundamental purpose, or essence, given by God.
It is simply a humanly constructed activity that will ultimately distract the
Christian from attaining his or her higher calling. In this respect Christians
are more closely aligned to the Rortian view of sport that sees no inherent
value in sporting activity.

As we will see in a moment other periods in the history of the church
have adopted similar stances where they are unable to view sport separated
from either the questionable practices surrounding the activity or the external benefits gained. This has left a vast opening in theological discourse
over a topic whose importance continues to grow in society. For that matter,
sport's importance continues to grow within the church and there still is
relatively little thought devoted to Christian theological reflection on sport.

The absence of Christian voices in the world of sport is astounding.
Shirl Hoffman poignantly addresses the "deafening silence" of the evangelical community by stating that it has been "eager to lead the charge in the culture wars but has remained largely uncurious about sports."[14] He continues,
"Christians frequently voice criticism about the violence in video games,
but the violence of sports such as football and hockey, which involves their
children more intimately and dangerously, rarely is questioned."[15]

13. Augustine, *Confessions of Saint Augustine*, X. 35, 241–42.

14. Hoffman, *Good Game*, 11.

15. Ibid., 11.

Surely Hoffman is correct to point out the blind eye of the contemporary Christian community. Christians are quick to condemn the violence produced in Hollywood then unquestioningly cheer for their favorite Mixed Martial Arts fighter as he bloodies the face of whoever will challenge him.[16] But Christians have not always been so swift to accept sports. In addition to seeing it as insignificant the church has traditionally taken the negative attitude that sports are immoral or the neutral attitude that says sports are instrumental and best used to serve some other purpose.

Sport as Immoral

Idolatry and Immoral Behavior

Condemning all forms of games as gruesome, immoral, and idolatrous, Christians were among the most outspoken critics of Roman and Greek games. As a means of strengthening their case writers offered specific details of the grotesque events to demonstrate how bad they were. In writing about the textual evidence of Roman spectacles sport historian Donald Kyle notes that "ironically, some of the most valuable evidence comes from Christian authors, who wrote highly charged polemics, apologies, and martyrologies in which they, as outsiders, condemned Rome's games as idolatrous rites they could not enjoy or abide."[17]

The foremost of these Christian texts is undoubtedly Tertullian's treatise *De Spectaculis*.[18] This short work is the harshest assessment of sport in early Christendom, though he does not restrict his criticism to athletic contests. He condemns all forms of theatre, games, and spectacles (hereafter summarized by "games"). Tertullian was initially concerned with the games' pagan origins. Of athletic competition he asserts that the "whole equipment of these contests is stained with idolatry" and that all behavior associated with the games is "incompatible with moral discipline." [19]

For Tertullian, the games were thoroughly anti-Christian though it was not only the pagan rituals that drew his criticism. In fact, roughly half

16. I am aware that sports like boxing and MMA are not the same in all respects as violent video games and movies but they do promote images of violence that are powerful enough to influence others toward violence especially when the athletes are cheered and adored for their violent behavior. Furthermore, I will argue in chapter five that Christians should be concerned about the injury risks of these sports.

17. Kyle, *Sport and Spectacle in the Ancient World*, 14.

18. For more cultural and historical insights on the whole of Tertullian's *De Spectaculis*, see Sider, *Christian and Pagan in the Roman Empire*, 80–106.

19. Tertullian, *De Spectaculis*, 263, 271.

of his treatise focuses on the immoral behavior surrounding the games. He begins by condemning games because of their pagan ritual origins and having found sufficient reason to reject them on these grounds alone he spends the second half offering a more impassioned moral criticism. Little more is said about the idolatry of the games, possibly because he felt he had exhausted the argument.[20]

A more likely explanation is that he was eager to begin addressing the more immediate problems with games. Even though they had pagan origins both Roman and Greek athletic contests had become largely secularized. Allen Guttman suggests "whatever religious significance remained was apparently overshadowed in the eyes of the mob accustomed to bread and circuses and blood."[21]

Tertullian did not believe the pagan origins would be enough to convince his Christian audience to avoid the games. Now he sets about the task of showing why the behavior of the games is inappropriate for followers of Christ. Even if the idolatry is no longer present (an idea Tertullian clearly did not accept) there are still many reasons for Christians to abstain from the games.

It is commonly assumed that Roman games consisted of gladiatorial contests where participants fiercely battled to the death while the Greek games were civilized, highly competitive contests that honored physical abilities. Kyle points out the stereotype that "Greek sport elevated but Roman spectacles debased human nature" held some truth but it would be more accurate to allow for each to have a significant amount of influence on the other.[22] Regardless of their distinctive natures, both Greek and Roman games were extremely popular in Tertullian's time.

Apparently they were popular among Christians as well thus explaining why Tertullian needed to write this treatise in the first place. He did not single out specific games or themes but considered all of them anathema and attempted to show why Christians should share his view. "You can never be pleased with injurious or useless displays of strength, nor with the care that develops an unnatural frame (outdoing God's handiwork). You will hate the type of man bred to amuse the idleness of Greece."[23]

---

20. Tertullian outlines five specific areas in which the games involve idolatry. Having dealt with the origins, names, equipment, places, and arts he states in chapter XIII that "enough has been said" to prove their relationship with idolatry. From here he begins his attack on the immorality of the games.

21. Guttman, *From Ritual to Record*, 24.

22. Kyle, *Sport and Spectacle*, 19.

23. Tertullian, *De Spectaculis*, 277.

Still, even after the heavy criticism of athletic contests by early church leaders like Augustine and Tertullian one might ask why, if the games are to be wholly rejected by Christians, would Paul use athletic imagery in the sacred scriptures? Stuart Weir's response is to suggest that, "if indeed sport is evil, it is surprising that the Holy Spirit, who inspired the scriptures, did not lead the writers to omit the sporting metaphors or indeed to warn their readers of the dangers of having anything to do with the games."[24] Weir makes an interesting point though it is imprudent to make an argument from omission. Holy Scripture can surely speak to the people in their social setting utilizing metaphors they would understand without necessarily condoning or condemning the actions found in the literary device. It is pure speculation to suggest reasons why the Holy Spirit would exclude further articulation of a point, aside from the questions it begs about the nature of the divine inspiration of Scripture.

Pfitzner is more helpful in pointing once again to the distinction between *image* and *content*. He answers,

> The image suggested itself not only as an illustration already popularized, but also as the most suitable since the conditions under which the athlete contested also applied, in a transferred sense, to the athlete of the Gospel. In no other image, not even in that of the soldier, was there such a wealth of parallels.[25]

This seems to conflict with the strongly anti-sport ideology of Tertullian who boldly states "it is above all things from this that they understand a man to have become a Christian, that he will have nothing more to do with games!"[26] To be sure, he was aware of Paul's use of athletic imagery but it does not stop him from condemning the games. "But if you urge that the stadium is mentioned in the Scriptures, so much I concede you. But the things done in the stadium—you will not deny that they are unfit for you to see."[27] To accept any part of the games is to accept that which comes from the devil. Tertullian further explains that the games "one and all were instituted for the devil's sake, and equipped from the devil's store (for the devil owns everything that is not God's or does not please God)."[28]

Is this strong language justified? Certainly Christian morality would condemn the pagan rituals, sexual promiscuity, and brutal violence of the

---

24. Weir, *What the Book Says about Sport*, 29.
25. Pfitzner, *Paul and the Agon Motif*, 193.
26. Tertullian, *De Spectaculis*, 289.
27. Ibid., 277.
28. Ibid., 289.

games, but is it fair to claim that all games do not please God and therefore come from the devil? Or did Tertullian, and perhaps Augustine, go too far in their dismissive and fervently antagonistic view of games? Is there something valuable in games that they missed?

It is doubtful that either of them saw inherent value in games since neither one gives much attention to games in their own right. Based on the few excerpts pertaining to games it is likely that they did not conceive of them in this way. Augustine rather flippantly dismisses them as distractions while Tertullian focuses primarily on the pagan affiliations and immoral actions surrounding the games rather than the games themselves. This adds credibility to the idea that they had dismissive attitudes toward sport.

Yet, Tertullian does allude to the possibility of certain activities being created with a godly purpose but corrupted by games. He says, "Equestrian skill was a simple thing in the past, mere horseback riding; in any case there was no guilt in the ordinary use of the horse. But when the horse was brought into the games, it passed from being God's gift into the service of demons."[29]

He does not elaborate as to whether he means the "ordinary use of the horse" to be for work or for leisure but given his sharp criticism of idle pleasures in the opening paragraphs, the most likely assumption is that Tertullian saw the purpose of the horse as a means for human beings to accomplish godly tasks rather than the mere enjoyment of horseback riding. Therefore, it is doubtful that he had leisurely activity in mind, further reinforcing the notion that early Christian leaders considered leisure insignificant and unworthy of theological discourse in its own right.

On the other hand, we find in Augustine a glimpse of value in leisure. He offers a brief comment on play in his short work on music. "I pray thee, spare thyself at times: for it becomes a wise man sometimes to relax the high pressure of his attention to work."[30]

Still, there is not much sympathy for leisure in the mind of Augustine. Leisure was a necessary evil that must be fought against continually. He illustrates this in his own struggle with eating and drinking. They are required to rejuvenate the body but it becomes sinful when one finds the activity pleasurable. He considered himself "at war" with this pleasure and strove to eliminate the pleasure of food so as not to become its slave. He attempted to make eating an emotionless activity. Just as there is nothing pleasurable about taking medicine, there too should be no pleasure in eating.[31]

---

29. Ibid., 255.

30. Augustine, *De Musica*, ii. 15, 4.

31. Augustine, *Confessions* X 31, 232–35.

It is in this context that Augustine makes his mention of games, only a few pages later in the same chapter of the *Confessions*. It is likely then that while he did recognize the necessity of relaxing from work, such relaxation should not be pleasurable. This pleasure would then become a threat to one's more important task of meditating on God.

Moreover, Tertullian offers an argument similar to Augustine's when he asks, "Do you think that, seated where there is nothing of God, he will at that moment turn his thoughts to God?"[32] The answer, for Tertullian, is clearly no. There is nothing for the Christian to gain by attending the games. Indeed, it is the mark of Christians that they no longer go to the games.

The Idleness of Mirth

Despite the best efforts of Christian leaders like Tertullian, Christianity became more and more accepting of sport, though it may be inaccurate to view the ascetic campaign as a complete failure. At the very least its proponents were successful in making it obvious to the laity that the practices surrounding the games were unfitting for the Christian. As a result, over the centuries Christians came to adopt many of the games into their own religious celebrations. While this may not have been the outcome men like Tertullian had envisioned, it is reasonable to suggest they were instrumental in bringing about the heavy involvement they sought to eliminate since the condemnation of immoral behavior served to reinforce the idea that if Christians want to play it must be on their own terms. No doubt games would have found their way into the life of the church anyway. Nor were the games adopted *in spite of* monastic opposition. Rather, since critics had little to say against sport as such, there was no substantial opposition to Christian versions of sport. As was the case in many of the pagan religions, games became foundational to a number of Christian religious festivals.[33]

However, by the time of the Protestant Reformation there was renewed vigor in some Christian circles to completely eliminate games from the lives of their faith's practitioners. Though key reformers, such as Luther and Calvin, were advocates of an instrumental view of sport and offered very few writings on the value of games, they sparked the next wave of "anti-sport" Christian thought that would become a prevalent attitude for the better part of the nineteenth and twentieth centuries.

32. Tertullian, *De Spectaculis*, 289.

33. It is questionable whether Tertullian and Augustine would have been likely to support Christian versions, even those done as part of a Christian celebration or festival since, as we have said, they were unable to separate pagan sin from the games.

In distancing themselves from the Catholic Church, Protestants also succeeded in reviving the animosity between their religion and sport. Just as many early Christians rejected all forms of games for their pagan affiliations, many Protestants, with their anti-Catholic sentiment, cast away all games associated with the Catholic festivals. The Protestant opposition to sport began as a statement against the Catholic Church but soon came to be perceived as an individual spiritual cleansing. On the Protestant view, not only were they tainted by the Catholics but the games themselves were a sinful waste of time. Christians had far more important matters to attend to than playing games, even if those games were in celebration of God's goodness.

The Protestant movement away from frivolity to a life of work was discussed at length in Max Weber's influential work, *The Protestant Ethic and the Spirit of Capitalism*.[34] Many of Weber's suggestions have been sources of intense debate but there are two key ideas relevant to our present topic.[35] First, the Calvinists Weber studied believed that a healthy commitment to work provided evidence of salvation. Their interest in work was not primarily for the financial gain, though they were pioneers in the idea that Christians could, in morally appropriate ways, seek the accumulation of wealth in good conscience. This was permissible so long as one's wealth came from honest labor with the motivation to glorify God. Instead, the powerful work ethic developed within their capitalist society found its inspiration in the freedom to pursue work of heavenly value.

While there has been much debate over whether or not Weber implied that Protestants are somehow the chief architects of capitalism, one thing is clear. Protestantism reasoned out a work ethic that flourished during that particular stage of modern capitalism's development. McGrath summarizes Weber's modern capitalism as, "rational, possessing a strong ethical basis."[36]

This ethical basis, Weber says, comes from a religious motivation to do good works. In talking about the ascetic views of Calvinism he focuses on the evidences of salvation. God's elect are only known by a life spent doing works that bring glory to God. Weber identifies this as a motive from fear to work hard. Christians are to engage in hard labor not to earn salvation but to prove it. "In order to attain that self-confidence intense worldly activity is recommended as the most suitable means. It and it alone disperses religious doubts and gives the certainty of grace."[37] It may be argued that Weber

34. Weber, *The Protestant Ethic and the Spirit of Capitalism*.

35. For theological discussions of Weber, see Ryken, *Worldly Saints*, 23–38, 57–72; McGrath, *A Life of John Calvin*, 219–46; Hudson, "The Weber Thesis Reexamined"; Milbank, *Theology and Social Theory*.

36. McGrath, *A Life of John Calvin*, 223.

37. Weber, *Protestant Ethic*, 83–84.

has misunderstood Calvinism on this point or at least failed to capture an alternative motive in doing good works. Not all Calvinists would agree that good works ought to be done to prove one's salvation. Rather, because of one's salvation there exists a genuine desire to do good works. In addition to strengthening their assurance of salvation the Westminster Confession states that Christians "manifest their thankfulness" by doing good works in obedience to God's commandments.[38] Whatever the motivation, Weber is correct in pointing to the Protestant emphasis on being productive.

In fact, a strong work ethic was a defining characteristic of Puritans. Their Creator and Savior demanded a life of worship and service, both of which were intrinsically tied to laboring in one's vocation. Time spent relaxing when one should be working was perceived as a direct disregard for the Christian's duty. It also ran contrary to numerous passages that underline the role work has in the life of believers. Dozens of references in Proverbs to the blessings of hard work versus the destruction of the lazy were often cited as were many of the New Testament scriptures warning against idleness, such as these words from Paul:

> Now we command you, brothers, in the name of our Lord Jesus Christ, that you keep away from any brother who is walking in idleness and not in accord with the tradition that you received from us. For you yourselves know how you ought to imitate us, because we were not idle when we were with you, nor did we eat anyone's bread without paying for it, but with toil and labour we worked night and day, that we might not be a burden to any of you. It was not because we do not have that right, but to give you in ourselves an example to imitate. For even when we were with you, we would give you this command: If anyone is not willing to work, let him not eat.[39]

Spending time playing was something non-Christians did. Laboring night and day is the example set in both the Old and New Testament scriptures for Christians. Ignoring this example had serious consequences in the eyes of the Calvinist community. Though specific writings on sport were few, several Puritan leaders were rather outspoken against idleness more generally. One of the most articulate detractors of idleness was Richard Baxter. On several occasions in his massive volume, *A Christian Directory*, he warns against sinful indolence. Particularly in reference to sport he says, "all sports are unlawful which take up any part of the time which we should spend in

---

38. Center for Reformed Theology and Apologetics, "Westminster Confession, Chapter XVI 'Of Good Works.'"

39. 2 Thess 3:6–10.

greater works . . . and all those that take up more time than the end of a
recreation doth necessarily require."[40] More generally he attacks the sin of
idleness when he says, "The rich he [the tempter] tempteth to an idle, time-
wasting, voluptuous, fleshly, brutish life; to excess in sleep, and meat, and
drink, and sport, and apparel . . . to waste their time in unprofitableness."[41]

Again, something more like the Rortian view than the MacIntyrean
view is evident in this approach to sport. Rather than seeing sport as a social
activity with internal goods, the pursuit of which develop moral virtues, the
immoral view sees it as a quest of individual desires that promote all man-
ners of sinful behavior.

However, Baxter's statements present an opportunity to clarify a
point about the unfortunate stereotype placed upon him and other Puritan
leaders. These statements are not an unqualified condemnation of these
activities. In fact, they are statements that exclude the possibility of these
activities being inherently sinful. While it is too presumptuous to say Baxter
is implying that it is no more possible to prohibit sport than it is to prohibit
sleep, it is clear from these assertions that he is allowing for the possibility
of sport being a morally appropriate activity. This provides a foundation
for Baxter to articulate what sports he believes to be acceptable (when they
meet highly specified standards) and sports that are never acceptable for
Christians to engage in.

The idea that Satan would tempt us to pursue these things in *excess*
suggests Baxter saw a proper role for leisure. Otherwise, he would have
condemned these activities unequivocally. Furthermore, he is not singling
out any of these items specifically as the context of this section is against
the wealthy wasting their time doing only these things rather than by, say,
helping the poor or serving God with their talents. Baxter was indeed critical of those who took sport too seriously. "You would little think that they
are speaking to the most holy God, for no less than the saving of their souls,
when they are more serious in their very games and sports."[42] Taking such
a serious attitude toward leisure is, for Baxter, nothing short of idolatry.
Clearly Baxter and other like-minded Christians recognized these activities as a potential area for temptation to sin but the manner in which they
criticize leisure suggests their quarrel lies in its improper use rather than
in using it at all.

Using the blessings of God to serve others rather than wasting them
selfishly is a constant theme in Puritan writings but has had the misfortune

40. Baxter, *The Practical Works of Richard Baxter*, 387.

41. Ibid., 278.

42. Ibid., 546.

of being interpreted as a prudish rejection of all things fun. This perception, says Puritan scholar Leland Ryken, is misinformed. The condemnation of leisure found in many Puritan writings when understood in context suggests their problem was not with sport and other leisurely activities, per se. Rather, "the statements of the Puritans occur chiefly in contexts where they are talking about the aristocratic classes who did not work for a living, monks who retired from the world, and the Catholic proliferation of religious holy days."[43]

True, they universally condemned some leisurely activities as unsuitable for a servant of Christ. They also prohibited participation in any sport on Sundays. One will also find a perpetual emphasis on seriousness, but to say Puritans were categorically against sport and leisure is misleading and untrue. Many found sport and other leisure events rather enjoyable and valued such activities as an important resource in the Christian life. However, this enjoyment was always to be restrained to its proper function so as not to lead to either idleness or idolatry. It is this warning that is so frequently cited in current discussions of Puritan attitudes toward leisure.

Another aspect to the Puritan stereotype that may give us more clarity on the issue is presented by historian Bruce Daniels. He poses the question of whether or not there may have been some discrepancy between what we have in the recorded writings of the Puritan leaders and the actual practice of everyday Puritans. He asks, "was there a divergence between the rhetoric expressed in literary evidence, and the reality reflected in the daily living habits of the general public?"[44] Indeed, it is my own assumption that the amount of literature and sermons by the articulate Puritan leaders suggests this discrepancy to be the case. If the Puritan community agreed whole heartedly with these critics of mirth then it hardly seems necessary for the leaders to continually plead their case.[45] On the other hand, it may be reasonably estimated that these outspoken critics saw many leisurely activities as a constant threat to their ideal standard of Christian living and in this case were "preaching to the choir."

43. Ryken, "The Puritan Ethic and Christian Leisure for Today," 35.

44. Daniels, *Puritans at Play: Leisure and Recreation in Colonial New England*, 10. Moreover, there were certainly discrepancies not only between clergy and laypersons but also between geographical groups of Protestants. For example, New England puritans were notoriously more rigid than their counterparts in the southern United States.

45. Perhaps they would be persistent if their targeted audience was non–believers, but it seems that the vast majority of these treatises are aimed at the sanctification of the believer and helping them avoid sinful behavior rather than offering evangelistic messages to non–believers.

In either case, the Puritan leaders' words were widespread enough to brand the majority of sixteenth to eighteenth century British and American Protestants as having a strongly negative view of sport and leisure. But as we have already pointed out, this notion is somewhat misleading. As Ryken again points out, "although the Puritans failed to grant sufficient credence at a theoretical level to the non-utilitarian side of life, in practice they valued their non-working hours more than we (or they) might think if we listened only to their pronouncements."[46] Even the most vocal opponents of many leisurely activities accepted some sports as instrumental to the Christian life. But their ideas about the usefulness of sport did not originate within the Puritan movement. To be sure, traces of instrumentalism can be found throughout the history of the church but we need to return to Aquinas in the thirteenth century who paved the way for a more robust account of sport's usefulness.

Sport as Instrumental

The pleas by early monastics for Christians to withdraw from the games continued and a number of Roman emperors who had converted to Christianity played an important role in dismantling the games. Two of the more significant events were the banning of the gladiatorial games by Constantine in 325 and the Olympics by Theodosius in 393. Both emperors were Christian but it would be inaccurate to suggest the Christian religion was solely responsible for ending all the games. Economic and cultural factors played their respective roles as well. There is evidence to suggest that even after their prohibition the games continued in some form or fashion well into the fifth century, often times in Christian cities and with Christian participants.[47]

While the Greco-Roman games came to an end sport never did. It merely took on other forms and actually gained in popularity among Christians. Theologians and clergy throughout the Middle Ages differed greatly on what role leisure should play in the Christian life. The church wanted to allow individual Christians the opportunity to be involved in games but without exposing them to the immoral behavior that seemed to follow large scale sporting events. This led to the church condemning the tournaments and hosting their own festivals. Leisure became an "integral part of medieval church life" as the church courtyards "provided some of the best places to play games."[48]

46. Ryken, "The Puritan Ethic," 43.

47. See, Kyle, *Sport and Spectacle*, 346; and Harris, *Sport in Greece and Rome*, 237. See also Hoffman, *Good Game*, 60.

48. Hoffman, *Good Game*, 61.

The Utility of Play

As the church became accustomed to participating in sporting events a theological problem ensued.

> One of the sticking points that prevented large-scale Christian ecclesiastical endorsement of sport was the seeming incompatibility between Christian teaching on the need for believers to be good stewards of their time (a godly gift) and carving out blocks of time to engage in what was considered largely frivolous activity.[49]

Aquinas offers a solution to this problem. He sees the merits of play and says, "Just as man needs bodily rest for the body's refreshment, because he cannot always be at work, since his power is finite and equal to a certain fixed amount of labour, so too is it with his soul, whose power is also finite and equal to a fixed amount of work."[50]

He did not share the ascetic views of Augustine and Tertullian. Leisure was, according to reason, a desirable thing. Just as the body is made for physical labor the mind is made for the labor of contemplation. In fact, since contemplation was a loftier goal than physical labor, the weariness of the mind would surpass the weariness of the body. If the body is wearied by its physical work, Aquinas reasons, how much more so will the soul be wearied when it is "intensely occupied with the works of reason?"[51]

For Aquinas, "the remedy for weariness of soul must needs consist in the application of some pleasure, by slackening the tension of the reason's study."[52] He clarifies this pleasure he refers to as "words or deeds wherein nothing further is sought than the soul's delight."[53]

Aquinas relies heavily on Aristotle in that he describes play as an autotelic activity. Aristotle says that play, or "pleasant amusements," seem to be choice-worthy activities in their own right rather than necessary for some other end.[54] It is also true, according to Aristotle, that in order for an action to be virtuous it must be aimed at some other end beyond the action itself. Furthermore, he believed "the happy life seems to be a life in accord with virtue, which is a life involving serious actions, and not consisting in

49. Ibid., 64.
50. Aquinas, *Summa Theologica*, II–II, 168, 2.
51. Ibid.
52. Ibid.
53. Ibid.
54. Aristotle, *Nicomachean Ethics*, X. 6, 162.

amusement."[55] If this be the case are we to conclude that games, which have no end but themselves, cannot be virtuous?

On the contrary, since relaxation of the soul is in accordance with reason Aquinas considers play to be an acceptable activity. He does so with a couple of stipulations. The pleasure "should not be sought in indecent or injurious deeds or words" and must be done in moderation so as not to become all-consuming.[56] When these words of caution are followed, Aquinas believed there could be virtue in games and play. In fact, he goes on to explain that both excessiveness and deficiency in playful actions are sinful. This is in accord with Aristotle's idea that the virtuous life is not spent in amusement. There is room for leisure, of course, but a life consumed by it cannot be a truly happy life. Christian thinkers like Aquinas and the Puritans would agree. A life of idleness cannot be a life pleasing to God.

This reinforced the attitude of acceptance of sport that had been building slowly within the church. It also laid the foundation for the instrumental view of sport that has dominated Christian thought since that time. Hoffman notes that the position adopted by Aquinas and other medieval theologians meant that "the pleasures of play became redeemable on the strength of their usefulness."[57]

This idea that sport could be used by Christians in service of their heavenly Father did not end with medieval theologians. Rather, it was a notion more forcefully pursued by post-Reformation Christians, particularly English Puritans such as Richard Baxter. Baxter approved of some leisure activities, giving the following definition to lawful sporting practice.

> No doubt but some sport and recreation is lawful, yea needful, and therefore a duty to some men. Lawful sport or recreation is the use of some natural thing or action, not forbidden us, for the exhilarating of the natural spirits by the fantasy, and due exercise of the natural parts, thereby to fit the body and mind for ordinary duty to God. It is some delightful exercise.[58]

Given the stereotype of Puritan attitudes toward sport it is surprising to read that one of the most prominent Puritans says sport is needful and in some cases a duty. But to label Baxter a sport enthusiast would be going too far. Upon closer inspection we find that he gives eighteen specific qualifications that must be met before a sport is acceptable to Christians. In addition

55. Ibid., X. 6., 163.
56. Aquinas, *Summa Theologica*, II–II, 168, 2.
57. Hoffman, *Good Game*, 67.
58. Baxter, *Practical Works*, 386.

to obvious restrictions, such as the prohibition of any sport that tends to promote sinful behavior, (i.e., violence, lust, etc.), sport is only acceptable when no better use of time can be found. The first and foremost qualification is that "the end which you really intend in using [sport], must be to fit you for your service to God; that is, either your callings, or for his worship, or some work of obedience in which you may please and glorify him."[59]

Three things merit our attention to Baxter's proposal for suitable play. First, his discussion of sport is in the context of his framework for appropriate Christian moral behavior. As such, he is outlining when it is morally acceptable for Christians to engage in sport. However, he takes it a step further when he says,

> the person that useth it, must be one that is heartily devoted to God, and his service, and really liveth to do his work, and please and glorify him in the world: which none but the godly truly do! And therefore no carnal, ungodly person, that hath no such holy end, can use any recreation lawfully; because he useth it not to a due end.'[60]

This line of thought about whether or not Christians should view sport differently than non-Christians is an idea worth pursuing further but is perhaps best left for the following chapter. Presently, it should be noted that Baxter was insistent that only Christians, when properly following his other restrictions, could participate in sport lawfully. All leisure, by anyone else, for any other ends, was immoral and unacceptable in God's eyes.

Second, even Christians, for whom sport was in some cases permissible, were subjected to a very detailed list of when and how it was appropriate. Such strict regulations lead one to ask whether or not there is anything left to enjoy about sport. His pious checklist makes it extremely difficult, if not impossible, to participate in lawful sport. The Christian will be so busy making sure not to violate a single letter of the law that it will be less like recreation and more like another form of labor. In other words, Baxter's requirements for lawful sport make leisure too much work. By his own definition leisure should be some "delightful exercise" but the structure in which he allows sport presents such a small window of enjoyment one may question how far he has moved from the ascetic view already discussed.

Finally, even if we allow that Baxter does not advocate a complex form of asceticism and that it is possible to truly enjoy lawful sport, he still presents an inadequate theological account of sport. The first qualification reveals an instrumentalist framework that finds no value in leisure as such. Instead, play

59. Ibid., 387.
60. Ibid.

is only valuable as a means to some other end, namely labor. Baxter does allow for different types of leisurely activity although he provides strict guidelines that emphasize the development of physical strength. People of different vocations have need of different types of leisure. Some need to recreate the body while others, the mind. While giving the appearance of acceptance to a number of sports he again eliminates most sports by default.

For Baxter, it is unlawful to engage in a sport when a more appropriate form of leisure is available. Since one's physical condition is of primary concern for being productive he structures his case in such a way as to make physical labor categorically more appropriate than many sports. This narrows the list of lawful sport even further. For instance, someone in a physically demanding job does not need the physical exercise of many sports so reading may be a more appropriate activity, whereas someone whose work does not require a great deal of physical labor needs to develop physical strength through more strenuous activity. Such sedentary persons (Baxter lists students and scribes as examples) have the greatest "need of exercise and recreation, and labour is fitter for you than sport; or at least a stirring, labouring sport."[61] So while some "labouring sport" is permissible, the spirit and context in which he writes this suggests that, for someone whose work does not include physical labor, the most appropriate form of leisure *is* physical labor.

Baxter describes sport in purely utilitarian terms. That is, sport is only good in so far as it brings about another good. For Baxter, the chief utility of sport is preparation for service to God. Many Christians have pointed to several ways sport functions in service to Christian values. In the final section of this chapter we will look at those most commonly promoted by sport enthusiasts.

The Positive Benefits of Sport

There are surely numerous benefits to participating in sport but each of them will likely fall under one of three major headings. First, sport provides a means to mental and physical health. Secondly, it promotes social benefits, including community identity and the development of friendships. A third common support given to sport is that it serves as a moral resource by teaching desirable character traits and provides alternatives to mischievous behavior by young people. We will look at each of these three benefits and assess their instrumental value as characterized by the majority of Protestant Christian thought. This chapter will conclude by suggesting that this

61. Ibid., 388.

common understanding of sport reduces the importance sport plays in the life of the believer.

First, sport is commonly used as a vehicle to a healthy body. Millions of people around the world engage in sporting activity on a regular basis as a means to get or stay in shape. From the Christian perspective this is beneficial because it enables the servant of God to be better fit for heavenly service. To quote Baxter again on the subject, "If it have no aptitude to fit us for God's service in our ordinary callings and duty, it can be to us no lawful recreation."[62] He does not intend this to be a universal condemnation of certain activities. He goes on to say that the same leisurely activity may be beneficial to those who have a different calling than ourselves. If it benefits others in the pursuit of their calling it may be acceptable for them but in so far as it provides no means of fitting oneself for service it is unacceptable.

Any activities that have "no higher end, than to please the sickly mind that loveth them" are unlawful.[63] Therefore, on Baxter's view, sport is to be done for the sake of physical health. This idea carried over to the late nineteenth-century Protestants as well, particularly those influenced by the Social Gospel, which emphasized glorifying the human body. Historian Clifford Putney writes that those in this tradition "considered upkeep of the body a virtue and its neglect a sin" and, as a result, "came perilously close to calling musclemen saints and the sick sinners. Exacerbating this tendency was the Social Gospel idea of salvation in this world, which seemed to require more doers than thinkers."[64]

Putney may be right that the movement intensified the Protestant emphasis on the value of the body but Social Gospel Christians were no more emphatic about the need for physical health than their seventeenth-century counterparts. Though the theological scene differed greatly between these two Protestant movements it seems there is relatively little by way of conflicting views on the functional nature of leisure and sport. One believed the body was inherently good and required physical activity to build up that goodness while the other favored a much more restricted view where the body was merely a vessel to be used in God's service. Both the Social Gospel and Puritanism found mutual ground in the idea that sport was an activity of instrumental value. The former saw it as a means to work out one's salvation through righting social injustice in the world while the latter sought to use sport as preparation for one's calling.

62. Ibid., 387.
63. Ibid.
64. Putney, *Muscular Christianity*, 57.

Current attitudes toward sport seem to have less of a theological basis for determining sport's value. Some Christians suggest little other reason beside the health benefits is needed to justify participating in sport. In her practical guide to involving young girls in sport Holly Page, a coach and physical education instructor, says that "the physical benefits alone of participating in athletics are so significant and compelling that all young students should be involved in athletics at least throughout their junior high years."[65] Page is reiterating the notion of universally mandating young people's involvement in sport that is currently enforced around the world. Nearly every state in the USA has legislation requiring varying levels of physical education courses in order to graduate with many in the medical field calling for an increase in such requirements.[66]

As a form of exercise sport holds value in the obvious way of physical health but it also contributes to the athlete's mental and emotional health. Learning to play the game requires, among other qualities, determination and commitment. Sport equips us with the means of developing these virtues. An individual's mental focus necessary for competitive athletics may "help the student-athlete perform better in academics and can carry over to other areas of adult life." Page goes on to say that sports can help its young participants "learn to deal with complex and sometimes confusing emotions brought on by success and by failure. Young athletes can also become more aware of their individual likes and dislikes, educating themselves on the subject of . . . themselves."[67]

Secondly, sport is frequently supported by the notion that it fosters positive social influences. The benefits to society provided through sport come chiefly in one of two ways, either as a form of cultural identity and community pride or in developing friendship. Virtually every level of sport is comprised of a geographical or ideological heritage that represents the members of that community. A football (soccer) team like Glasgow's Rangers not only competes for the sake its players but in many respects represents certain religious factions in Scotland, (i.e., Protestant vs. Catholic). In baseball, the Chicago Cubs are comprised of more than the nine players on the field. They are part of a cultural tradition, a practice, which extends from and contributes to a narrative that is distinct to that sports team.

Perhaps the grandest sporting venue of them all is also one that highlights the different cultural representations more than any other. The

65. Page, God's Girls, 28.

66. Cawley et al, "The Impact of State Physical Education Requirements on Youth Physical Activity and Overweight."

67. Page, God's Girls, 29.

Olympics brilliantly contrast the diversity of cultures with the unifying spirit of sport. Sport is valued, in part, because it is able to transcend all cultural, political and religious boundaries. There is a uniqueness to sport that draws upon some of our most fundamental connections as human beings.

In his comments during the opening ceremonies John Furlong, CEO of the Vancouver Organizing Committee for the 2010 Winter Olympics had these poetic words to say about the unifying capabilities of sport.

> The Olympic flame has touched many millions and prompted spontaneous, peaceful celebration. Reminding us all that those values that unite and inspire the best in us, we must never abandon. As the Olympic Cauldron is lit—the unique magic of the Olympic Games will be released upon us. Magic so rare that it cannot be controlled by borders. The kind of magic that invades the human heart touching people of all cultures and beliefs. Magic that calls for the best that human beings have to offer. Magic that causes the athletes of the world to soar, and the rest of us to dream. Tonight, here in the glow and wonder of the Flame, we can all aspire to be an Olympian. From whatever continent you have come we welcome you to Canada, a country with a Generous Heart. We love that you are here. You are among good friends.[68]

In addition to geographical borders many Christians see opportunity to reach across religious borders. Some view the unique dynamic sport presents as an opportunity for evangelism. Stuart Weir comments, "sportspeople have the opportunity to demonstrate the image of God in an environment which is often lacking in sacrificial and unconditional love." He goes on to add, "Christians have found opportunities to share the gospel in gyms, golf courses, tennis courts and sports fields the world over. The lost may not come to church but, by seeing the sports club as your mission-field, you can take Christ to them."[69]

This was part of the motivation in the nineteenth-century movement known as "muscular Christianity." In response to what was perceived as the feminization of the church this movement sought to recast the image of a Christian as someone who was very physically fit, athletic and masculine. It was active in sport-related activity in an attempt to draw men and young boys inside the church walls. It was also used as a tool for recruiting masculine missionaries. By the end of the nineteenth century more than half of American Christian missionaries were women. Using sport to build up the image of

68. Mahlmann, "Welcome to Vancouver: Stirring Speech from John Furlong."
69. Weir, *What the Book Says about Sport*, 36–37.

the church as something muscular and work-oriented was a central strategy for increasing male participation in global and domestic missions.

Today, a number of sports mission organizations exist throughout the world including ones like the International Sports Federation. ISF has partnered with more than seven hundred missionaries and sent over eight thousand volunteers to more than one hundred and twenty countries. They state their instrumental view of sport very clearly when they say,

> We believe that sports is merely a tool that we can use for a specific purpose. It is not our goal to leave behind better, stronger or faster athletes resulting from participate with our volunteer teams. Our goal is to use the tool of sports to build a relationship that can hopefully lead to an open sharing of the Gospel of Jesus Christ with those who will listen and want to hear.[70]

Another social benefit of sport often tied to the first is the unique atmosphere in which friendships can flourish. Page again applauds sport for, "being a great place to start building healthy, long-lasting friendships that will assist a young person in making a smooth transition through all the developmental stages of the teenage years."[71]

However, it does not hold true that sport always results in such healthy relationships. Often time the competitive nature of sport fosters animosity and even hatred toward other players. In spite of this, it does appear to be the case that sport is more conducive to developing friendships and strengthening the sense of community than it is to corrupting it. As Michael Novak notes, there is a unique bond between players on the same team (and to a lesser extent the fans of that team). "For those who have participated on a team that has known the click of communality, the experience is unforgettable, like that of having attained, for a while at least, a higher level of existence: existence as it ought to be."[72]

Such a close-knit bond results from teams functioning in the proper manner. To achieve this level of functionality individuals must learn certain key elements of good social behavior. A mutual relying on each other, a commitment to do one's best for the sake of the other team members, and developing a group personality idiosyncratic to that particular team are all socially good benefits present in sport. "The point of team sports," Novak says, "is to afford access to a level of being not available to the solitary individual, a form of life ablaze with communal possibility."[73] The sense of

70. International Sports Federation, "Why Sports Missions?"
71. Page, God's Girls, 30.
72. Novak, The Joy of Sports, 144.
73. Ibid., 149.

possibility here is inspiring and perhaps signifies more than an instrumental value. Unfortunately, it is often seen as just that, a tool in service of good social etiquette.

A third area of benefit sport is purported to supply comes from the contributions to the individual participant's moral development. The moral pedagogy of sport is developed in both active and passive forms. It actively promotes virtues such as teamwork, commitment, fairness, and hard work. Passively, sport serves as a deterrent, especially for young people. Involving children in sports is a way to occupy their time, leaving less opportunity for mischief.

The idea that sport provides a double-edged sword in the attack against improper and immoral use of one's time was, not surprisingly, championed by the Puritans but the notion of sport as a tool for moral character was not. A primary reason for this is because Puritans believed divine revelation alone was the source of morality. Sport offered nothing of ethical value that could not be attained through Scripture and other Christian sources. In fact, as we have seen, it was most often the case that sport destroyed moral behavior rather than encourage it. Despite this, the Puritan misgivings about the moral elements of sport have given way to a Christian account that praises the moral characteristics believed to be essential to most sports.

Growing these virtues often goes hand in hand with the passive use of keeping trouble at bay. Page claims, "sport can and should be used like a pressure-release valve to positively discharge and direct youthful energy that might otherwise be misguided or misused for destructive purposes."[74]

On the other hand, countless examples can be readily found that suggest sport also cultivates less favorable moral traits. Aggression, violence, and selfishness are just a few of the behaviors typified by many athletes. In the next chapter we will look more closely at the serious challenge these attitudes present to the Christian athlete. Presently, we simply need to recognize that moral transference in sport can have both positive and negative effects. As a result Christians should be cautious about how heavily they rely on the moral benefits of sport as a defense of its practice.

The physical, social, and moral benefits provided in sport have praiseworthy aspects that Christians should embrace. However, as we have seen there are also negative expressions in these same areas. What I am calling the Rortian view is most clearly evident in the instrumental view just discussed. Christians frequently cite the development of certain habits (for better or worse) as the reason to participate in or avoid sport. It becomes, then, a simple means to achieving some other end. Depending on whether

74. Page, *God's Girls*, 28.

the moral aspect of sport is viewed positively or negatively it is either a way of becoming a more virtuous person or a more sinful person.

My conclusion is that these arguments fail to give consideration to the internal qualities of sport. They are either incompatible with one's value system or they may be accepted if they can produce a desired result. That is, one is a negative view that condemns sport as immoral or a waste of time. The other is a neutral view that assigns value to sport only when it leads to some external good.

The moral approach to sport defended in the previous chapter, which sees sport as a social practice with its own internal goods, rejects all three of the dominant views that have been employed by the church. Through each of the next three chapters I will demonstrate three necessary steps that will help in our development of an account of sport that is more adequately informed by Christian theology. These include reconciling Christian ethics with participating in sports, recognizing our human limitations as foundational to the nature of sport's purpose, and recovering the spirit of play in a sports culture driven by the corrupted desire to win above all else.

—————— 4 ——————

Reconciling Christian Ethics and Sport

AMONG THE INSTRUMENTAL PURPOSES of sport cited in the previous chapter there are three that stand out as the most frequently used to praise sport. Sport provides the benefits of competitive motivation and camaraderie, contributes to a healthy body, and develops moral character. However, no coin is one sided. As we have seen, there are also some serious theological concerns with the actual effect these practices have in the lives of Christians. At the heart of his recent book on Christianity and the culture of sports Shirl Hoffman challenges the assumption that these qualities are automatically good for the believer. While many promote these benefits of sport he suggests they often times are more damaging to traditional Christian commitments than they are to their development.

Hoffman's book is one of the most thorough treatments available on Christianity and sport. It is a refreshing exposition that details both the historical context of and theological challenges in the relationship between Christianity and sport. In this chapter I will engage Hoffman's work on the moral and theological challenges encountered by Christians who wish to participate in competitive sport. I will explore his arguments for why Christians should be cautious about modern sport and the dangers presented in three major categories.

Curiously, these major areas of concern are the same three categories the instrumental view of sport typically promotes as beneficial outcomes of participating in sports. Hoffman finds fault with the divisive nature of competition, the degradation of the body, and the corruptive influences on Christian morals found in many sports. As a result he sees a large portion of the sports culture, in some cases entire sports, as incompatible with the

Christian life and urges Christians to abstain from these practices. I will argue that he is to be credited with drawing attention to some very important issues in sport that many Christians neglect but that the extent of his caution reaches further than it should. He is right to condemn many of the practices and attitudes which plague contemporary sports but his pessimism is perhaps too extreme. For continuity's sake I wish to address each issue in the same order as does Hoffman by beginning with the concern over competition. Then I will look to the ways sport necessitates a disrespectful attitude toward the human body and conclude with the issue of whether sport teaches or corrupts moral character. These three are by no means the only concerns Christians should have with sport though they are three of the most serious.

Christians and Competition

Starting with the concern over competition seems fitting since it is a foundational aspect to most any sport. Indeed sport without competition would no longer be sport at all. Many of the world's most beloved sports would become an altogether different type of activity or perhaps even cease to exist. One may question whether sports without competition could collect enough interest to sustain its survival. But endorsing competition for the sake of supporting the existence of sport is hardly a defense of its practices. What it does help clarify is the inseparable connection between sport and competition. More importantly it makes plausible the argument that if competitive attitudes can be shown to be morally suspect then the ethical nature of sport may rightly be called into question. This is the line of inquiry pursued by Hoffman in his chapter on the killer instinct, in which he criticizes Christian participation in competitive ventures.

Winning at All Costs and the Selfish Goals of Sport

While many within the church suggest competition is inherently good and in a constructive way pushes people to be better than they currently are, Hoffman insists that competition in modern sport is incompatible with Christianity. Christian concerns over the effects of competition are not new. In fact, he believes the problem of competition has been the greatest source of alarm among Christians. Says Hoffman, "A fair reading of the history of the relationship between sport and the church suggests that it was the fruits of competition, more than anything else, that sparked moral outrage."[1] He does not explicitly clarify what he means by "fruits of competition" but presumably he is referring to what he sees as the chief problem with competition, namely that competition sets one's own interests ahead of other competitors.

My own reading of the history puts forward an alternative conclusion. Competition, as such, does not seem to stand above any other moral criticism. Pagan rituals, violence, sexual immorality and a grave misuse of time appear at least as frequently as anything that might be described as the fruits of competition. They are sure to overlap in many instances but linking competition as the root cause of each issue is problematic.

The moral unease with which Christians have viewed each of these separate issues was shown in the previous chapter to be emphasized differently in different time periods of historical Christianity. However, if one issue stands above the others it was certainly the disquiet of wasting time; a view expressed from Augustine to Baxter to present day. Christian theology from the patristic period to today has emphasized the scriptural mandate to "redeem the time" found in Ephesians 5:16. In specific relation to sport this criticism seems to be a more uniting and common theme throughout church history.

Even if there is some question about the status he gives to competition Hoffman may be right that in a more generalized way competition is an activity that divides people by setting personal interests against each other. This certainly would gather a unified criticism from the church that is called to "love others as you love yourselves." It is the antithesis of this idea that Christianity finds so appalling about many competitive activities that possess an inherent reward system for putting yourself before others. "For the Christian, the fact that sport plays to this urge to put ourselves at the front of the line may be its most troublesome aspect."[2]

However, as Hoffman points out throughout his chapter on competition, these anti-Christian attitudes are not as appalling to modern Christian sport enthusiasts, particularly evangelicals, as perhaps they should be. "Evangelicals implicitly recognize their spiritual obligation to shun sinful temptations, but under the guise of sports they seem more often to organize them, sponsor them, and celebrate them."[3]

He is critical of evangelicals and Christians from all traditions for that matter, who in his view, set aside their Christian convictions to enjoy the excitement of competitive sports.

1. Hoffman, *Good Game*, 145.
2. Ibid., 147.
3. Ibid., 148.

Viewed from a strictly objective standpoint, the picture of
Christians deliberately suspending concern for one another
(even in this limited sense) and engaging in deception, cunning,
and physical domination in an effort to further their own interests is a very troubling one indeed. True, players only suspend
mutual sympathy in an illusory sense as part of play, but even in
pretending to be motivated by self-interest, they are pretending
not to be the Christians that they claim to be.[4]

In my view there are three key components to Hoffman's critique of
competition. One issue with the viewpoint he expresses is his treatment of
the fundamental nature of competition. He sees competition as incompatible with Christianity in part because he sees competition not as an innate
part of human nature but as a corrupted form of community.

The second and third issues are very closely related and make up a
substantial portion of his critique of competition. The second aspect of his
argument that I wish to address is the extent to which play suspends moral
responsibilities in "an illusory sense." Briefly stated, my concern about Hoffman's position is that even though players suspend some sympathies it is done
in a mutually agreeable way that can immediately be resumed if need be. If a
player is injured, athletes do not continue to play around the fallen competitor. They pause until the injured player can be removed from the playing field
before resuming the game.[5] To put it concisely, suspending certain elements
of mutual sympathies during play does not necessarily translate into a total
removal of concern for other competitors. Wanting to best our competition
at a game does not mean we are pretending not to be Christian.

This affords us the opportunity to make an important distinction between three levels of attitudes toward competition in an illusory world. These
attitudes have been identified elsewhere as sportsmanship, gamesmanship,
and Christmanship. I will explore these concepts in more detail a little later.
Some have argued the former two are incompatible with Christian theology
while the latter transcends the illusory world and develops proper Christian
responses to others in a competitive environment.

---

4. Ibid., 147.

5. I am aware that some sports do not stop the contest when a competitor becomes
injured. If a runner falls out of the race with a pulled muscle the rest of the field does
not stop running until he or she is able to race again. They continue on until the race
is finished. However, in these types of cases there is no further threat to the runner
with the injury and he or she may withdraw from the competition without affecting
the other competitors. In most sports, especially team sports, if an athlete falls to the
ground with an injury all competitors will temporarily cease playing while the injured
player is attended to.

Also under the umbrella of social implications is the third idea where Hoffman criticizes competition as an activity that explicitly disobeys the Christian mandate to always put others before oneself. He attempts to place the burden of proof on those involved in competitive activity to show how they are not behaving selfishly. However, the responsibility is Hoffman's to show how competition implies a suspension of "concern for one another" in any morally or theologically meaningful sense. What makes Christianity incompatible with the culture of competitive sports, in his view, is the impossibility of justifying this suspension. On the contrary, I will argue that viewing the activity from a Christian perspective does justify participation by virtue of competition's nature as an intricate web of cooperation, proper respect for co-competitors, and personal development.

Is Competition Part of Human Nature?

It is a legitimate question to ask whether competition is part of our human nature. Is the desire to compete against others inborn or is it conditioned through culture? Hoffman favors a development through nurture theory due in part to the fact that different members of a culture have such diverse attitudes toward competition. "If competition is part of humanity's created essence, then we might expect all humans to share the urge to compare and test themselves against each other, and by extension, all societies would incorporate competition as a way of organizing their social relationships."[6] But such unity is not found, he claims. Not only do societies place differing emphases on competition, but individuals within any given society are likely to express a range of thoughts about the value of competition. "We are left to explain why there is wide variation in individual attraction to it: some enjoy testing and comparing their efforts against others while others shun it at every opportunity."[7] This raises interesting sociological and anthropological questions about the ways in which certain human behaviors are acquired and carried out but Hoffman's point does not close the book on the naturalness of competition. Human behavior and attitudes, such as competition, are sure to see different individual expressions, whether they are innate or conditioned. Those who loathe the competitive dimension of sport may be more accepting of competition in other areas of life, such as competing for a promotion at work or competing against other suitors for the affection of a potential partner.

6. Ibid., 158.
7. Ibid.

It also seems that competition, at least in a generalized form, is evident throughout creation. In an article putting forward an ethic of competition in a church setting Greg Linville argues that competition is not as morally dubious for Christians as Hoffman would suggest. Instead, Linville believes competition is created into the fabric of our being as a gift from God. Not only do humans have an inherent tendency to compete against one another, many inanimate objects express the created sense of competition as part of God's order in the world. Trees grow tall competing for sunlight while their roots spread deep and wide competing for water. Animals compete for food and water. "Competition," says Linville, "is part and parcel of the universe that God created."[8]

Hoffman disagrees with competition being part of God's design since "to accept this hypothesis, one must presume that God intended his creatures periodically to dedicate themselves to their own interests in the pursuit of fun, ignore the interests of others, and seek opportunities to compare and display their achievements before throngs of onlookers."[9] There does not seem to be anything inherently wrong with wanting to display one's achievements in a public setting unless you are also willing to condemn musicians, artists, even scientists and academics presenting their research. Pride could certainly become an issue but it is not inevitable. Similarly, selfishness can easily result from competition, particularly at higher levels, but it is not unavoidable.

Additionally, Christians are sure to oppose the idea that God intends for us to ignore the interests of others in favor of our own. But as Hoffman sees it, because it is a distorted form of another created good it is inherently corrupted. This means competition is an activity that holds no value for the Christian believer. If sport is to be redeemed and made appropriate for Christians then the competitive element must be sharply re-evaluated and the emphasis returned to human relationships. It is true that competition all too frequently leads to its extreme form of a "win at all costs" mentality but competition itself is not the root of the problem. Watson and White suggest that, "the idea and application of the 'win at all costs' ethic becomes the soil in which the personal (of athlete, coach, parent or fan) and structural sins (of institutions) of pride and idolatry are borne."[10]

The competitive drive in sports, as well as other areas of life, often places one's own interests ahead of others. However, I would argue that it is incorrect to label competition as a fundamentally corrupted exercise on

---

8. Greg Linville, "Ethic of Competition in a Church Setting," 175.

9. Hoffman, *Good Game*, 157.

10. Watson and White, "'Winning at All Costs' in Modern Sport," 67.

the basis of this tendency. It is the sin of pride that corrupts competition and persistently tempts competitors to subvert the more laudable aspects of competition in favor of selfish and dubious forms of competitive conduct. Like Watson and White, Linville also maintains that competition is not inherently sinful. He agrees that it is possible to conceive of competitive sports in a way that does not necessarily encourage self-indulgence. But neither does he take the opposite end of the spectrum and say competition is inherently good. He suggests competition is an amoral activity that is made good or bad by the way the competitor reacts to the pressure. It is a God given tool to help believers become the type of individuals God wants them to be. Competition is capable of bringing out the best or worst in people but "we cannot blame competition if athletes fail morally, emotionally, or psychologically."[11]

After stating the moral neutrality of competition he touches on an interesting thought. What would society look like if competition were removed? What impact would it have on the church if there were no competitive sport? The outcome would be more negative in Linville's view than in Hoffman's. According to Linville, competition is part of God's design for character formation, an issue we will discuss in a later section. What is important presently is Linville's assertion that "any attempt to remove competition from our lives will only hamper our spiritual development, not enhance it."[12] The focal point of the character building aspect of sport, if indeed there is one, is to be found in the fundamental nature of competition as God intended.

However, there seems to be a disconnection in what he says here and the position from neutrality argument he presents just a few paragraphs earlier. The latter comment suggests at least an implicit understanding of competition as intrinsically good, rather than neutral, since the removal of competition all together would have a negative effect. Linville sees competition as a created good that can be corrupted whereas Hoffman sees competition as a corruption or distortion of the created good of human relationships.

> To believe that sports as played in modern society actually teach such virtues, [love, patience, compassion, and self-sacrifice] one must overlook not only an extensive body of literature on character development in sports but the fundamentally egocentric impulses inherent in competition itself.[13]

11. Linville, "Ethic of Competition," 175.
12. Ibid., 176.
13. Hoffman, *Good Game*, 162.

Again, the focus here is not on the character development language as much as it is on these two different theological conceptions of the nature of competition. I am more sympathetic to Linville's theory since his allows the merits of competition to be recognized though I would suggest he eliminate the neutrality language and suggest competition plays a valuable role in human flourishing. Further articulation of Linville's view moves us to the second issue in Hoffman's summary of competition.

Gamesmanship and the Fear of Losing

Hoffman is mistaken to suggest that we must overlook the negative influences of sport to see the positive. In doing so he seems to be guilty of his own practice. His thorough examination of sport's negative character development discounts the ways in which sport teaches the positive virtues he lists. It is indeed a more accurate picture of sport to note both the good and bad attitudes it can encourage. As we will explore in the next chapter, competitive sport reveals to us that sport is as much about losing as it is about winning. It demonstrates the frailty and vulnerability of human beings by teaching us that sometimes to lose is to be human. In this sense sport provides an endless source of teachable moments as losing can help develop a certain kind of humility.

But Hoffman does not see the attitude of humility being taught in sport. Instead he identifies at least part of the essence of competition as having "fundamentally egocentric impulses." The promotion of self-glorification is truly a challenging aspect of competitive sport that Christians must wrestle with. Hoffman is right to criticize Christians, for ignoring the seriousness of this offence. He notes that often times it not so much ignored as redecorated and given a new name. Phrases like "a commitment to excellence," "hard work," and "determination" are all part of the terminology used to justify competitive sport though slightly more common is the notion that athletes competing against themselves is superior to their competing against each other. "The problem with such suggestions is that they try to convert competition into an individual, isolated experience that it can never be; *they deny the relational essence of competition.*"[14] He correctly recognizes the fallacy of promoting sport as an exercise in self-betterment. Such an approach neglects the required cooperative element of all competitive sport. This leads Hoffman to believe that if competitive sport cannot be primarily about self-betterment then it must be about being better than others; an idea not easily accepted in Christian practice.

14. Ibid., 160; italics original.

There is little disagreement that faith in practice supersedes winning an athletic contest. No doubt there are instances where a commitment to modeling the selflessness of Christ requires athletes to lessen their chances at victory or even forfeit entirely. But it is not necessarily true that the two are mutual exclusive. We should not equate the desire to win with the sin of selfishness. The apostle Paul recognized the merits of competing to win in the epistle to the Corinthians. "Do you not know that in a race all the runners run, but only one receives the prize? So run that you may obtain it."[15] Surely Paul would not have used such an illustration if competing to win necessitates selfishness and a lack of concern for others. Yes, there will be times when the desire to win exceeds its appropriateness and athletes act outside of proper competitive rules.

When this happens we typically refer to such actions as lacking in sportsmanship.[16] Virtually all Christians can agree that this behavior is wrong. Sportsmanship is certainly laudable but is it enough to govern Christian participation in competitive sport? Both Hoffman and Linville would deny this and Linville provides a constructive distinction between three ethics of competition. He begins with sportsmanship and notes its benefits but also points out its shortcomings. It carries with it the ideas of specific "characteristics, skills, and ethics that sports people bear upon themselves as they compete" and includes notions of "having fun, playing fair, using skills, maximizing abilities, and being a gracious winner or loser."[17]

However, the problem with sportsmanship according to Linville is that "these ethics are determined by popular opinion of a society, which has no permanent mooring."[18] He goes on to explain that sportsmanship can mean a number of different things to different groups of people. Therefore the abstract elements valued in competition are fluid, changing as the players, coaches, and spectators change.

Linville's concern is that while the ideas valued within sportsmanship may change there is one aspect that always stays the same. "The final authority or ethic of sports is to win, and the ethic of sports is not determined by the philosophy of sportsmanship but rather by the pragmatism of gamesmanship."[19] As he describes it, the ethic of gamesmanship is far more dangerous than sportsmanship. The latter recognizes the importance of the

15. 1 Cor 9:24.

16. Sportsmanship and similar words are used here in a gender neutral sense as accepted nomenclature in the field. It is used in an inclusive way meaning both male and female athletes.

17. Linville, "Ethic of Competition," 162.

18. Ibid., 163.

19. Ibid.

skills and attitudes society values within the context of the competition. The former sees winning as the most important element of competition. The trouble, says Linville, is that "sportsmanship always devolves into gamesmanship."[20] He believes this to be the case since sportsmanship is not anchored in anything more solid than societal whims. As social values change the principles of sportsmanship will as well. The only immutable aspect of sport, the force that drives all sport, in all cultures, according to Linville, is the desire to win.

An obvious problem at this point is deciding "what is the point of a distinction in terminology if sportsmanship always becomes gamesmanship?" Linville does not address this directly but instead begins his contrast with a third approach. For him, neither sportsmanship nor gamesmanship presents an ethic of competition compatible with Christianity. What is needed is an ethic that reflects who we are as Christians. "Christmanship embodies the best of sportsmanship (fun, fairness, being a good loser, etc.) and the best of gamesmanship (giving one's best effort within the rules to win), but it transcends and surpasses them both."[21]

Again, it is worth asking why we see the "best of sportsmanship" as having any value since, on his account, it will ultimately collapse into gamesmanship. Linville's view is that gamesmanship is a moral wasteland with the only goal being to win. Societies try to build a bridge across the cesspool of selfishness by inserting culturally acceptable standards of behavior. However, since these are also designed by sinfully fallen human being they too will ultimately be consumed by gamesmanship's ego-centrism. The only way to redeem sport, says Linville, is to adopt a Christmanship attitude toward sport. This approach is founded on Christ rather than our own corrupted conduct.

Linville is right to draw our attention to the tendency for competitive athletics to degrade into self-centeredness. However, he may be going too far to say that sportsmanship is based on social whims and always turns into gamesmanship. Winning is an essential part of the game but he is mistaken to suggest it is always the final authority. His argument leads to the conclusion that only Christians are able to participate in sport without making winning the final goal. It is not difficult to think of non-Christians who play sports "just for fun" and are not guided by the ethic of winning. Additionally, athletes can participate in sport with a desire to win without falling into Linville's description he calls gamesmanship. There is a sizeable distinction between playing to win and playing to win *at all costs*.

20. Ibid., 166.
21. Ibid.

I am sympathetic to his attempt to make Christ the centre of our sporting behaviors and attitudes. I would add that Christians can have a more fulfilled experience in sport and a richer understanding of its purpose. He goes on to outline seven areas of competitive sport where Christians should reflect attitudes of Christ-likeness that are distinct from the sports culture of gamesmanship. Jesus Christ should shape how Christians treat teammates, coaches, officials and opponents. He also provides the foundation for how to think about competition, winning and losing, and success. The first set of categories includes the way Christians ought to handle the social or cooperative aspect to competition. The second set addresses the internal struggles facing the athlete. All of these areas should be shaped by a proper understanding of competitive sport. Gamesmanship's primary focus on winning excludes a healthy appreciation for the importance of these seven components.

Rejecting an ethic of gamesmanship certainly is not unique to Christian theology. In an article without any religious overtones Leslie Howe cites several criticisms of the attitude. "The decisive element in gamesmanship is the attempt to gain competitive advantage either by an artful manipulation of the rules that does not actually violate them or by the psychological manipulation or unsettling of the opponent."[22] This description could be considered a weak form of gamesmanship since she keeps its behavior within the rules of the game.

I would agree with Linville that an ethic of gamesmanship actually goes further than this by making it perfectly acceptable to deceive, intimidate, or cheat an opponent in order to win. Cheating may often be done in an artfully manipulative way but it still blurs the boundaries of fairness. Murray Hall states, "As long as winning remains more important than *how one plays*, there is little chance for fair play. Cheating, or at least bending the rules, is condoned if not often accepted outright, and practices which were previously regarded as cheating are accepted as an integral part of the game."[23]

Included in the often overwhelming desire to win is an equally strong fear of losing. The idea of "win at all costs" is typically painted in a positive way where the reward of winning, be what it may, is the focal point. Athletes want to win so that they receive x. The other self-serving extreme in a structure of gamesmanship is the negativity associated with losing. It is something to be avoided at all costs. We are cautioned though by Edwin Delattre that "success in competitive athletics is not reducible to winning, nor failure to losing."[24] In gamesmanship there is no merit in losing. Excellence becomes

22. Howe, "Gamesmanship," 213.

23. Hall, "Christian Ethics in North American Sports," 228; italics original.

24. Delattre, "Some Reflections on Success and Failure in Competitive Athletics,"

synonymous with winning that is, as Howe also notes, a false conception of reality. Winning often is the outcome of an excellent performance but winning does not define excellence. She reorients the mindset of gamesmanship by shifting competitive sport's goals from winning to excellence.

> If the more substantive goal of sport is excellence, and excellence is about process rather than result, and thus the athlete rather than the score line, then we need to consider what effect gamesmanship has on the pursuit and the pursuer of excellence. If and insofar as gamesmanship subverts excellence in favor of winning, it must be considered antithetical to the athletic endeavor.[25]

Howe goes on to argue that with excellence rightly in its place as the purpose of sport we can offer a clearer picture of the role of competition. It becomes a catalyst for a holistic improvement in the athlete. "It is a test of the whole athlete—not just his or her physical skills, which could be tested just as well in training or in the lab, but their psychological and moral skills, as well."[26]

So for Howe competition then is relegated to a form of self-betterment; a dangerous idea for Christians since it implicitly reduces one's opponent to a means. Additionally, from a Christian point of view her emphasis on the self is too strongly stated when she identifies the problem with gamesmanship as a "failure of self, of self-respect, and of commitment to oneself in sport."[27] Hoffman sees the risk in Christians adopting a self-enrichment theory of sport.

> Maximizing one's potential is fine, of course, but when "being all that one can be" is elevated to a Christian virtue, the reality of the opponent on the other side of the net or field or in the adjacent lane can get lost in the process. It denies the real possibility that there may be occasions when faith puts a heavy constraint on athletes, compelling them at times to "be less than what they could be."[28]

If Hoffman is right, then Howe's framework of competition cannot be fully accepted. To do so would mean that being less than one could be in order to follow principles of the faith actually denies, at least in those instances, participating in sport according to its purpose, (i.e., as God

133.

25. Howe, "Gamesmanship," 216.
26. Ibid., 219.
27. Ibid., 216.
28. Hoffman, *Good Game*, 161.

designed it). Following God's design for the treatment of fellow persons in a particular activity may result in a rejection of God's design for that activity in the first place. If this is indeed the case then Hoffman is right to argue that competitive sport and Christianity are incompatible. Christians are better off abstaining from such activities.

Making as the aim of sport "being the best that one can be" dangerously resembles gamesmanship, an attitude Christians will do well to reject. But "being less than what one could be" in certain instances is hardly antithetical to competition. Even the most competitive athletes recognize some things to be more important than sport. In the 1988 Summer Olympic Games Canadian rower Lawrence Lemieux was nearing the finish line for what would have been, in all likelihood, a second place finish when he saw a boat from another race capsized. Both sailors in that boat were in the water fighting to stay above the surface. With an Olympic medal easily within his reach he forsook his own race, charging through thirteen foot waves and winds of thirty-five knots to save the lives of these two injured and endangered sailors. Once rescue crews arrived he continued his own race finishing in twenty-first place.

Sacrificing an Olympic medal to help fellow athletes is an easy example of respecting the reality of other competitors. Lemieux's actions have been called many things including morally praiseworthy and self-sacrificing but it is doubtful whether anyone would consider what he did uncompetitive.[29] He knew when it was appropriate to set aside his competitive desires for victory and attend to more important matters. Examples like this one challenge Hoffman's understanding of competition since "being less than what one could be" is not explicitly an indictment against competition as such. Rather it is revealing of the character of the competitor. Nor does competition deny occasions for such behavior when athletes place respect for other competitors above the fear of losing.

Christian Virtue and Competition

Hoffman would still be critical of competition since he believes the proper ordering of respect for competitors is rare indeed. Far more common is the divisiveness and conflicting interests at play. He is doubtful whether or not Christians can in fact participate in competitive sports in a way that is not

---

29. Verstraete, *At the Edge*, 60–61. Lemieux was awarded the rare Pierre de Coubertin medal for sportsmanship citing his "sportsmanship, self–sacrifice, and courage." The International Yacht Racing Union bestowed an honorary second place silver medal, the place he was in when he stopped to help the other sailors.

reduced ultimately to self serving goals. Here I wish to suggest a new assessment of such claims that takes into account the narrative from which we understand competition. By that I mean Hoffman has taken competition as it is displayed in a secular sports culture and compared it with the beliefs of the Christian faith and found that they are not compatible. This is only half of the equation. Beyond simply comparing Christian values with the standard of secular society I wish to reverse the order and advocate a more thorough evaluation of competition from a distinctly Christian perspective that is then applied to the sports culture. One way of going about this task is to look at the difference between Christian and pagan understandings of virtue. The pagan model, championed by Aristotle, is predicated on the notion of *agôn*. His understanding of virtue is informed by the sense of a struggle between two parties. Critics like John Milbank argue Aristotle's notion of supreme virtue, as demonstrated through the magnanimous man, "seeks to outshine others in liberality, which implies a competition for limited economic resources."[30] Since generosity is one of the virtues displayed by the magnanimous man, he cannot be virtuous unless he has resources with which to be generous.

This implies two things. First, the materially poor do not have the means to become virtuous, an idea Christians rightly reject. Secondly, it stands to reason that the more resources one has, the more generous he can be and the more generous he is, the more virtuous he becomes. This means, as Milbank notes, that even virtues such as generosity are affected by competition with others. We rightly find it troublesome when generosity becomes a matter of who can give the most. Even though material goods are transferred and people in need benefit from the giving, it is true that some important aspect of the giving act has been corrupted.

Indeed, Christians would join Aristotle in looking favorably on the virtue of generosity. However, there is a significant difference between the two when it comes to the nature of that virtue (among others). Christians look askance on Aristotle's foundation of *agôn*. In their helpful work, *Christians Among the Virtues*, Stanley Hauerwas and Charles Pinches articulate a Christian criticism of Aristotelian virtue. They point out that a community that honors agonistic virtue will inevitably be at odds with a Christian community. They write, "Pride and a properly severe anger are the keepers of excellence and, concomitantly, the guarantors of the perpetuity of the pagan community."[31] Obviously, pride is not a virtue in the Christian tradition, but a vice and therefore ought never to be a key value within the community. At

---

30. Milbank, *Theology and Social Theory*, 352.

31. Hauerwas and Pinches, *Christians among the Virtues*, 109.

the heart of this contrast between Christian and pagan virtue is the fundamental issue of the aim or "noble end" of virtue.

Nowhere is this distinction more evident than in the virtue of courage. For Aristotle, courage is best modeled in war. "Death on the battlefield," notes Hauerwas, "stands as the paradigm of courage for Aristotle precisely because it gives the genuinely courageous person the chance to offer the one great good which unifies all other particular goods, that is, his life, for an even higher good, namely the common good of the state."[32]

He and Pinches go on to compare Aristotle's version of courage with that of Aquinas. They are similar in many respects, not the least of which is that fear of death is a key source for courage. They conclude there is one major difference between these two conceptions and that is the reason for facing death. In Aristotle's view, giving one's life on the battlefield serves the higher good of the state. For Aquinas, it is possible to see a soldier's death as courageous but there are other forms of facing death that surpass that of war. Something very different from the pagan courage of war is the Christian courage of charity. Hauerwas argues that the Christian community shifts the paradigm for courage from one of war to one of martyrdom. "The world of the courageous Christian is different from the world of the courageous pagan. This is so because of their differing visions of the good which exceeds the good of life itself."[33]

He goes on to explain that the Christian community is informed by love, not *agôn*, and its members "are required patiently to persevere in the face of persecution, since they have the confidence that enduring wrong is a gift of charity."[34] Therefore, courage still is about facing death on the battlefield. It is simply a different kind of battlefield for Christians. Rather than mutually engaging in violence, Christians through a display of charity, withstand the violence by placing their trust in God rather than in their own might. Samuel Wells agrees that, "whereas Aristotle's ultimate purpose, and that of his courageous soldier, is the good of the nation, Aquinas' purpose is friendship with God."[35]

How does this radical paradigm shift affect the way the Christian community addresses competition? One response would be to argue, as Hoffman has, that if courage is exemplified through martyrdom then members of the Christian community should not reciprocate the agonistic attitude in sport. Christian courage is demonstrated in the ability to stay out of highly

32. Ibid., 156.
33. Ibid., 160.
34. Ibid.
35. Wells, "The Disarming Virtue of Stanley Hauerwas," 84.

competitive activities. It is doubtful Hauerwas, since he is an avid baseball fan, would apply Christian courage in this way. Instead, it would be helpful to draw out the basic distinction Hauerwas is after. Wells clarifies the issue in this way. "The heart of the matter is that the life of [secular] virtue calls for people to be heroes, whereas God calls his people to be saints . . . a hero is at the centre of a story; a saint is a character in God's story."[36] He further explains that while both Aristotle and Hauerwas provide narrative accounts of virtue the difference is in the place of individuals within that story. "The Christian story is always told for the greater glory of God, rather than the glory of a hero or even his virtues."[37]

What this suggests, then, is that as Christians we ought to recognize our place in the narrative. The modern sports culture encourages agôn informed self-promotion. The Christian story makes it possible to see redemptive qualities in competition. Christianity is right to confront any narrative that attempts to withhold for itself any of the glory God rightfully deserves. To that extent Christian athletes must push back against the predominately agonistic, overly competitive culture so prevalent in modern sport. As we saw in the previous chapter, one of the most common ways Christians have attempted to challenge this culture was by condemning its practices entirely. I wish to suggest an alternative approach that sees Christian athletes being an example of how to fit competition within the broader context of a God glorifying narrative. More so than abstaining from sport, Christian courage is needed to participate in sport in the right way. What the modern sports culture, which is focused on self-made heroes, needs is a course corrective that is led by saintly athletes.

Scripture guides us in this respect and, ironically enough, Paul uses a sporting metaphor to make his point. We saw earlier how 1 Corinthians 9:24–27 contains two different sports analogies. It was suggested that while Paul certainly would have rejected many of the practices surrounding the sporting events of his time it is doubtful he would have used this illustration if he believed sport to be inherently corrupt. Conversely, neither does this passage necessarily argue in favor of sport. Instead, Paul's use of a sporting metaphor was a culturally relevant way of making a larger point. Paul uses two key verbs in the first two verses of this passage, ἀγωνιζόμενος and ἐγκρατεύεται, which complement each other. Paul recognizes the intense striving and self-control athletes demonstrate in a race. Yet not only do the exhibit these qualities during the race but in their preparations as well. Robertson notes that "Training for ten months was required under the direction

36. Ibid.
37. Ibid., 85.

of trained judges. Abstinence from wine was required and a rigid diet and regimen of habits."[38] Paul knew that both of these attributes needed to be present for the winning competitor. One who does not strive will not win. Similarly, without the self-control to forfeit simple pleasures like wine and specific foods the athlete will not be fit enough to win the prize, no matter how the athlete strives.

However, Paul does not write this to praise the athletes for their dedication and abilities on the race-course. He uses their commitment to attaining a perishable wreath as instruction for the believers at Corinth. They are committed to a pine wreath that will crumble and fade away. How much greater should Christ's followers be to that which is eternal? Yet the illustration is more than surface deep. There are two implied ideas in Paul's use of the contestants. First, that winning provides meaning to sport. As N.T. Wright suggests, Paul is saying for both the athlete and the Christian, "There's no point entering the race unless you are going to go all out to win."[39] The point is more about the Christian than the athlete as made clear by Paul's "them/us" distinction tied to the perishable and imperishable prizes. Paul is more concerned about the devotion to Christ displayed by his followers than he is about any of them winning an athletic competition. This clearly suggests to Christians that behaviors and attitudes that might lead to victory on the race course must be made subject to the principles and values of the Christian faith.

Paul is saying that Christians ought to behave, or "compete", like they are in it to win. Wright clarifies what the prize is when he says, "The Christian is called to live in the present as someone who will inherit that incorruptible, deathless new body when God makes the whole world new."[40] Moreover, Paul's illustration makes clear to the Corinthians that if they want to follow Jesus they ought to strive, or agonize as the Greek word implies, after Him. To do so Christians must display self-control. Just as the athletes sacrificed certain luxuries for a chance at the prize, so must Christians be willing to forfeit anything that hinders them from winning. Morris notes, "The strenuous self-denial of the athlete in training for his fleeting reward is a rebuke to all half-hearted, flabby Christian service."[41] Paul wants his readers to understand the importance of self-control in the life of a Christ follower. He does not run aimlessly. He runs with discipline, completely focused on the prize. It is here that he introduces his second sporting

38. Robertson, *Word Pictures in the New Testament*, Vol. IV, 148.

39. Wright, *Paul for Everyone: 1 Corinthians*, 119–20.

40. Ibid., 120.

41. Morris, *1 Corinthians*, 139.

metaphor. Boxing the air, or shadow-fighting, was done "when practicing without an adversary."[42] Shadow-fighting was easy because there was no one to return the punches. By contrast, Paul says the Christian life is difficult. "The discipline of the Christian life requires strenuous moral effort. You have to learn how to play this game. It's no use just getting into the ring and hoping it will all work out."[43]

A second implication of Paul's metaphor involves who the winners are. The greatest difference between the athlete and the Christian is the prize that each receives. A second way the two are dissimilar is by the number of winners. Obviously, only one runner wins the prize but as Christians this is not so. John Calvin takes up this point, "but our condition is superior in this respect, that there may be *many* at the same time. For God requires from us nothing more than that we press on vigorously until we reach the goal."[44] It is here that the Christian story can account for competition in a God glorifying way. Calvin continues, "Thus one does not hinder another: nay more, those who run in the Christian race are mutually helpful to each other."[45] It is in the context of community, particularly Christian community, where individuals mutually submit to the goals of that community and help one another grow. To this end, the Christian tradition honors friendship with each other as we strive toward the ultimate goal of friendship with God.

If all of this is the meaning of Paul's teaching then it would seem that for our present purposes his use of sporting metaphors is fitting. It not only teaches us the importance of self-control and striving for the prize in a context of community, but the metaphor itself speaks to the need for Christians to be self-controlled, disciplined Christ-followers in the sporting arena. But to what extent is friendship possible in an activity with winners and losers?

Alienation or Friendship?

Shirl Hoffman insists that competitive sport sets individual's desires against one another in a selfish and immoral way. He makes a strong accusation that participating in the modern culture of competitive sport, an activity with an innate tendency to promote one's self-interests, is patently unchristian. He believes this to be the case since the only outcome of competition is a desire to place oneself ahead of other competitors.

42. Robertson, *Word Pictures*, 149.
43. Wright, *Paul for Everyone*, 118–19.
44. John Calvin, *Calvin's Commentaries*, vol. 20, 308.
45. Ibid.

"How evangelicals, mindful of scriptural exhortations to 'unity of spirit, sympathy, love of brethren, a tender heart, and a humble mind,' can momentarily claim release from this obligation is not easily explained (1 Peter 3:8)."[46] One may be tempted to respond that participation in a game of sport does easily explain this "momentary release" since all parties involved are mutually agreeing to subject themselves to the rules of the game. Hoffman rejects this idea since consent does not remove any existing moral or spiritual duties.

This is similar to the traditional Christian view that sex is not necessarily morally acceptable just because both parties consent to the act. From this perspective even if there is mutual agreement some sexual behavior is still worthy of condemnation. Hoffman himself does not use this example but the parallels are easily noted. Just because multiple participants agree to compete in a "pretend world" it does not excuse them from honoring others appropriately as Christians ought always to do.

According to him, "the quandary is not lessened for evangelicals simply because they, along with their opponents, willingly accept this risk in exchange for the fun of the game. Acts of dubious morality are hardly cleansed of the obliquity when perpetrated as part of a mutual agreement entered into for the purposes of entertainment."[47]

This risk is not the physical or psychological risks of sport but what Drew Hyland refers to as the risk of alienation. Hoffman's choice to enlist Hyland as an ally on this point seems peculiar since Hyland's argument in its entirety stands in opposition to the point Hoffman is trying to make. Hoffman is critical of sport here because, in his view, it intentionally and necessarily divides competitors by setting self-interests in opposition to one another. From his perspective, one of sport's fundamental characteristics is to seek one's own gain at the expense of others. No doubt he is right to label this a risk of sport. Examples of selfish behavior in sport abound and many sports organizations implicitly, if not explicitly, encourage and reward selfish behavior by their athletes.

That Hyland is not blind to this reality is attested to by Hoffman's passing reference in which both writers agree that competition far too frequently results in alienation. Both are rightly convinced that sport risks unfriendly encounters. But I think Hyland's viewpoint in its broader context needs to be explored more intentionally. It is more important to this conversation than Hoffman gives it credit for. Hyland's article is on competition and friendship. He asks whether competition is fundamentally a causal force

46. Hoffman, *Good Game*, 147.
47. Ibid., 155, 156.

more in favor of friendship or alienation. As part of his argument he points out the root of the word for competition implies a social connection or relationship. Meaning "a striving *together*," he states the word competition "suggests an affinity more with friendship than with alienation."[48] Hoffman takes an opposite approach. In the same sentence in which he references Hyland he comments "under any rubric, mutually striving for excellence necessarily involves creating social distance between competing parties."[49]

While he does acknowledge that it often happens, Hyland does not see alienation as an inescapable reality in competitive play. In fact, Hoffman's view is a distant one from the position taken by Hyland where competition, being rooted in our human nature, drives us to the mutual pursuit of human fulfillment. "In competing with others," he claims, "our chances for fulfillment are seen as occurring within a framework of positive involvement with, a cooperation with, or a friendship with others. Far from being opposed, competition and friendship are seen to be founded together in our natures as erotic."[50]

Erotic here is used in the sense of a Socratic view of human nature in which "the human soul is decisively characterized by eros (love)."[51] Hyland briefly summarizes this view of eros as consisting of three parts. First, human beings are not whole. Second, eros is the experience or recognition of this incompleteness. The third aspect of eros is the "striving to overcome experienced incompleteness, the striving for attainment of wholeness out of partiality."[52]

This teleological view provides the foundation for his approach to competition that allows for a fundamental orientation toward friendship. Hyland comments, "I am saying that competition, as a striving or questioning together towards excellence, in so far as it most adequately fulfils its possibilities, does so as a mode of friendship."[53] Competition in its most ideal form, Hyland would say highest form, produces friendship. It is ideal in the sense that friendship is the standard by which we are to judge the proper functioning of competitive sport. He adds that friendship is not only the proper expression of competition but its natural or fundamental orientation as well. Sport or any other form of competitive play, when done right, says Hyland, will always result in friendship.

48. Hyland, "Competition and Friendship," 34.
49. Hoffman, *Good Game,* 155.
50. Hyland, "Competition and Friendship," 34.
51. Ibid., 31.
52. Ibid.
53. Ibid., 35.

I hold the *highest* possibility to be the truly *natural* situation, in the light of which other manifestations of competition, specifically that of alienation, are to be judged defective. According, then, to my teleological account of competitive play, all competitive play which fails to attain its highest possibility, that of friendship, must be understood as a "deficient mode" of play. This could even be interpreted as implying an ethical injunction: we *ought* to strive at all times to let our competitive play be a mode of friendship.[54]

This conclusion is rather different than the one postulated by Hoffman where he insists that there is an undeniable "unique psychological transformation" *required* of sporting participants that ultimately results in an "inherent friction between the ethos of competitive sport and Christianity."[55] Hyland clearly does not endorse the same dim view of sport as does Hoffman, or at least not to the same extent. Both agree that alienation, due to conflicting self-interests is an unfortunate, even morally condemnable outcome too frequently experienced in competitive sport. However, there is separation between the two over sport's fundamental nature. Hoffman's view of competition that sees inherent friction with Christian values is far more negative in that, for him, selfish behavior is inescapable.

For Hyland, competitive sport's highest aim is the good of friendship. When that is not achieved something has gone wrong in both the purpose of the game and in the competitors. Like the view expressed by Linville he believes competition is not inherently corrupt but can easily become so. However, he goes further than Linville, as I have, and believes competitive sport is fundamentally good and every case of improper competitive action is a distortion of that good. Hyland suggests that "alienation in our competitive play is in every case a failure of the telos of competition, and indirectly of our very natures as erotic."[56]

Sports will often set political tensions aside for the duration of the match as we often see with India and Pakistan in cricket or Israel and Palestine in football. Perhaps the grandest sporting venue for friendship and solidarity is also one that highlights the different cultural representations more than any other. The Olympics brilliantly contrast the diversity of cultures with the unifying spirit of sport. Sport is valued, in part, because it is able to transcend all cultural, political and religious boundaries. There is a

54. Ibid.

55. Hoffman, *Good Game*, 155, 156.

56. Hyland, "Competition and Friendship," 36.

uniqueness to sport that draws upon some of our most fundamental connections as human beings.

However, cultural identity in sport is not always good. Many teams identify with cultural or political ideals and when conflicting views meet on the pitch it often causes extremely high tension. During the Soviet era Dinamo Moscow FC was the state sponsored club for the KGB. Their rival, Spartak Moscow was a team for the working class. It became one of the largest rivalries in the world. "The Spartak-Dinamo rivalry was the greatest in all of Soviet sport. On a global stage, it seemed to be as rich in political implication as the clash of the Spanish giants Real Madrid and Barcelona, the Glasgow 'Old Firm' of Celtic and Rangers, and the Buenos Aires derbies of Boca Juniors and River Plate."[57]

The unifying spirit advertised by sports fans can quickly diminish into dissension and even violence. Hooliganism, riots and vandalism are often the result of excessive allegiance. George Orwell's essay on "the Sporting Spirit" came about after he witnessed an international football match between an English and a Russian team. Highly critical of the flagrant social elitism he was disgusted by the uncivil behavior of both the athletes and the spectators but also of the national backing by both countries. "But the significant thing is not the behaviour of the players but the attitude of the spectators: and, behind the spectators, of the nations who work themselves into furies over these absurd contests, and seriously believe—at any rate for short periods—that running, jumping and kicking a ball are tests of national virtue."[58]

A division between groups of people over allegiance to different sporting teams is an un-Christian practice. Unfortunately, Christians have not exempted themselves from participating in such rivalries. One of the most looming examples is the Catholic and Protestant segregation that is embodied in the football rivalry between two of Scotland's best known teams, Celtic and Rangers. The former is comprised of Catholic fans while the latter represents a Protestant constituency.

Other fans are separated by a geographical barrier such as the two professional baseball teams in Chicago. Those who live on the north side of the city are typically Cubs fans while those who live on the city's south side support the White Sox. When games are played between the two teams there is an increase in police presence and security measures since the rivalry sparks a lot of tension. This is clearly a case of the problem Freud called

57. Edelman, *Spartak Moscow*, x.
58. Orwell, "The Sporting Spirit," 196.

the "narcissism of minor differences"[59] where there is constant feuding between groups of people for no other apparent reason than that they live in close proximity to each other. These two teams compete in different leagues within professional baseball and have relatively little to do with each other throughout the course of the season. The same could be said for New York's Yankees and Mets.

There is nothing inherently wrong with competitive rivalry so long as it is practiced in an agreeable manner. Unfortunately, there is a lot of disagreeable behavior when it comes to rivalries. This is when it becomes important to remember not to take sport too seriously. Hooliganism is a worldwide problem in sport and seems to show no signs of fading away, though Christians can make concerted efforts to avoid this behavior themselves by rejecting a "win at all costs" mentality.

Friendly rivalries can be healthy expressions of sporting practice and need not always result in the alienation or separation Hoffman and others fear. In fact, rivalries can come from or may result in friendships as is the case with downhill skiers Lindsey Vonn and Maria Riesch. Two of the top Olympic skiers in the 2010 Winter Games, Vonn and Riesch were fierce competitors, each representing her country of USA and Germany, respectively. They also are best friends. Their friendship is a source of motivation for competing with one another and it was in competition that their friendship began six years before they met in the Winter Olympics in Vancouver.[60]

Theologians might not want to say as Hyland does, that the purpose of competitive sport is to fulfill some incomplete form of love through the development of friendships. Certainly friendships are a benefit of sport and the cooperative element of competition is usually neglected. But in a Christian theological framework it makes more sense to say that the development of friendships is an outcome of sport, not the purpose. The prominence Hyland places on the social dimension is a bit extreme but he is to be credited for pointing to an oft ignored facet of competitive sport. Too commonly are opponents set against each other rather than respected in a way that edifies both competitors.

Despite this tendency so prevalent in modern sports culture Linville asserts that Christianity remains compatible with competition and makes an insightful comment concerning the treatment of opponents that is the part Hoffman finds most troubling. He points out that the term "opponent" is an unfortunate term for sport since it connotes something similar to "enemy." Instead of viewing opponents as enemies that must be defeated, which

59. Freud, *Civilization and Its Discontents*, 98.

60. Moore, "For Lindsey Vonn and Maria Riesch, Friendship and Rivalry Blur."

gets us close to the problem Hoffman has with competition, they ought to be seen as "co-competitors" worthy of our support. He says, "encouraging one's opponents sounds ludicrous until church leaders, athletes, and coaches examine their premise for competing."[61]

The tendency to alienate other competitors comes not from an inherent flaw in competition but out of viewing competition from an ethic of gamesmanship. If winning is the chief goal of sport then seeing co-competitors as enemies is completely justifiable. To prevent this mentality Christians ought to be mindful of how the desire to win can influence the way competitive sports are played. We have already identified a conceptual framework for one way Christians can think about sport.

Viewing sports as MacIntyrean practices provides the benefits of seeing sport as a practice with internal goods that are to be sought for their own sake. In this view sport is fundamentally good and as Christians play in competitive sport they can express thanksgiving to God for both the ability to play and for the gift of sport itself. Appreciating sport will help keep the Christian athlete alert to the powers that can corrupt the practice. MacIntyre terms these corruptive influences institutions and sets them in a paradoxical contrast to practices. Institutions play a unique role in social practices in that they at the same time sustain and endanger said practices.

> Indeed so intimate is the relationship of practices to institutions—and consequently of the goods external to the goods internal to the practices in question—that institutions and practices characteristically form a single causal order in which the ideals and the creativity of the practice are always vulnerable to the acquisitiveness of the institution, in which the cooperative care for common goods of the practice is always vulnerable to the competitiveness of the institution.[62]

Appearing at times to be nearly indistinguishable from each other it can be easy to intend a critique of institutions and end up being critical of the practice. That is why MacIntyre's framework is so crucial to this understanding of competitive sport since making the distinction between institutions and practices, between external goods and internal goods, Christians can condemn the corruption of institutions while participating and enjoying the internal goods of the practice. It is worth being reminded that external goods are still in fact goods. They do not necessarily and essentially entail corruption. Earning money for winning an athletic contest is not in itself wrong. It is when the prize of winning, (i.e., external goods) becomes

61. Hoffman, *Good Game*, 173.
62. MacIntyre, *After Virtue*, 194.

more important than pursuing the standards of excellence contained in the practice, (i.e., internal goods) that the integrity of the practice is in jeopardy.

The ethic of gamesmanship has as its end the external goods that are distributed by the institutions. The ethic of sportsmanship identifies with the values of the practice that the institutions are entrusted to sustain but as we noted earlier they are not safeguarded against the corruptive influences of external goods and will ultimately be assimilated into an ethic where winning is the *raison d'être*.

Randolph Feezell recognizes the game itself as a social practice that "changes the ethical tone and atmosphere of sports participation" when he says, "in sport it is the game that binds the community together, and the game is a larger reality that generates the standards of excellence over against which the individual defines his own achievements and his sport-related identity."[63] Viewing sport in a framework of MacIntyrean practices allows one to go beyond oneself and see the larger implications of being involved in a community oriented activity. Sport is not about one athlete versus another. It is about both athletes performing in service of the game itself. "It is the game that demands the attention of the players attempting to achieve a particular kind of goodness, and it is the game that benefits when achievements are understood as shared goods."[64]

If Christianity is to be compatible with competitive sports then it must adopt something like what Linville calls Christmanship, an attitude toward competition that reduces the importance of winning, is respectful of co-competitors, and celebrates the goods internal to the practice.

Opponents do not stand in the way of victory and as such are not obstacles that need to be removed. From this view opponents prevent an athlete from achieving their goal. Instead they are helpful in reaching those goals. Not least of all reasons is because co-competitors push each other to be better.

Athletes can encourage one another since victory is only fulfilling when the victor knows his or her rival competitor gave it their all. Winning because one's opponents did not try their best is hardly rewarding. When the fear of losing is removed athletes are freed to support opponents knowing that they can make each other better. Playing one's best not only satisfyingly tests the limits of his or her own physical abilities but improves the opportunity for opponents to do their best. This mentality serves as a safeguard against seeing an opponent as an enemy to be humiliated.

63. Feezell, *Sport, Play, and Ethical Reflection*, 146.

64. Ibid.

Hoffman is doubtful that cooperative striving toward excellence is enough to redeem sport since there still must be winners and losers. He admires former tennis professional Andrea Jaeger who quit playing tennis when "she realized that her faith could no longer allow her to play her hardest when doing so brought so much disappointment and suffering to those who were victims of her talent."[65] Jaeger's own moral dilemma was not the result of cheating, intimidation, or the like. It was simply that she could not stand the "suffering" she inflicted on opponents. However, the extent to which one "suffers" from losing a sporting contest perhaps reveals an existing attitude of gamesmanship that needs to be altered. One also may question whether it is worse to disappoint an opponent by displaying greater talent in a fair contest or disrespecting an opponent by giving less than one's best.

"If athletes do not compete to their fullest potential, they are making a statement that their co-competitors are not worthy of their best effort . . . A true competitor never insults a co-competitor by not giving his or her best effort."[66] There are two attitudes toward co-competitors that will lead an athlete to give less than his or her best in a competitive event. The athlete is either patronizing the opponent or is arrogant about his or her own abilities.[67] Both lack respect to co-competitors and are outside of the proper attitude of competition. Attempting to humiliate an opponent is condemnable behavior but so is the elimination of competitive zeal. Underselling the competitive element of sport at the same time disrespects the unique talents of one's opponent as gifted to them by the Creator and spells the demise of the sporting activity.

After being highly critical of competition Hoffman concludes by somewhat softening his tone. "Sport that does not involve opposition and is not framed in the possibility of winning is not sport."[68] Believing competition is an activity that can be redeemed he points to the need for evangelicals to "appreciate how their public witness can be undermined when they elevate competition to anything other than the simple organizing principle for playing games" and cautions that "anything competitive is always treacherous ground for Christians to tread, for it threatens to realign human

65. Hoffman, *Good Game*, 163.

66. Linville, "Ethic of Competition," 174.

67. A third possibility is that a club could choose not to play their best team. This often happens near the end of a league's regular season in order to rest and protect the best players so that they will be better fit for the playoffs. However, these are relatively rare exceptions and openly accepted practices. For our purposes we will use the two alternatives listed above in the context of a typical competition without these added implications.

68. Hoffman, *Good Game*, 164.

relationships and sever bonds of fellowship that their faith enjoins them to protect and nurture."[69]

He is too critical on some of the finer points of competition but Christians would do well to pay more attention to the general concerns Hoffman raises. Competition can be very dangerous to the faith, especially when the corruptive powers of institutions remain unchecked. Christians must engage in competitive sport aware of these dangers and keep a proper perspective of competition as a measuring stick and a motivator, both for our own abilities and the abilities of others. Marvin Zuidema summarizes competition from a Christian perspective in the following way. He says,

> A Christian response to competitive play is focused competition which encourages the athlete to be an expressive player in celebration to the Lord, to give God thanks for the gift of play, to play intensely, to pursue excellence and test the limits of abilities, and to develop and act with Christian commitments.[70]

Unfortunately, as Hoffman correctly points out on multiple occasions, Christians have done a poor job thinking about competition in a theological context. Studies have shown that church sport leagues in general and individual Christians in particular have developed their attitudes toward competition not from theological convictions but from their local sports communities and watching competitive sports on television.[71] Perhaps then the criticism should not be aimed at competition per se, as much as it should be at Christians for their failure to engage the culture of sport with principles of the faith. Christianity can be compatible with competition but it will require a large portion of its adherents to re-evaluate their understanding of the purpose and goals of sport in a Christian context.

Conceptions of the Body

In addition to the challenges Christians face because of corrupted views of competition Hoffman develops a second criticism of the modern sports culture. He devotes a chapter of his helpful book on Christianity and sports to the dangerous ways sport is involved in "building and sacking the temple." There he makes the case that Christians too blindly encourage the thrill and excitement of dangerous collisions and injury-prone routines while failing to face the reality that our enjoyment is at the expense of a biblical mandate

69. Ibid.

70. Zuidema, "Athletics from a Christian Perspective," 197.

71. Keller et al., "Competition in Church Sport Leagues."

to honor the body. In this section I will relay the theological concerns Hoffman has about the physical dangers of sport and argue that his unease serves as a well founded caution to Christians and should be considered very carefully. His assertion is not that all sports are inherently wrong but that "any reasonable person of any theological persuasion would conclude that in some sports, the risk of injury is simply too substantial to justify participation."[72]

Any theological discontent over health issues in sports may be reduced to one of two potential pitfalls. In order to justify participation in sport Christians must overcome two common errors. Athletes and spectators are often inclined to either glorify the body too much by placing unmerited worth in a particular physical appearance and/or performance or they may neglect proper respect and admiration of the human body as created in the image of God.

Sport's Proclivity to Body Worship

Seeking theological justification, advocates of the nineteenth-century Muscular Christianity movement placed more emphasis on one's physical abilities than had previously been given. In his historical account of Muscular Christians Clifford Putney notes that, "at their most extreme, 'body as temple' men completely dropped the traditional Christian emphasis on confessing weakness in oneself and forgiving it in others."[73] At least within this circle of Christians there was a shift in attitude from "the meek shall inherit the earth" to "only the strong survive."

As we saw in the previous chapter, Muscular Christians were concerned about the feminization of the Church and saw a need for a manly, rough and tumble renewal in Christian leadership. Putney reveals the agenda of these Christians as one that used a number of reasons to involve Christians in sport, including the promotion of healthy bodies, as a means to making bigger, stronger, more masculine believers. But they were also motivated by deeper theological issues. "Most likely, churches kept gyms for a variety of reasons: to 'save' citified children, to raise church membership, and to ensure healthfulness. But behind all these reasons was the liberal religious notion that salvation lay as much through the body as through the soul."[74]

Not only is the emphasis on the body as having a central role in salvation but ultimately this movement was guilty of rejecting the orthodox

72. Hoffman, *Good Game*, 192.

73. Putney, *Muscular Christianity*, 57.

74. Ibid., 63.

doctrine of salvation as being a work of God. "For despite their stated intention of giving boys religious and ethical values from the past, boys' workers in essence preached the virtues of modernity: regulation, socialization, and reliance on oneself rather than God."[75]

Putney may have overstated his case on this point. To be sure, some adherents would have taken the view of the body to this extreme but it would be unfair to label the entire movement as having done so. For many, it was not an effort to replace God but to restore the masculine appearance of power to the faith. The modern sports culture often makes it easy to overvalue the human body. The "no pain, no gain" attitude reflects ideas consistent with the Muscular Christian view of a physically healthy body as the normative standard for all human beings. If a body was not big, strong, and physically fit it was not a body that honored God.

While most of the Muscular Christianity movement has faded away there are still traces of its influence in contemporary Christian circles. Watson has articulated how the Muscular Christianity movement has contributed much to modern sports ministry.[76] Many of the ideals in the movement were adopted by revivalist protestants in Britain and, to a greater extent, in America. These were utilized as means of proselytizing and gave some protestant groups a platform for promoting their faith. Watson states, "the force of American protestant revivalism has reshaped and redirected its modern counterpart. This has resulted in a utilitarian 'work-based ethic' that seems to characterise *some* of what sporting evangelical organisations do."[77] One case in point is Bruce Gust. He has developed a program that combines Bible study tools and an intense exercise regimen to promote both spiritual and physical fitness. Giving the program the same name as its parent movement, Muscular Christianity, tells of the scriptural commandment to be like God. Based on Ephesians 5:1, Gust presents the argument that Christians are to be imitators of God. Even though the context of this passage refers to walking in love and avoiding immoral behavior, Gust reads into it the idea that we are to be imitators of God in all respects. This includes having the same level of physical fitness that, presumably, Jesus himself had. Given the cultural diet, his profession as a carpenter and the need to walk dozens of miles between cities suggests to Gust that Jesus was a very physically fit man.

> To imitate Jesus, then, is to recognize fitness as a matter of more than just wellness or aesthetics, it's a matter of obedience. And when you look at it from that standpoint, fitness is no longer

75. Ibid., 126.
76. Watson, "Muscular Christianity in the Modern Age."
77. Ibid., 93; italics original.

just an extracurricular activity. Rather, it's a part of your walk with Him. And with that Reality comes a sense of urgency and inspiration that goes beyond simply wanting to look good.[78]

Another advocate of a contemporary Muscular Christianity is P. G. Mathew. In a sermon dated February 2007, he said that what is needed to understand the doctrines of the Bible are "muscular, not mushy, Christians" and stressed that muscular Christians are developed through endurance and discipline.[79] He does not explicitly address certain sports or appropriate ways of becoming physically fit. He keeps his focus on attacking those he sees as weak Christians who are not as morally dogmatic as he believes they should be. His criticism is aimed at those who are accepting of a range of moral issues from abortion to divorce to laziness. He makes clear his position that the physically healthy possess spiritual wisdom so obviously lacking in those not willing to condemn these actions. "Such people, however, refuse to become *athletic* muscular Christians of great discernment and judgment, competent to make correct decisions and counsel in every life situation."[80] Why must one be athletic to have discernment? This claim lacks theological merit and is guilty of idolizing a particular physique. It implicitly suggests an athletic body is the normative standard for all Christian bodies and is somehow fundamental to good moral decision making.

Mathew, like Gust, is to be commended for stressing the importance of the Christian's obedience and dependence upon God but certainly takes the case too far by believing physically and mentally fit bodies are the keys to enduring in the Christian faith. They take the other side of the same coin used by the nineteenth-century Muscular Christians. Both are guilty of adopting a form of body worship that makes sport and physical exercise an essential requirement for spiritual development. One views a strong, healthy body as a necessary component of salvation while the other see physical fitness as a requirement for obedience to God.

Both views fail to capture any notion of inherent good in the physical activities they so strongly advocate. As a result they do not escape the instrumental view of sport previously criticized. To be fair, they are not academics concerned with parsing every theological aspect of physical exercise. They are more interested in the practical application of their perceptions of what it means to be obedient to God. However, it does not excuse the neglect of theological reasons for why a specific fitness activity is so fundamental to the Christian faith. It may be the case that such a routine

78. Gust, "Muscular Christianity Overview."
79. Mathew, "Muscular Christianity Sermon Transcript."
80. Ibid.; italics added.

is more self-serving than Christians like Gust care to admit. This proves the point Watson is making in his assessment of modern sports ministry. There is a disparity between practitioners and scholars. Watson proposes a more unified approach. He suggests that those involved in sports ministries to be open to critical scholarship and at the same time scholars "should also be very careful not to disparage or alienate those working 'in the field' but rather, offer encouragement and support through collaborative projects, sound biblical exegesis and systematic theological study of their work."[81]

I affirm Watson's appeal to more collaboration between theological scholarship and sporting practices. The neo-Muscular Christian ideology promoted by Gust, Mathew, and the like provide examples of opportunities to think more critically about athleticism while engaging in sport from a Christian perspective. For instance, might these sports ministries be affirmed for their devotion to God and promotion of physical health, and at the same time reassess their insistence on sport/physical fitness being the avenue to true Christian fidelity? Hoffman is helpful in developing a more thoughtful approach when he writes, "For all of its practical benefits, exercise can be a singularly indulgent and selfish experience. Perhaps redirecting the physical energy invested in treadmills or stationary bicycles to vigorous acts of public and private service would be a more profitable and justifiable way to glorify members' bodies."[82] How are Christians to justify spending their time in a gymnasium when, say, helping to build a house for the homeless would result in the same contribution to one's physical well-being? Hoffman adds, "While there is little question that Scripture teaches Christians to care for their bodies, there are many ways of fulfilling this spiritual obligation; it hardly requires replication of commercial gymnasia or programs that divert time, energy, and money from missions and other spiritual matters traditionally vouchsafed to the church."[83]

Millions upon millions of people around the world engage in sporting activity on a regular basis as a means to get or stay in shape. Sport provides a suitable form of exercise that is at the same time enjoyable. The enjoyment found in sport provides an answer to Hoffman's criticism though it is likely insufficient. Hoffman's response may be to say that we, as Christians, are not called to a life of enjoyment but to serve others and show them the love and grace God has shown to us. Or he may rightly question the genuineness of a Christian's attitude who seeks personal enjoyment over the alleviation of another's suffering and hardship. This rationale is difficult to accept,

81. Watson, "Muscular Christianity in the Modern Age," 90.
82. Hoffman, *Good Game,* 173.
83 Ibid.

particularly when the Christian's excuse for exercising is to become a more able body for doing God's work; work that would have the same result on the body's development as playful exercise. Hoffman's point is not to condemn all sports and exercise routines but to make Christians aware of how often their attitudes are self-serving. Sadly enough, physical exercise and participation in sport "to be better fit for service" can be a blanket of false piety used to cover up one's own self-indulgence.

This is not to say that all the time available to a Christian should be spent in spiritual matters. Neither Hoffman nor I make such a claim. Indeed there are appropriate times and places for sport. As should already be evident, sport is an expression of play that is a basic good of human well-being. Instead, I suggest that what Hoffman is doing is trying to do is caution Christians about the danger of forsaking our role as representatives of Christ's kingdom so that we may have a good time.

Moreover, he is calling out the ulterior motives in many who would argue that they participate in sport as a means of becoming better servants of God. Surely Hoffman is right to conclude that "if there is a theological justification for sport, it will be found in its appeal to players' spirits, not as a health-inducing experience."[84]

The Degradation of the Body

Hoffman's critique reveals a second pitfall Christians ought to be aware of when it comes to views of the body in sport. This view is more prevalent in contemporary Christianity and in some sense forms the basis of the previous pitfall. The error is to view the body as a means to an end. Christian commitments to a healthy body, both physical and mental, form the basis for the acceptance of some forms of sport. In fact, as was shown in the previous chapter sport is sometimes viewed as a necessary activity for better fitting one's body to the service of God. This was the approach advocated by Richard Baxter. There are times when sport can be beneficial to our physical health that more appropriately enables us to fulfill our spiritual calling.

Yet it is often the case that participation in sport results in as much physical harm as good. Sometimes such harm is dangerous enough to require serious medical attention. For Baxter, this sends us a step in the wrong direction. If sport is allowable only when it results in a more fit body then any sport making a player unfit is to be prohibited. Physical injuries impede upon one's ability to fulfill his or her calling. Therefore Baxter states that, "all those are unlawful sports, which really unfit us for the duties of our callings,

84. Ibid., 174.

and the service of God; which laying the benefit and hurt together, do hinder us as much or more than they help us!"[85] It is clear, at least to Baxter, that even though the sport may provide some benefit to our higher purpose, if it could result in unfitting our bodies then it is to be avoided.

This is a difficult notion for many modern Christians. The full contact sports that are so popular in contemporary society are often extremely dangerous. In fact, while there are health benefits to be found in sports it is the case that participating in the most popular sports of our day means subjecting oneself to the very real possibility of bodily injury.

Participants of European football, rugby, hockey, boxing and the American big three sports (football, baseball, and basketball) all are at very high risk of serious harm. This is a distinct possibility of professional sports but is also very widespread in amateur and youth sports as well.

A number of government programs have emerged encouraging people, particularly children, to participate in sports rather than television and video games. These initiatives promote athletics for their physical health benefits. While it is true that involvement in sport helps fight obesity and encourage overall health it does open new possibilities for injury.

The National Center for Sports Safety reports that more than 3.5 million children under the age of fourteen are medically treated for sports related injuries every year in the United States meaning nearly forty percent of all sports related injuries are children in this age range. It also claims that twenty-one percent of all traumatic brain injuries are sport related.[86] There are also so called "extreme sports" including mixed martial arts, skateboarding, parkour and the like, which increase the risk of injury exponentially.

Baxter believes participating in these sports to be unacceptable for Christians since an injury may prevent the athlete from carrying out the labor of his or her calling, although it is not just Baxter and other Puritans sympathetic to this view. Hoffman notes the precedent in theological thought predates the Puritanism of the sixteenth and seventeenth centuries. "There has been no more consistent theme in the theological literature related to sports over the past 600 years than the teaching that Christians should avoid sports that are dangerous to themselves and others."[87]

The most notable reason for this unity is the Christian emphasis on the image of God in humanity coupled with the notion of the body as the temple of the Holy Spirit. How can a Christian be committed to these doctrines and at the same time condone participation in a sport where the temple

85. Baxter, *The Practical Works of Richard Baxter*, 387.

86. Lemak, "Sports Injury Facts."

87. Hoffman, *Good Game*, 176.

will most likely be heavily abused? One attempt to diffuse this criticism has been the cliché "No pain, no gain." This mentality suggests that in order to advance one's status as an athlete, one must be willing to subject his or her body to physical pain.

"In the culture of risk", says Hoffman, "sprains, broken and dislocated limbs, and other disfigurements of the *imago Dei* become emblems of moral conviction and strength rather than an unnecessary maiming of a sacred vessel."[88]

One response to this would be to note the different cultural environment in which Baxter penned his words of warning against sport. A physical injury in the sixteenth century was likely to be more serious than a similar injury in the twenty-first century. The ability to treat serious injuries as well as the typical recovery time has drastically improved since the sixteenth century resulting in minimal consequences to the course of one's calling. What real affect would, a knee injury, for instance, sustained in a game of football, have on a minister's ability to fulfill his or her calling? It is doubtful that most injuries would carry any lasting implications that would hinder Christian obedience.

It is true enough that many participants do not experience moderate or severe injuries while playing any sport. Many will play sports and never become injured and so fail to see the strength of this criticism. Moreover, the players are not intending to get injured. It happens accidentally and the risk is not sufficient enough to merit prohibiting all participation.

The accidental nature of most injuries is not sufficient justification for overlooking the dangers to the body. As Hoffman argues, "when humans of massive proportions collide at breakneck speeds, when runners subject their bodies to multiple marathons, when the knees and hips of gymnasts endure tens of thousands of crushing dismounts, their bodies surely will pay the price."[89] Just because athletes do not intend to get hurt does not take away from the fact that they are likely to be injured.

However, if it is the case that we are meant to avoid sport because of the inherent risk then we must avoid other activities in life as well. For instance, one should not drive a car since, even though there is no intent to be injured, statistically there will be thousands of car related injuries each year. Commercial fishers and construction workers work in highly dangerous professions yet there does not seem to be an outcry of Christian voices condemning such work. Perhaps this is because of a distinction between the types of activity in question. One is a form of work. That is, it is a means

88. Ibid., 184.
89. Ibid., 177.

by which someone earns a living. Sport, in their view, is a frivolous activity with no lasting impact, which makes the risk not worth taking.

What are we to make then of the professional athlete whose source of income is provided by participating in the sport? Now it seems the distinction is one of types of professions, not a categorical difference. Instead it may be argued that the worker is contributing to society in a meaningful way, by providing food or creating buildings, etc. The athlete provides no benefit to the community and therefore the risk is not justified. However, such a response can only be made from the framework we have already rejected, which denies any inherent value in sport as a basic good for human well-being. If sport is to be rejected for its inherent risks then so too must other ventures in life be prohibited.

The point is not to condemn these professions but to draw attention to the fact that life is full of risks. The fact that one *might* sprain an ankle in a game of football is no reason to abstain from playing in the first place. Football and other physically demanding sports are perfectly acceptable forms of recreation for Christians, as are professions such as construction work, so far as risks against the body are concerned.

A second response to Hoffman would be to question in what sense the doctrine of the *imago Dei* truly affects the physical risks to which we subject our bodies. This concept has less to say about humanity's physical likeness to God than it does our non-physical likeness. Many have argued it refers to humanity's unique position in creation as exhibited by our reason, free will and moral decision making. Others suggest we are made in God's image in that we are relational beings. Theologians have offered numerous perspectives on what the imago Dei best represents but few of them build a defense of our physical bodies based on this doctrine.[90] Wayne Grudem comes close when he says our bodies, "have been created by God as suitable instruments to represent in a physical way our human nature, which has been made to be like God's own nature."[91] He goes on to say,

> In fact, almost everything we do is done by means of the use of our physical bodies—our thinking, our moral judgments, our prayer and praise, our demonstrations of love and concern for each other—all are done using the physical bodies God has given us. Therefore, if we are careful to point out that we are *not* saying that God has a physical body, we may say that our

---

90. For a discussion on the various interpretations of *imago Dei*, see Culver, *Systematic Theology*, 248–57.

91. Grudem, *Systematic Theology*, 448.

physical bodies in various ways reflect something of God's own
character as well.[92]

In what way does this understanding of our physical bodies and the
imago Dei inform our decisions about the risks to which we subject our bodies? With the possible exception of "thinking" none of the other examples
Grudem uses for how our bodies can reflect God's image are in any danger
by participating in sport. If this is as near a defense of our physical bodies as
the *imago Dei* gets us, then I remain unconvinced that the doctrine should
be used in criticizing potentially harmful sporting activity.

Yet as Hoffman rightly suggests, Christian theology does provide
direction in the uses of our physical bodies. For instance, Paul says, "Or
do you not know that your body is a temple of the Holy Spirit within you,
whom you have from God? You are not your own, for you were bought with
a price. So glorify God in your body."[93] This passage is frequently used to
steer Christians away from activities that would be harmful to them. However, the context in which Paul is speaking refers to sexual immorality, not
risking physical harm. Moreover, the phrase "your body" in each verse is an
interest construct with "your" in plural form (ὑμῶν) and "body" in singular
form (σῶμα) suggests the text is more focused on the broader church body.
As Kenneth Bailey points out, "Paul is not merely interested in the personal/
bodily health and destiny of the individual, but also in the health of the
whole body of Christ."[94] Even if the purpose of the passage is to confront
the sexual immorality of some Corinthian believers, the context does lend
itself to an application for all believers to honor our bodies since they were
made for, belong to, and are intended to glorify the Lord. Christian theology
recognizes a purpose in our physical bodies that reaches beyond risking
physical harm to win a contest or entertain a crowd.

Moderate to serious injuries, such as a concussion or torn anterior
cruciate ligament (ACL) present a more difficult case than do minor sprains
and bruises. These, two of the most common serious sports injuries, often
temporarily restrain the full range of human activity but allow for a complete recovery. However, depending on the severity of the ACL tear it may
result in permanently reduced strength and mobility of the athlete's knee.

Similarly, research suggests repetitive head trauma may contribute to
memory loss and dementia up to thirty years later. The 2010 season of the
National Football League (NFL) was marked by a growing concern for the

92. Ibid.

93. 1 Cor 6:19–20.

94. Bailey, *Paul through Mediterranean Eyes*, 190.

long term effects of concussions brought on by severe head to head contact.[95] More strict regulations, extended recovery times, as well as, increased fines and suspensions for dangerous hits are some of the steps being taken to increase the safety of NFL players.

The fact that such extreme measures are necessary suggests that the risks of football are more serious than a sprained ankle. Even with the new safety protocols it is reasonable to assume serious head trauma will still occur. Steps can be taken, perhaps should have been taken years ago, to improve the safety of players but the danger remains. The danger, says Hoffman, is more than the physical risks. A degradation of the body is required to participate in dangerous sports. "Willful submission to the violence in sports like boxing, football, and hockey may be possible only when athletes disassociate from their bodies, relating to them as though they were athletic equipment, or imagining that they occupy a separate space from the rest of their being."[96] He continues,

> Bodies have little intrinsic worth in the world of sports; their value is in the uses to which they can be put for the team. Recognizing that bodies frequently fail, the sports culture inculcates a casualness toward arms, legs, backs, fingers, and skulls. They are regarded not only as separate from souls, but as expendable appendages of athletic production. Injuries are the cost of doing business.[97]

Hoffman is correct that an attitude that degrades the body into a tool for the purpose of winning the next match is incompatible with Christian theology. Yet, the bleak picture he paints fails to capture the good of sport on three different accounts. First, he exaggerates the risks of bodily injury by drawing an unfair comparison between modern sport and the infamous gladiatorial games. "In the end, it may be no more possible for modern sports aficionados to appreciate the bodily abuse that occurs in competition than it was for ancient Romans to view the death battles in the arena as blood-thirsty cruelty."[98] Certainly Christians ought to condemn the "injuries are the cost of doing business" mentality and should do more to bring awareness to such dangerous attitudes toward the body. But to equate the injuries sustained in modern sport with those experienced in the Roman arena simply lacks credibility.

95. Farmer, "NFL Is Taking the Long–term Impact of Concussions Seriously."
96. Hoffman, *Good Game*, 184.
97. Ibid., 187.
98. Ibid., 188.

To begin with, there is the issue of intentionality. We have already seen how Hoffman gives less merit to this idea than I believe he should. While it is true that some athletes will be injured there remains a moral distinction between accidental and intentional injuries. The modern athlete(s) seeks to overcome obstacles within clearly defined rules, some of which are designed to prevent injuries, and do so in a way that is more effective, faster, or more plentiful than his or her opponent(s). When injuries occur in modern sports they are the result of unfortunate accidents that occur as competitors vie for the goals of the sport. The gladiators' goal was to cause fatal harm to other gladiators. The two cannot be compared as it serves an injustice to both athlete and spectator of modern sports. A fan may cheer at a violent collision of football players (wearing protective equipment of course) and still wish for the well-being of the players. This is very different from the spectators of the Roman games who cheered as gladiators were mauled to death by wild animals.

The second reason Hoffman's criticism against sport is insufficient is because it focuses on the inherent risks associated with sports but declines to praise the ways in which the body may be honored in sport. He depicts an entirely negative approach to the body in sport by focusing solely on the physical dangers. He makes no mention of ways sport honors the body. Sport is an activity with intrinsic respect for the human body and the feats it can accomplish. It is designed in such a way as to allow the body to fully explore the gifts God created in it. The attitude toward the body he describes is far more evident in professional level sports than in the grassroots games that the average person would participate in. Again, as was the case in his argument against competition, Hoffman's theological disquiet pertains more to the institutions that sustain sport than to sport itself.

Yet, there are aspects of his position that are helpful. His critique of modern sport viewing the body as a machine or as a tool to be used in competition provides a helpful argument against biotechnological enhancements in sport. "When athletes are reduced to scientific specimens to be manipulated in a relentless assault on human limits, it becomes easy to think of them as soulless packages of muscle, bone, and nerve rather than human beings with feelings, emotions, and an eternal destiny."[99] He is correct to point out this wayward view of the human body to which sport so easily succumbs. Christians are standing on dangerous ground but it doesn't mean we should never tread the terrain.

99. Ibid., 188.

Character Formation

The third aspect of Hoffman's argument I wish to address is his position on sport's negative influence on the development of an athlete's moral character. The MacIntyrean distinction we made earlier, between practices and institutions has been helpful in identifying the points of sport worthy of moral criticism. It has defended sport against charges of inherent competitive corruption and has been useful in recognizing different attitudes toward the body and sport that are incompatible with Christian theology. Here again the distinction will be helpful in our discussion of the moral nature of sport. Randolph Feezell says, "it is within this structure [of MacIntyrean practices] that respect for the game can be understood, and such an attitude seems naturally to arise among members of the practice community who become serious about the possibilities related to becoming a good player."[100]

The images of progression Feezell uses are instructive. The development of attitudes as well as skills suggests the learning of a practice is a process. Certainly this is in line with MacIntyre's own description of practices as they involve "sequences of development" and "progress towards and beyond a variety of types and modes of excellence."[101] No doubt some would include the development of moral excellences through sport. The rigorous demands of athletic activity combined with the strict adherence to a specified set of rules makes sport a prime candidate for bestowing moral character on those who enter its arena.

> No one who has engaged in athletics at a serious level can doubt that they teach us something about the value of concentrated effort, how to handle disappointments, and how to keep calm under stressful situations, or that they provide us with valuable experience in testing our psychological and physical limits.[102]

Many have suggested that sport offers a platform for developing moral character. The list of traits attributable to sport includes, but is not limited to teamwork, determination, fairness, commitment, and respect for rules. These teachable qualities are most commonly cited as reasons for involving young people in sport. "In the heat of competition," notes Judi Jackson, "values are not just taught to adolescents; they are built into their personality and decision making."[103] These deep-seated morals supposedly instilled by

---

100. Feezell, *Sport, Play, and Ethical Reflection*, 146.

101. MacIntyre, *After Virtue*, 189.

102. Hoffman, *Good Game*, 198.

103. Jackson, "Introduction to Recreation and Sports Ministry For All Ages," 193.

sport will fundamentally shape how these youth think, how they act, and ultimately who they will become.

Does Sport Encourage Positive or Negative Moral Behavior?

As a way of emphasizing these virtues many organized sports honor individual athletes for their selfless acts and demonstration of good sportsmanship. The behavior of those who receive such awards is certainly commendable. There ought to be, especially in Christian sports such as church leagues, more recognition of those who display virtuous behavior in competitive sport. Often these awards are given to athletes who encourage opponents, are humble in victory and gracious in defeat, or who demonstrate a high commitment to fair play. While it is important to point out those whose actions go above and beyond that which is required in sport Hoffman makes an interesting claim. He says, "by singling out these acts of elemental decency for awards, the NCAA [National Collegiate Athletic Association] implicitly acknowledges that most of its coaches and athletes, faced with the same set of circumstances, probably would not have acted in the same honorable way."[104]

More than this, it is worth asking why virtuous behavior is singled out for acknowledgement if sport so basically teaches such behavior. Instead, it seems that recognition is given because, while known to be desirable, that behavior is actually rather *un*common in sports. One would not visit a pub and give an award to anyone with a pint in his hand. Furthermore, it hardly seems meritorious to do what so many would do naturally in other activities. Bumping into someone on the street and then refusing to help her off the ground back on to her feet would be rude and rightfully invite moral criticism. Bumping into someone on the pitch and refusing to help her up again is just being a "good competitor." The fact that truly praiseworthy behavior is so recognizably infrequent suggests that sport may not be the beacon of moral transference some claim it to be. Perhaps sport does not pass along virtue quite so readily to those who participate.

Part of "the problem is that this dual ethic—so vital to the playing of games—can easily be generalized to an entire ethical scheme so that sports become answerable only to their own internal moral code."[105] Affording sport a separate ethic other than "real life ethics" makes it easy to compartmentalize one's ethical behavior so that when participating in sport an athlete can

104. Hoffman, *Good Game*, 206.
105. Ibid., 204.

ignore the virtues he or she would display in any other setting such as helping a person off the ground when bumping into her on the street.

Allan Bäck recognizes this disparity and believes it means that sport as a competitive enterprise is not a source of transferable moral instruction. "If we take sport in the classical way, as a type of play in contrast to the serious business of work and survival, then it is somewhat strange to talk of producing virtues for our whole life in a sport."[106] He links the source of this trouble to the corruption of competition and suggests that if sport has any redeeming moral qualities they are to be found in non-competitive athletic activities, particularly in the martial arts. However, Bäck seems to be in the minority as a great many number of people advocate the moral lessons learned in sport that have served them well later in life.

Conducting interviews of dozens of highly successful individuals Brian Kilmeade has composed two volumes that credit sport with laying the groundwork for their accomplishments.[107] Virtues like hard-work, determination, courage, strength in the face of adversity, and the like are frequently associated with the ability to compete at the highest levels but most people never make it that far in sports. Most become professionals in some other area of life.

However, as Kilmeade points out, the lessons learned from childhood participation in sport are formative experiences that contributed to successes later in life. His interviews include several United States presidents and other politicians, actors and television personalities, as well as highly successful corporate CEO's and a few professional athletes. He begins these interviews by stating, "I have come to the conclusion that sports is the best classroom for life."[108]

Citing just one example of the appreciation for sport captured throughout both texts he quotes professional golfer Ben Crenshaw. "Looking back at my life, I realize I learned to respect rules in golf, which, in turn, taught me to respect the rules of life. I've learned from the sport to act honourably, even when no one else is looking . . . I guess you can say I learned that first life lesson on the green."[109]

106. Bäck, "The Way to Virtue in Sport," 226.

107. See Kilmeade, *The Games Do Count*; and Kilmeade, *It's How You Play the Game*.

108. Kilmeade, *It's How You Play the Game*, 2.

109. Ibid., 211.

Sport Among the Christian Moral Pedagogues

There is little doubt that sport has its teachable moments. Any number of qualities has the *potential* to be developed through participating in sport but two words of caution must be heard before accepting its moral nature. First, these traits are not exclusive to sport. Virtues like respecting rules and teamwork can be learned in other activities. Hoffman notes that sports can provide some moral development, "but given the ticklish questions that so often surround our games, it is legitimate to ask whether Christians might better seek these effects in other, less ethically complicated human activities."[110] He has a valid point in so far as one views moral pedagogy a chief purpose of sport. If Christians are going to argue for the validity of their involvement in sport on the grounds of its character formation then they must also demonstrate why one is not better off developing those qualities elsewhere. But simply because something is "ethically complicated" does not mean it should be avoided. Learning to navigate around and through the moral complexities may itself be one of sport's many values.

Like Hoffman, George Orwell points out that high level competitive sport is laden with these disagreeable behaviors. "Serious sport has nothing to do with fair play. It is bound up with hatred, jealousy, boastfulness, disregard of all rules and sadistic pleasure in witnessing violence: in other words it is war minus the shooting."[111]

C.S. Lewis was also cautious about the idea that sport was a conduit of moral virtue. "Not, indeed, that I allow to games any of the moral and almost mystical virtues which schoolmasters claim for them; they seem to me to lead to ambition, jealousy, and embittered partisan feeling, quite as often as to anything else."[112] Despite this he was not willing to say participating is unchristian. On the contrary, he lamented over the fact that he himself was not predisposed to sport. "Yet not to like them is a misfortune, because it cuts you off from companionship with many excellent people who can be approached in no other way."[113]

In addition to teaching character sport is becoming a large evangelistic platform for Christians in which they can openly share their faith.[114] A major contributing factor to this is the common interest that people share. Sport provides a non-threatening way to get to know others and opens avenues of

110. Hoffman, *Good Game*, 198–99.

111. Orwell, "The Sporting Spirit," 198.

112. Lewis, *Surprised by Joy*, 124.

113. Ibid., 124.

114. For two differing views on the merits of sports evangelism see Krattenmaker, *Onward Christian Athletes*; and Solc, *Communicating on the Playing Field*.

communication that were previously unavailable. However, for purposes of our present conversation the focus is less on faith sharing and more about how sport is able to reveal personalities in a unique and speedy way.

Former professional basketball player and United States Senator Bill Bradley has commented on the ability of sport to quickly display characteristics of people that otherwise would take long periods of time to see. He says, "I can learn more about people by playing a three-on-three game with them for twenty minutes than I can by talking with them for a week."[115] Mutual interests and getting to know people are certainly helpful in spreading the Christian message but, again, the more relevant point here is that sport has a way of exposing behavior in an effective and efficient manner.

In this way, athletic competition can be used to teach, correct, and improve an athlete's predispositions. It can be instructive on how to avoid moral pitfalls as well as pointing the way toward morally healthy behavior. As one Christian author observes, "an emphasis on the positive outcome of respecting authority, playing by the rules, and other issues pertinent to the life lessons of sports can ensure a child's exposure to the right type of influence on his moral development."[116]

However, this is obviously easier said than done. Even the most devoted fans see the complexities of character formation in sport. Despite his zealous attitude toward sport Michael Novak does not accept the idea that there is "some simple transfer of values learned in sports to other areas of life."[117] As an example he uses the virtue of learning to follow rules well. This quality does not take shape in other areas of life simply because it is learned in sports. An American football player learns to respect rules because it is the only way to play the game and there is strict oversight by officiating crews to ensure the rules are properly followed. Moving from the football field to the corporate office the rules become less articulated and in many cases less governed.

Sport possibly will teach us something about rule-following and respecting authority but expecting those lessons to be conveyed in the exact same fashion to other spheres of life is unrealistic. Just because an athlete has learned to follow the rules of the game does not mean he or she will exhibit the same adherence to rules in the corporate, academic, or any other realm of life. Someone who understands the value of teamwork on the pitch may be a very selfish individual the rest of the time.

115. Bradley, *Values of the Game*, 19.

116. Jackson, "Introduction to Recreation and Sports Ministry," 189.

117. Novak, *The Joy of Sports*, 234.

Instead, says Novak, sport helps shape the athlete through teaching more generalized principles that can be transferred in a non-specified way. He identifies two primary virtues that he believes stand out above the rest. "Perhaps what one learns best in sports are habits of discipline and poise under fire. Having faced often the prospect of the death that comes through defeat, one tends not to panic when things go badly."[118]

Another writer from a Christian perspective sees two very similar virtues at the forefront of sport's moral pedagogy. "God has given us the gift of sports so that we might learn endurance and perseverance."[119] The notion of endurance is commonly associated with the physically demanding requirements of sport but could no doubt be expanded to include the mental and moral demands of sport as well. Respect for officials who continue to make bad calls and refusing to cheat even when your opponent does so are examples of how sport habituates moral endurance and those lessons are fully transferable to other areas in life.[120]

The second point is that even if such virtues can be developed through active involvement in sport it does not mean the activity on the whole will always be morally constructive. As Paul Davis reminds us, "a positive moral flavor clearly is attached to notions such as courage, fairness, and self-control. But it does not follow that any manifestation of them is morally commendable."[121] Determination, for example, is a respectable quality in the right context and in the appropriate measure. The self-centered athlete aimed only at acquiring wealth and fame can show just as much determination as his or her competitors. Determination may also be taken to an extreme and result in an unhealthy obsession. Simply because the potential exists for moral formation does not mean the development of an athlete's character is a foregone conclusion.

Unfortunately, there are numerous examples where the opposite is true. The habits acquired through sport, often times in the name of so called virtues like determination, end up being undesirable or immoral traits. An attitude of determination, if not kept in balance, can result in over indulgence. Many athletes and coaches have become obsessed with winning and

118. Ibid., 235.

119. Altrogge, *Game Day for the Glory of God*, 45.

120. Since sport is so physically and mentally challenging, endurance and perseverance are requisites of achieving sport's standards of excellence. Yet, perhaps even more important to the Christian than the development of endurance and perseverance are the dimensions of humility and vulnerability. It is precisely because it is so difficult that those who participate in sport are made keenly aware of their own physical shortcomings and must come to terms with their finite capabilities.

121. Davis, "Ability, Responsibility, and Admiration in Sport," 210.

will push themselves or their players to physically and morally unhealthy levels in the name of victory.

Moral Concerns of Excessive Financial Spending on Sport

Spectators are also obsessed with sport as made evident by their bank accounts. Some estimates place the annual spending on sport and sport related activity in the United States alone to be more than $400 billion.[122] That is roughly fourteen times the amount of federal aid given to developing countries around the world. The inordinate amount spent on a single ticket to the biggest sporting event in America is astounding. USA Today reports the average ticket price for a seat at the Super Bowl in 2008 was over $4,300.[123]

In his fascinating account of travelling with University of Alabama football fans, journalist Warren St. John tells the stories of several fans who each have spend hundreds of thousands of dollars on recreational vehicles and countless hours on the road to travel to every Alabama football game.[124]

The book does not detail the religious affiliations (if any) these fans have but there is no reason to doubt that Christians cling to similar spending practices. Whether it is for travelling to watch their favorite team or sending their children to a high priced sports camp, modern Christians have not excluded themselves from emptying their wallets in the name of sports. Some estimates place the annual spending for the average American family's annual spending on sports for their children above $2,000 with some parents paying out more than $10,000 each year.[125]

It is not just Americans willing to spend large portions of their cash on sports. In 2008 a BBC survey found the average season ticket for middle-priced stands to a Barclay's Premier League club was nearly £600 with many clubs scheduled to raise that price by up to seventeen percent before the 2009 season.[126] Combine this with the hours spent watching, playing, and talking about sport each week and the global obsession becomes very clear.

In some parts of the United States devotion to a local university football team trumps even the priority of family. Warren St. John writes about a Mr. and Mrs. Reese who missed their own daughter's wedding to attend a University of Alabama football game. When asked why he would do that St. John

---

122. Plunkett Research, "Introduction to the Sports Industry."
123. Weisman, "Super Bowl Tickets are Way Over Price of Admission."
124. St. John, *Rammer Jammer Yellow Hammer*, 15.
125. Kadet, "Parents Spare No Expense in Children's Sports."
126. Taylor, "Premier League Clubs Hit Fans with Massive Price Rises."

reports that Mr. Reese had to pause as if he had never considered the question. He finally replied, "I just love Alabama football, is all I can think of."[127]

Serious concerns arise when one's loyalty to a sports team takes priority over family milestones. Fortunately, this is a rather extreme example but similar, less radical measures of obsession occur on a daily basis. Furthermore, Hoffman is right to question whether such large amounts of money and time are best spent on sports when there are so many situations where that money would provide food, clothing, and medicine to starving children or other humanitarian efforts. The Christian imperative "to visit orphans and widows in their affliction, and to keep oneself unstained from the world"[128] should be at the front of a Christian's mind when deciding how much time and money to put into sport instead of different noble causes. Again, this is not to condemn participation in sport but to point out the error of excess so frequently found in Christian sports fans. As Christians we must discover a healthy balance that sees more effort put into charity and less into the self-gratifying world of sports.

The Potential for Character Formation

More than just our time and money, the obsession with sport presents a danger to the Christian mission to love others as oneself and to show compassion to those in need by exalting the conception of sport to something necessary for a fulfilling life. In fact, some have gone so far as to argue for the fusion of a human being's worth with the love of sport. Christian philosopher Michael Novak in his tribute to sports claims, "I have never met a person who disliked sports, or who absented himself or herself entirely from them, who did not at the same time seem to me deficient in humanity."[129] He pushes the issue even further when he states, "such persons seem to me a danger to civilization."[130]

Novak represents an extreme line of thought that results from an unhealthy obsession with sport. The notion he articulates is common among many Christians in the local church. It is hard for them to understand how anybody can not like sports. Rather than trying to grasp the possible reasons for apathy, fanatics simply conclude that there must be something wrong with those people. Whatever else it may be, sport is not an essential

127. St. John, *Rammer Jammer Yellow Hammer,* 15.
128. Jas 1:27.
129. Novak, *The Joy of Sports,* 44.
130. Ibid.

requirement for being human, nor is anyone who is entirely uninterested in sports somehow a deficient person.

In his experience, those not involved lack certain qualities developed in sport like discipline and an understanding of the "role of chance and Fate in determining human outcomes" and end up being people whose view of the world is "far too rational and mechanical."[131] But these qualities are not exclusive to sport. They can be learned elsewhere and as a result do not automatically limit their acquisition to the realm of sports. Novak's point that sport adds a unique dimension to human flourishing is fair enough but it is difficult to see how the uninterested present a danger to society or are somehow less human than an avid sports fan.

C.S. Lewis would surely have disagreed with Novak since in his comments about sport he says that it is a "misfortune" that he personally disliked sport. Pointing out his aversion to sport he notes it is "not a vice; for it is involuntary. I had tried," says Lewis, "to like games and failed. That impulse had been left out of my make-up."[132] Lewis is not alone. It is undeniable that sport pervades virtually all aspects of western society. But to say that those who do not like the practice are in some way dangerous is unfair and untrue. This kind of a statement reveals the unhealthy obsession with sport and should serve as a reminder to Christians that even if we can avoid the common pitfalls in the sports culture we just explored that our affinity for the activity can stretch too far.

To elaborate further on a point Novak makes I would submit that if *everyone* disliked sports then the world would be in danger of becoming too rational and mechanical. Eliminating sport all together would indeed make the world a little bit shallower. What Novak fails to recognize is that if everyone shared his passion for sport then here too one would find a similar lack in depth. Those whose interests are not in sport are free to focus their energies and talents to the ends of music, art, science and so on.

Perhaps it would be more advantageous to broaden Novak's point from one about participation in sport to participation in play. For play gives us the qualities Novak insists are important for human well-being, adding depth to an otherwise mechanical and shallow human existence and at the same time includes those individuals who have no interest in sports. Even though the purpose here is to demonstrate the importance of sport in the life of the Christian community it must be accepted that many within that community may rightfully find the activity unappealing. As is most often the case, each extreme has something to learn from the other. The apathetic

131. Ibid.
132. Lewis, *Surprised by Joy*, 124.

can learn to appreciate the significance of sport in the lives of so many fellow believers while the fanatic can be made aware of the dangers of over indulgence.

When properly measured, determination and withstanding adversity are admirable traits many athletes learn. Determination means not giving up too early and also knowing when to quit. We can expand the list, as Kerrigan does, to include the virtues of honesty, integrity, and justice. "Learning the rules of the game, fostering respect for the values of honesty, integrity, and fair play, along with developing skills to deal with adversity on the playing field offer potential for positive formation of life skills in other areas such as family, community, and work."[133] There is no reason to stop here though. Various other values can be instilled through sport, such as humility, courage, and prudence, all of which can contribute to Christian ideals of a good life.

Among other things, Pope John Paul II was known for his love of sport. In 2000 he held an international convention with the theme of "During the Time of the Jubilee: The Face and Soul of Sport" in which he stated, "the potential of sports makes it a significant vehicle for the overall development of the person and a very useful element in building a more human society."[134]

A few years later he reiterated the value he placed on sport when he addressed the European Championship club Real Madrid. He said,

> The Church considers sports as an instrument of education when they foster high human and spiritual ideals and when they form young people in an integral way to develop in such values as loyalty, perseverance, friendship, solidarity and peace. Because they jump over cultural differences and ideologies, sports can be a good opportunity for dialogue and understanding among peoples to build the desired civilization of love.[135]

In the preface to the publication of the proceedings for an international seminar on sport as a field of Christian mission *Stanisław Ryłko* said that Pope John Paul II saw sport as an activity with both individual and collective formative capabilities. "He was deeply convinced that . . . practising sport must be considered not only as a source of physical well-being but also as an ideal of a courageous, positive, optimistic life, and as a means whereby individuals and society can fully renew themselves."[136]

133. Kerrigan, "Sports in the Christian Life," 25.

134. John Paul II, "Jubilee of Sports People."

135. John Paul II, "Address of John Paul II to the Players, Trainers and Directors of Real Madrid."

136. Ryłko, "Preface to the Publication of the Proceedings for 'Church and Sport.'"

Ryłko continues, "John Paul II always forcefully emphasised the educational value of sport, which can inculcate such important values as love of life, spirit of sacrifice, fair play, perseverance, respect for others, friendship, sharing and solidarity."[137] It is clear from the addresses of Pope John Paul II and the other Christian sources cited here that Christians will do well to engage in and emphasize the positive values associated with sport.

However, Christians should be admonished concerning sport's negative moral influences. Finding Christian voices in today's world who will praise the character building qualities is easy. To date, Shirl Hoffman remains one of the few who unabashedly issues warnings to churches and other Christian groups who would advocate the use of sport as a tool for developing character in our children. He reminds Christians that the modern competitive sport culture tends to favor the exploitation of an athlete's moral weaknesses more than furthering the development of his or her moral strengths. He says, "to imagine that a sense of fairness and sensitivity toward others will bloom from an experience that is by nature self-concentrated and self-absorbed is to expect that oranges will grow where one has planted apple seeds."[138]

Tossing them into the arena where moral ills abound may not be the most constructive way to pass on ideals of virtuous behavior. This is as much a criticism of how Christians have expressed themselves in the sports culture as it is of the culture itself. "Evangelicals have 'entered into' and 'pervaded' sports, but have yet to seriously take on the burden of transformation. Consequently, evangelicals in the sports community have too often been followers rather than leaders, adopters of the dominant ethos rather than trendsetters who challenge it."[139]

There are valuable lessons to teach our children through sport but they will be difficult to learn if Christians are unable to distinguish themselves from the "win at all costs" mentality of modern competitive sport. Such distinction is not for lack of opportunity. In her practical guide to parents of adolescents involved in sports Page reminds her readers that, "there are daily opportunities for a Christian athlete to show love, joy, peace, patience, kindness, faithfulness, gentleness, and self-control when she is dealing with teammates and coaches."[140]

These and other virtues may be taught and developed through sport but it is unlikely that they will flourish if the sport's paradigm is governed by

137. Ibid.
138. Hoffman, *Good Game,* 212.
139. Hoffman, "Sports Fanatics."
140. Page, *God's Girls in Sports,* 32.

an overwhelming desire for victory or external gain. Such mentalities will corrupt the nature of the practice, which is why the virtues are so essential to that practice. Recall that MacIntyre argues the virtues act as safeguards against the corruptive influences of institutions. "For the ability of a practice to retain its integrity will depend on the way in which the virtues can be and are exercised in sustaining the institutional forms which are the social bearers of the practice."[141]

On MacIntyre's account moral virtue is a prerequisite of social practices. "The integrity of a practice causally requires the exercise of the virtues by at least some of the individuals who embody it in their activities; and conversely the corruption of institutions is always in part at least an effect of the vices."[142] He cautions that virtues relate differently to external and internal goods. "The possession of the virtues—and not only of their semblance and simulacra—is necessary to achieve the latter; yet the possession of the virtues may perfectly well hinder us in achieving external goods."[143] If an athlete is to experience the internal goods of a sport it will be through virtuous behavior. The same behavior may result in missing out on goods external to the practice.

A common example would be the virtue of honesty. Required for a fair contest, honesty also compels an athlete to admit when he or she violates some rule, even when it is not spotted by the officials. Acknowledging being the last player to touch the ball before it went out of bounds and owning up to the fact that you did not catch the ball but instead let it hit the ground are common instances where honesty demands a less advantageous outcome for an athlete and his or her team. In some cases it may result in defeat.

Instead, "playing along" with the incorrect call or even trying to persuade the referee to rule in one's favor despite knowing it too be the wrong verdict have become nearly obligatory tactics and are generally accepted as "part of the game." Such a mentality is precisely the type to which Hoffman points his criticisms.

Prioritizing competitive advantage and the desire to win above all else incites corruption in both the sport and the athlete. "As long as performance and technical achievement remain the yardstick by which excellence is measured, and as long as newspaper headlines and financial jackpots go to those blessed with technical but not necessarily moral skills, moral uplift will be at best an accidental outcome of sports."[144] If sport is to be redeemed Chris-

141. McIntyre, *After Virtue*, 195.

142. Ibid.

143. Ibid., 196.

144. Hoffman, *Good Game*, 214.

tians must emphasize the morally formative qualities advocated by Pope John Paul II and other Christian leaders while at the same time keeping in check the corruptive powers of the institutional external goods.

In this chapter I have sought to answer the three major theological challenges facing Christians who participate in the world of sport. Sport has the potential to corrupt one's adherence to Christian values. It often leads to bitterness, jealousy and hatred. Athletes are tempted to place their own interests ahead of others resulting in animosity and alienation. Athletic competition can influence people to trivialize the body, causing oneself tremendous physical harm for the sake of victory. Furthermore, these actions can become so common in sport that athletes who have learned the bad habits begin displaying these behaviors in other areas of life.

Despite these pitfalls sport remains an activity of immense value when pursued in a proper manner. Sport does have a place in the life of Christian discipleship. That is, one can simultaneously participate in sport and grow in his or her understanding of and actions on the teachings of Jesus Christ. The cooperative aspect of competition, a non-instrumental view of the body, and an awareness of the need for moral excellences are theological convictions that guide the Christian athlete. Within these principles sport can become a source of joy and inspiration. It insights admiration for one's physical abilities and at the same time makes one mindful of humanity's physical limitations. Sport provides opportunities to teach our children (and ourselves) how to behave in the face of adversity, to develop character through emphasizing the physical and moral excellences of sport, and can be a fruitful place to share one's Christian faith. Above all, it provides endless opportunities that remind followers of Jesus that discipleship does not come easily in this fallen world. There are no paved pathways to holiness. We Christians would be foolish to expect to find one through sport. Instead, like all other aspects of human life, sport is swarming with sinful temptations.

In this realization is a distinguishing mark of the Christian athlete who knows the Holy Spirit is also present in our sporting activities and Christ's sovereign rule is at work on earth as it is heaven. Taking seriously God's kingdom on earth means, as N.T. Wright puts it, "an agenda in which the forgiven people are put to work, addressing the evils of the world in the light of the victory of Calvary. Those who are put right with God through the cross are to be putting-right people for the world."[145]

I have argued here that in addition to the negative, there are positive influences found in sport as well. However, these will be far and few between if Christians acquiesce to the many corruptive behaviors that dominate the

---

145. Wright, *How God Became King*, 244.

modern sports culture. Christians will do well to exhibit the moral qualities of their faith, even if doing so places them in a less advantageous position. If the moral excellences of sport are to be displayed it will not be as a result of the prevalent "win at all costs" doctrine. It will be in displaying an attitude in line with "putting-right people" who belong to a different kind of kingdom than the modern sports culture promotes. In the next chapter we will explore further the transformative nature of sport through a theological lens that sees sport as a God-created gift, inextricably tied to who we are as human beings.

5

Recognizing the Human Essence of Sport

ONE OF THE THEOLOGICAL challenges to a Christian ethic of sport reminded us that sporting behavior is to be grounded in morals that transcend the practice itself. It is dangerous to allow current social whims to govern the acceptability of actions within a game. Likewise, a dual ethic where certain behavior that is immoral in the "real world" is permissible in the sports world should not go without scrutiny. A lack of moral grounding to competitive sport easily gives way to corruptive behaviors that will quickly degrade the activity as a whole.

In an ethic governed solely by the competitive drive to win one can see how easy it would become for biotechnological enhancements to be accepted in sport by a biotechnological society. This is not the same as saying social norms make up the criteria for determining an action's moral worth. Rather what I am suggesting is simply the observation that in a society obsessed with biotechnological enhancements *and* an ethic of competition that is determined exclusively by that society's norms, widespread acceptance of biotechnologically enhanced athletes will be easily achieved.

It is not a stretch to say modern Western societies like the United States and the United Kingdom fit this description. These cultures have strong anti-doping policies in sport organizations but also are pervaded by psychopharmacology, sexual enhancements, and physical enhancements in many other areas of life. The implementation of these practices may at least be partially attributable to an underlying mentality that mildly resembles a form of eugenics.[1] In response to criticisms of its most blatant forms the

1. There are numerous resources available on this topic. Several important treatments of the issue include: Agar, *Liberal Eugenics*; Kuhse and Singer, *Bioethics: An*

eugenics attitude has taken on a more passive approach that seeks to improve the "normal" of society rather than an outright removal of the "weak."
As the availability of biotechnological improvement measures increases so
does the extent to which their use becomes the norm. One can only wonder
how long it will be before physical enhancements become part of the status
quo of competitive athletics.[2]

Indeed there are already signs that the mainstream media, arguably
at one time the most vicious of watchdogs against enhancements, are beginning to entertain the idea that maybe steroids should be permitted in
competition.[3] If it is morally inappropriate to use performance enhancing
substances in sport based on reasons outside of the sport itself, (i.e., more
than a concern for cheating) then athletes and fans are justified in at least
giving further consideration to whether or not such enhancements can
rightfully be used in other avenues of life. If it can be concluded that they are
prohibited in sport but not other activities then one must be able to explain
the differences. What is it about sport that makes it unique?

Leon Kass and Eric Cohen write, "we may condemn our athletic heroes
for using performance enhancing drugs, but we are in fact complicit in their
corruption, for we have created a culture that encourages the use of cosmetic
surgery, Botox, Viagra, and other tools in our growing arsenal of bio-magic
to remake our bodies in the image of our fantasies."[4] My contention is that
using biotechnological enhancements in sport to gain a competitive advantage can be nothing other than a further phase in the commodification of
human activity and the objectification of the human body.

The second step in developing a Christian ethic of sport is to recognize the human essence of sport. It is a valid question to ask whether

---

Anthology, 179–398; Lawler, *Stuck with Virtue*; Sandel, *The Case against Perfection*,
63–83; Song, *Human Genetics*, 47–51; Swinton and Brock, *Theology, Disability, and the
New Genetics*.

2. I am not condemning all forms of doping in sport from a slippery slope argument that says once we allow some forms of enhancement we will be unable to prevent
any form of enhancement. I am simply pointing out the logical progression of technology's gradual acceptance into various aspects of human activity and how they begin
to shape all future endeavors within that activity. This is not necessarily restricted to
biotech drugs and other substances. The advancements in video replay technology have
produced "official review" rules recently implemented, most notably, in American football and has seen subtle changes arise in the structure of game play that has already resulted in altering strategy and the way the game will be played from this point forward.

3. Brent Musburger, a highly respected sports journalist, recently told a group of
university journalism students that under medical supervision steroids could be used
in a morally permissible way to improve athletic performance. See Associated Press,
"Report: Brent Musburger Talks Steroids."

4. Kass and Cohen, "For the Love of the Game."

enhancements can honor the body in ways that are consistent with Christian theological convictions. How would the use of biotechnology bring honor to the body without either worshipping the body or reducing it to a means to victory or some other end? It is the external goods of competitive sport that persuade athletes to adulterate the component of sport's fundamental nature that involves the demonstration of physical abilities given to the athlete by God. Introducing biotechnology would serve only to corrupt the practice making it less than what it was intended to be.

In this chapter I will argue that a Christian conception of sport sees the practice as an activity rooted in the acceptance of our human limitations. Sport is an activity to be enjoyed for its intrinsic qualities. We should reject the ethic of the sports culture that maintains that sport is fundamentally about winning. I will also make the case that this dominant view fails to recognize dual standards of giftedness and effort as the most human aspects of sport. In the first section I will critique the culture of sport for its obsession with winning, records, and the adulteration of physical perfection.

I will suggest a new paradigm is needed that fundamentally shifts our conception of sport from a venue where being the best is all that matters to an attitude that recognizes our physical limitations and finds the athletes' mutual striving for excellence to be an equally honorable and praiseworthy aspect of sport. It is this striving, the effort of being human, that unites all who participate in sports. To demonstrate this I will use the example of Special Olympics to show how that organization exemplifies the theory of sport I am seeking to draw out in this work.

The new framework of sport proposed here reorients our appreciation for sport from an achievement-based view to one that values multiple aesthetic dimensions of athletic activity.[5] The beauty of sport is not necessarily captured by the most physically appealing or best performance. While they do not produce the fastest times or the most fluid and graceful bodily movements in the sports world Special Olympians display the highest of sport's aesthetic qualities, a combination of physical talent and human striving and aspiration. One of the most beautiful aspects of sport is that it calls us to recognize our essential humanity by demonstrating our finitude and dependency on one another. In this alternative sporting paradigm the striving toward sport's standards of excellence evokes far deeper admiration than does the outcome of one's effort.

---

5. In this chapter I admittedly will use the term "aesthetic" in a very vague sense. The purpose is to capture all aspects of sport that are pleasurable to the senses (including our emotions and imaginations) and to emphasize our appreciation of and response to the overall beauty of sport (versus a purely intellectual or mechanical response to specific athletic achievements).

Performance versus Results:
A Contrast of Attitudes in Sport

Records and The Quantification of Sporting Activity

Sport historian Allen Guttman has identified seven distinct characteristics of modern sport that have been developed throughout history. Modern sport differs from its primitive ancestors in the contemporary emphasis on secularity, equality, specialization, rationalization, bureaucracy, quantification, and records.[6] The final two of these distinguishing features are perhaps the most germane to the present discussion. The need to quantify everything is not lost on contemporary sport. Guttmann says, "modern sports are characterized by the almost inevitable tendency to transform *every* athletic feat into one that can be quantified and measured."[7]

He is correct to say that ours is a society greatly concerned with numbers and that mindset has been greatly influential on our approach to sport. That in itself is not necessarily a problem. It certainly satisfies the curiosity to know how contemporary athletes measure up to their predecessors. But as Guttmann notes, modern sport's obsession with quantifying results is sharply different than the attitude of the ancient Greeks. "For them, man was still the measure of all things, not the object of endless measurements. To wear the victor's leafy crown, to be the best of those who had on that cloudless day contested for glory and fame at Olympia or Corinth —that was sufficient."[8]

He continues by noting an extreme difference between the Greeks and modern athletes in that the former were not only uninterested in comparing themselves against athletes at other games but also against athletes in years gone by. "Whether or not the victor of one Olympiad sent his javelin farther than the one thrown four years earlier seems to have been a matter of indifference."[9] Guttmann makes it clear that the difference is not due to the ancients' inability to measure or time events. They certainly had the tools to do so but the noticeable absence of any such records indicates their apathy toward quantifying the games.

Fans and participants of modern sports have assumed a very different attitude toward athletics. Guttmann identifies a primary reason for this in the highly competitive culture of modern sports. "Combine the impulse

---

6. Guttmann, *From Ritual to Record*, 15–56.

7. Ibid., 47; italics original.

8. Ibid., 49.

9. Ibid.

to quantification with the desire to win, to excel, to be the best—and the result is the concept of the record."[10] No longer is it enough to know who the fastest runner was on a particular occasion. Records transcend time to tell us who is the fastest runner of all time. Some sports are not so easily quantifiable. In fact, it is a common discussion among sports enthusiasts to debate who should own the title of the greatest athlete or team of all time.

Would the greatest offence the world has ever seen be able to defeat the best defense of all time? The 1972 Miami Dolphins completed the first and only perfect season in the National Football League by winning Super Bowl VII. Would that undefeated team be able to keep its perfect record against the defensive-minded 1985 Chicago Bears who put together a very impressive season to win Super Bowl XX?

These nostalgic debates spark passionate discourse yet are unable to ever be settled. But surely it is odd to think that they were meant to be resolved. While it can be entertaining to imagine a game in which time is not a boundary and we are able to witness an unstoppable force colliding with an immovable object, measuring a team's greatness depends on more than the sum total of its victories. Yet the need to quantify the entire world of sport and the desire to compare the results has lead to the definition of greatness becoming synonymous with finishing in first place. What is more, finishing in first place can only be considered great when the victory's measurable aspects are better than those of previous winners. No doubt a victory is the result of a good performance but often times greatness is only something considered when the athlete or team has broken a previous record.[11] This attitude is particularly evident in the "big three" American sports of baseball, basketball and American football where statistics and percentages become the chief standards of measurement for athletic superiority.

Athletes not only want to be great but to be *the* greatest and so when greatness is determined by how one measures up in the annals of time it is easy to see why the culture of modern sports continues to push the physical limits of the human body. But Guttmann raises an interesting question. "What will happen to our obsessive quest for records when athletes finally do begin to reach, as eventually they must, the limits of human possibility?"[12] Certainly one way to expand those limits is the use of biotechnological enhancements. As we have seen, these enhancements will result in markedly

10. Ibid., 51.

11. Lending support to the extreme emphasis on record–breaking (At least in the United States) is the fact that both television viewership and admission prices dramatically increase for a competition where there is reasonable likelihood that a record will be broken.

12. Ibid., 53.

increased results but surely they too must have limits. Progressively stronger
and more invasive enhancements will at some point, and there is great debate over where this line is drawn, cross over the boundaries and become to
a greater degree the result of technological capabilities than of human effort.

Guttmann's question then becomes, "Will we accept sports in the
Greek sense, content with the dramatic contest of man against man (or
woman against woman), or will we imagine new ways to satisfy the Faustian
lust for the absolutely unprecedented athletic achievement?"[13] Biotechnology seems to be the easiest path for these new forms of achievement to arise
since they are already so prevalent in high level competitive athletics. Yet
it is not only biotechnology that could lead to new horizons for athletes.
Technological innovations in the venue and in the equipment used also feed
the desire to see records broken.

Using technology to improve sporting equipment helps the athlete to
push the limits of the human body further than ever before. The obsessive
pursuit of breaking world records leads to an ironic situation in which the
technology used to achieve such accomplishments at the same time weakens
the comparison to previous achievements. Without doubt many of the new
records being set are at least in part attributable to better equipment and a
better scientific understanding of the obstacles that comprise the games.

The Summer Olympics of 2008 in Beijing was a case in point as virtually every swimming event set a new record. In an impressive display swimmers set twenty-five new world records and replaced the existing Olympic
records in all but two of the thirty-two events. The advanced design of the
Beijing National Aquatics Centre included several key alterations from previous Olympic sites. In an interview with National Public Radio, Olympic
columnist Christine Brennan of USA Today stated, "It's physics and it's not
sports, but it makes sense . . . You make a deeper and a wider pool, and you
. . . give all of those waves and all of that splashing and all of that moving
water a chance to move away from the swimmers and get out of their way,
which makes them go faster. It's as simple as that."[14]

Not only was the pool given certain enhancements but the swimsuits
worn by the athletes are far more advanced than those worn by previous Olympians. Of the twenty-five world records broken the winner of
twenty-three of those races was wearing Speedo's newly released LZR, a
suit that makes the swimmer's body more compressed and buoyant. This

13. Ibid., 54.
14. Berkes, "China's Olympic Swimming Pool."

lead to some claiming the suit gives an unfair advantage and is a form of technological doping.[15]

While not technically unfair since in 2008 all athletes had access to the suit and swam in the same pool it certainly does call into question the validity of those results when compared against the swimmers from previous Olympic games. Michael Phelps dominated the 2008 Games by winning eight gold medals (itself a record) but is it fair to say he would have beaten another American swimming legend, Mark Spitz who won seven gold medals in the Munich games of 1972?

It is clear that as technology advances the games we play and how we play them evolve as well. To some extend this diminishes the value of the records the sports culture is obsessed with. Would Spitz have won if he were able to compete in his prime against Phelps in 2008 using the same equipment, in the same pool and had access to the same training and diet? It is an impossible question to answer though Spitz himself thinks it would have been a tie.[16]

Being mindful of the distinct differences the evolution of technology has made on the way a sport is played can add a deeper level of appreciation to records that have not yet fallen. When records were first kept in the pole vaulting event in 1912 the world record was 4.02 meters. Over the next eighty-four years there was a new record set seventy-one times with the current record set in 1994 at 6.14 meters by Sergey Bubka of the Ukraine. He dominated the event for more than ten years by setting, then breaking, his own world record a total of seventeen times.[17]

There can be no doubt that Bubka is one of the greatest vaulters of all time, in terms of production, especially in light of more than fifteen years worth of technological improvements since setting that record. Newer pole vaulting poles are made from advanced material and are designed to send the vaulter higher than ever before. Despite these improvements however great or small they may be no one has been able to beat Bubka's record. It could be the case that humanity has reached its limits in this particular event. The progression of record breaking from the early twentieth century through today began with a steep increase but then since Bubka pole vaulting seems to have hit a plateau.

At least one group of researchers believes the levels of human achievement are nearing their apex. After analyzing the development of world

15. BBC, "Fina Extends Swimsuit Regulations."

16. Schapiro, "Mark Spitz: Michael Phelps Couldn't Have Beaten Me."

17. This is for the outdoor event. He broke the indoor record a total of eighteen times, with his best effort clearing 6.15 meters—a record that stood for over 20 years.

records in Olympic sports since the modern Olympics began in 1896 Geoffroy Berthelot and others have calculated that world records have already progressed to ninety-nine percent of their asymptotic value. They predict that, "present conditions prevailing for the next 20 years, half of all [world records] won't be improved by more than 0.05%."[18] They are careful to qualify their predictions with the caveat that performance doping could alter their calculations but are also quick to suggest that stricter punishment against doping by the International Olympic Committee combined with the fact that some events have not seen their records challenged in nearly twenty years indicates that those records "may not be challenged anymore."[19]

Their research seemed to underestimate the influence artificial enhancements would have on athletic performance as evidenced by the numerous records broken during the summer Olympics of 2008 that would take place six months after the publication of their work. In an article published two years later the authors would revisit their predictions clinging to the general principles of their previous work while removing specific dates for the end of world records. They also would account for enhancements in equipment that contributed to the large number of swimming records, though they point out that swimming too may have reached a plateau since the buoyant suits used in 2008 have since been banned from Olympic competition.

Instead they state the facts of their research, which shows that the rate of new world records has slowed considerably since the 1988 Games, most noticeably in track and field events. They state that "this present halt of performances and the previously demonstrated stagnation of [world records] emphasize that our physiological evolution will remain limited in a majority of Olympic events."[20] They continue, "present performances may now be enhanced through extremely exceptional individuals at the frontier of our genomic condition or with the artificial help of technology."[21]

Berthelot's outlook on sporting performance is nothing new. Running a mile in less than four minutes was a feat many people thought to be humanly impossible until Roger Bannister did it in 1954. Since then dozens of athletes have beaten his time. In fact, Bannister's time in the 1,500m race that earned him a fourth place finish at the 1952 Olympics is ten seconds slower that the Olympic qualifying standard for the 2008 Games. This shows that the limits of the human body are not always what experts in

18. Berthelot, et al., "The Citius End," e1552.

19. Ibid.

20. Berthelot et al., "Athlete Atypicity on the Edge of Human Achievement," e8800, 6, 7.

21. Ibid., e8800, 7.

human physiology say they are. Still, it is difficult to ignore the evidence presented by Berthelot that most track and field events are not progressing as they once were.

The sports culture's emphasis on record setting raises important questions about what will become of sports once the fans and the athletes begin to realize that our human limits have been reached. However, these questions are far more relevant in a context where the role of records is overvalued. If breaking records and the competitive drive to be the absolute best is what motivates, defines, and gives value to sport then once the physiological limits are reached sport will go into decline or it will find new ways of pushing the limits. On the latter alternative there are two possible solutions. New games can be invented that test human capabilities in newly discovered ways or biological agents can be introduced that will significantly expand the human body's horizons.

The Spectacle of Sport

Right now sports seem to be pointing down the path of artificial enhancements. Presently, sport's governing bodies are encouraging equipment enhancement and prohibiting biological modifications. But eventually even the technology must reach its pinnacle of performance. For instance, a javelin must have an optimal combination of aerodynamics, weight, size, and flexibility that cannot be surpassed. Once that has been discovered the only area of improvement is in the biological agent.

So if pursuing records is the main goal of sport then doping will at some point become a necessary step in discovering new frontiers. Yet it is not only at this last stage that something is lost in the way we participate in sport. Journalist Paul Kix notes a link between technological and biotechnological improvements that show both to be harmful to the games we admire. He says the process currently used to improve performance,

> whether through an increasing reliance on computers, or NASA-designed swimsuits, or steroids that regulators can't detect—changes the work we once loved, or the sports we once played, or the athletes we once cheered. It may not always be for the worse, but one thing is certain. When we address our human limits these days, we actually become less human.[22]

The obsession with records and the unquenchable desire to quantify everything about sport contributes to a less human activity and more to a

22. Kix, "Peaked Performance."

mechanical exercise. In his social critique Christopher Lasch argues against what he calls the degradation of sport. By this he means reducing sport to nothing more than a spectacle. The reduction of sport to such a state places the emphasis not on the performance but on the results. What matters in the eyes of much of Western society is simply an issue of who wins and who loses. The excitement and the tension involved in a close contest provide the added flair but, as Lasch sees it, victory is ultimately all that matters to the modern sports culture. "The accumulation of elaborate statistical records arose from management's attempt to reduce winning to a routine, to measure efficient performance. The athletic contest itself, surrounded by a vast apparatus of information and promotion, now appeared almost incidental to the expensive preparation required to stage it."[23]

It is in the staging of sporting events where Lasch is most critical of society. Transforming the beauty of the game's intricacies into an entertainment show degrades sport into spectacle. "In a society dominated by the production and consumption of images, no part of life can long remain immune from the invasion of spectacle."[24] Sport has become in large part a spectacle as a result of what Michael Novak refers to as the "entertainment ethic" promulgated by television.[25] Lasch agrees with Novak that television has had a negative effect on sports. "Television has enlarged the audience for sports while lowering the level of its understanding; at least this is the operating assumption of sports commentators . . ."[26]

The result is that commentators become entertainers and dominate the televised event. Pregame and postgame shows provide hours of analysis and entertainment in addition to their constant commentary as the game is being played. Employing their showmanship to explain the fundamentals of the game, argue Lasch and Novak, reduces the need for the spectator to learn about and gain appreciation for the sport on their own. This has contributed to the attitude captured by former Major League Baseball player and manager Wes Westrum who said "baseball is like church. Many attend. Few understand."[27]

I am not as certain as they are that commentators lead to the depreciation of sport by spectators. It is certainly the case that the entertainment ethic's influence in sport has created a self-perpetuating reality that keeps spectators coming back for more while at the same time giving them less

23. Lasch, *The Culture of Narcissism*, 120.
24. Ibid., 122.
25. Novak, *The Joy of Sports*, 334.
26. Lasch, *The Culture of Narcissism*, 106.
27. Hye, *The Great God Baseball*, 6.

and less of the sport's substantive value. Furthermore, there is a danger in presenting sport from a purely entertainment perspective. Lasch notes, "as spectators become less knowledgeable about the games they watch, they become sensation-minded and bloodthirsty."[28] But commentators do in many occasions provide helpful information about particular rules of the sport and share insights that teach spectators about more effective ways to play the game. Perhaps it would be more accurate to say that broadcasters reduce the need for spectators to learn and appreciate the game experientially.

In no other case is the sensation more celebrated that when records are being broken. The viewership for athletic events significantly increases when record-breaking is a distinct possibility. For example, nearly forty million Americans tuned in to watch Michael Phelps earn his eighth and final gold medal in Beijing. The following day lacked such record breaking thrills and the American viewership dropped by more than thirty percent.[29]

It is perfectly natural for fans to be more attentive when history is about to be made. Accomplishments like these justifiably draw our admiration as we witness some of the most impressive physical performances ever seen. Unfortunately, for many spectators it is only the greatest of results that draw their attention as the beauty and grace exhibited by most other athletes virtually goes unnoticed. Further to the point, commentators typically ignore the style or skill of competitors who are not among the top few, giving praise only to the winners. This further solidifies the psychological emphasis placed on winning and winning alone.

Yet the involvement of spectators seems to be just as much a part of the game as the participants. They temporarily put on the illusion of identifying with another person. Roger Caillois notes,

> The audience are not content to encourage the efforts of the athletes or horses of their choice merely by voice and gesture. A physical contagion leads them to assume the position of the men or animals in order to help them, just as the bowler is known to unconsciously incline his body in the direction that he would like the bowling ball to take at the end of its course.[30]

The mimicry that takes place in sporting events by the fans adds a dynamic element to sports that is irreplaceable. Many sports draw such a large crowd that there is a significant home field advantage. The term Twelfth Man comes from an American football game held in 1922 between Centre College and the University of Texas A&M. The defending national

---

28. Lasch, *The Culture of Narcissism*, 107.

29. Schapiro, "Mark Spitz: Michael Phelps Couldn't Have Beaten Me."

30. Caillois, *Man, Play, and Games*, 22.

champions were heavily favored to defeat Texas A&M. Adding to the un-favorable conditions, A&M suffered several injuries in the first half of play and the coach was afraid he would not have enough players to finish the game. He called on E. King Gill who had played football for the Aggies but was now a member of the basketball team. Gill voluntarily suited up and awaited the coach's call. Gill never played in the game, which the Aggies went on to win, but he was the only player remaining on the A&M sidelines. Since there were eleven players on the field, Gill was the twelfth man and his willingness to support his team has inspired fans ever since.

Now the Twelfth Man is a familiar practice to both soccer and Ameri-can football fans around the world. Though they do not technically play in the game spectators are an important part of the game. When the game ends they return to ordinary life but during the game the thousands of fans take on the role of a single team member playing a part in the team's march to victory. Disapproving of modern sports because of how intimately involved the spectator has become seems to be misguided. On the whole, fans do not degrade sport but instead contribute to it.

Furthermore, being a sports fan can have a lasting, meaningful impact on a person. This can be seen on any school or park playground. Children often pretend they are their favorite professional athletes when they are playing that sport. What American boy playing baseball in his childhood has not playfully considered himself to be Babe Ruth or Mickey Mantle? In one sense this is simple childish mimicry but in another it holds important nuances for those our children pattern themselves after. Sport has such an important place in the lives of most citizens that the celebrity spotlight cast on professional athletes can put them in the precarious situation of influ-encing countless citizens, both children and adults, without ever knowing any of them. To be sure, children are more moldable but I include adults here because any adult sports fan can recite numerous athletes whose stories or actions have inspired them and continue to influence or inspire them at some level.

Special Olympics: A Paradigm for Sporting Practice

Leon Kass and Eric Cohen offer additional commentary on the negative influence the consuming desire to win has had on sport.

> Over time, athletic excellence becomes defined solely in terms of outcomes: winning rather than losing, breaking previous records, and compiling a stellar *statisticum vitae*. Some old-fashioned connoisseurs may still watch sports for the love of a

game well played; but most fans, encouraged by sports media's mania for keeping score, pay and watch largely to learn and celebrate the result.[31]

In professional and mainstream amateur sports techniques are perfected with the goal of shaving off hundredths of a second from their time. The "win at all costs" doctrine often produces mechanical routines that are celebrated only when it results in victory. There is nothing wrong with desiring to see one's favorite team win a championship. But the singular motivation to win is a far cry from the attitude of the Special Olympics organization, which offers over thirty Olympic style events to persons with intellectual disabilities. They hold regional, national and worldwide athletic competitions. The most recent summer world games held in Shanghai, China in 2007 drew more than 7,500 athletes from 164 countries.[32]

These athletes demonstrate a healthy view of sport that balances the games' competitive aspects with the values that transcend the practice. As an organization Special Olympics is committed,

> to provide year-round sports training and athletic competition in a variety of Olympic-type sports for children and adults with intellectual disabilities, giving them continuing opportunities to develop physical fitness, demonstrate courage, experience joy and participate in a sharing of gifts, skills and friendship with their families, other Special Olympics athletes and the community.[33]

Using sport as its niche, the organization is doing amazing work to eliminate discrimination and empower persons with intellectual disabilities. For Special Olympics, sport is an ideal tool that is useful in helping them achieve the agenda set forth in their mission statement and elsewhere. It provides a way for athletes with intellectual disabilities "to create a better world by fostering the acceptance and inclusion of all people."[34]

To be sure, there are many semblances between the ways in which they promote their goals and the approach to sport in this work. The work of Special Olympics is compatible with and strongly encouraged by the theologically informed notions of sport defended here.[35]

31. Kass and Cohen, "For the Love of the Game."

32. Special Olympics, "The History of the Special Olympics."

33. Ibid.

34. Ibid.

35. Eunice Kennedy Schriver, founder of Special Olympics, was a member of the Kennedy family, who aside from their legacy in American politics is known for their strong heritage in the Catholic Church.

The organization does not escape the instrumentalist view of sport I criticized earlier, nor do they intend to. Their mission is to use sport to achieve a lofty set of goals that is not necessarily related to athletics. They are very clear about the fact that they use sport as a means to other ends. "Special Olympics sports provide a gateway to empowerment, competence, acceptance and joy."[36]

Though I am critical of an instrumental view of the purpose of sport I am not opposed to taking advantage of sport's external goods so long as we do not lose sight of the internal goods that comprise the core of the activity. Special Olympics does this well as they utilize sport for other ends but have carefully safeguarded themselves from the corruptive influences of intense competition. However, they still are focused on external goods even if those goods seem more praiseworthy than those external aims of elite competition.

Here I will argue that attention to athletes with intellectual disabilities not only complements the ethic of sport I advocate but challenges the mainstream sports culture to fundamentally alter its conceptions of normative sporting practices. By virtue of their attitude, which diminishes the importance of winning, and by their distinct emphasis on human striving as a key component of athletic activity, I will show how the sports culture needs to reshape its understanding of what sport should look like.

As a point of clarification in the following sections I will often distinguish between Special Olympics and the modern sports culture. It is my contention that as athletic contests Special Olympics are part of the sports world. Unfortunately, there are significant distinctions, in theory and practice, which separate Special Olympics from the mainstream culture of sports. My distinction between the two ideologies is not intended to claim that Special Olympians are not athletes or a part of the sports culture as will be made clear in the following sections.

One of the most glaringly obvious differences between the contests found in mainstream sports and Special Olympics is the latter's diminished emphasis on winning. The organization does not set qualifying standards as is found in the Olympics and other elite level organizations. The games are open to anyone with an intellectual disability. This speaks to the natural inclusivity of sport as a human activity that welcomes all. The Olympics are an appropriate venue for demonstrating the talents of the most physically elite of our species but Special Olympics strikes a more fundamental chord in that sport is not exclusive to age, gender, race, socio-economic status, or ability.

36. Special Olympics, "Special Olympics Mission."

Consequently, there is a shift in emphasis from athletic victory to personal victory. The Special Olympics athlete oath states "Let me win. But if I cannot win, let me be brave in the attempt." Winning is still important but of greater consequence is the courage instilled in these athletes to perform to the best of their abilities. "Special Olympics is not about 'swifter, higher, stronger'; it is about achieving one's personal best."[37]

The contrast here between the purpose of Special Olympics and the Olympic motto of *citius, altius, fortius* is telling. It reveals the influence record setting and quantification has had on sport since the motto was adopted by the founder of the modern Olympic Games, Pierre de Coubertin. Records for various events in Special Olympics are not advertised or promoted since the substance of the events is found in the participation itself not the results. On the other hand, records for the fastest and strongest Olympic athletes are well documented.

Even greater separation exists between the value placed on personal striving and the solitary focus on winning found throughout most of the sports culture. The spectacle of modern sport has been reduced to the simple purpose of winning as demonstrated here by the mission statement of one of the teams in Major League Baseball. "The Chicago Cubs' *singular goal* is to reward generations of Cubs fans' support and loyalty with a World Championship."[38]

Special Olympics is not guilty of completely devaluing athletic victory. Athletes spend months and even years in rigorous training regimens with the help of coaches. The organization structures each event by grouping athletes into divisions based on their abilities so that competition will be as fair as possible. Each division is then contested as a final event where the most outstanding performances are honored as the top three competitors of each division are presented on a platform and awarded gold, silver, and bronze medals, respectively.

The athletic spirit found in Special Olympics is representative of the attitude captured by Kass and Cohen when they argue that "the dignity and worth of athletic activity are not defined only by winners and losers, faster and slower times, old records and new. It is not simply the separable, measurable, and comparative result that makes a performance excellent."[39]

If these metrics were the criteria by which sport's value was determined then surely we would be on our way to a sports world with legalized doping and even more invasive biological enhancements. But there seems to

37. Special Olympics, "Sports and Competition at the 2009 World Winter Games."
38. Chicago Cubs, "Mission Statement"; italics added.
39. Kass and Cohen, "For the Love of the Game."

be something intuitively problematic about going to any and all lengths to run faster, jump higher, and throw farther. As Kass notes, "no sane person would choose to be the fastest thing on two legs if it required becoming an ostrich."[40]

Instead, there are far more meaningful components to an excellent athletic performance besides the results. They explain,

> It is also the humanity of the human performer. Excellent athletic activity seems to have a meaning—the human body in action, the grace and rhythm of the moving human form, the striving and exertion of the aspiring human athlete—that is separable from competition, even when the athlete is competitively engaged. What matters more than the measurable outcome is the lived experience, for doer and spectator alike, of a humanly cultivated gift, excellently at work, striving for superiority and with the outcome in doubt.[41]

It is doubtful that the humanity of the performer is anywhere shown more clearly than in the case of Special Olympics. The results may not be as glamorous. The times are not as fast or the distances as far. The movements are not as graceful. But to say the efforts, aspirations, and strivings of Special Olympians are of a poorer quality than those of other athletes is wholly unfair. The mental or physical limitations of certain athletes do not make their athletic endeavors any less praiseworthy or any less human. A common perception in the sports culture is that Special Olympics are inferior to "normal" Olympics or professional sports. I wish to argue that this is an inaccuracy rooted in faulty social construction of both the importance of athletic results and, more importantly, improper normative judgments concerning the disabled.

Bernd Wannenwetsch is helpful in this regard as he presents a reshaping of the issue of disability and personhood within a Christian framework that places the disabled at the centre personhood rather than at the margins. He rejects the approach that seeks to identify reasons why the disabled should be included in discussions of personhood. The shift, he says, begins with moving from *including* the disabled as persons to *recognizing* their personhood. "In other words, they provide not just a test-case but the very paradigm for our recognition of any person."[42]

In the same way we will begin to see the value of sport when we cease trying to create an "us/them" category of athletes. Wannenwetsch

40. Ibid.
41. Ibid.
42. Wannenwetsch, "Angels with Clipped Wings," 184.

adds that it is the disabled who "effectively bring us (back) in contact with our own humanity" through a "revelation-like discovery and personal transformation."[43]

Wannenwetsch draws on the work of Robert Spaemann who argues that it is the disabled who "constitute the paradigm for a human community of recognizing *selves*, rather than simply valuing useful and attractive *properties*."[44]

Spaemann believes this means the disabled bring out the best in us though Wannenwetsch takes a slightly more nuanced approach in which our own humanity is evoked through recognizing their personhood. As Robert Song succinctly summarizes, the disabled "clarify that human dignity is fundamentally a matter of the humanity that is summoned forth in us as we recognize that we belong together and are called to be with each other."[45]

Wannenwetsch continues by pointing out the way walls of separation have been constructed to distinguish "us" from "them." "It is precisely to the degree, in which the lives of [the disabled] emphasize human dependency and need, that they unfailingly shock and perplex us, since we have invested a whole world, both individually and culturally, to cover our existential nakedness with the cloth of achievement, power and control."[46] He goes on to suggest that society chooses to ignore the message of dependency carried by the disabled. "The wings of these angels are clipped to the degree in which we, ideologically or practically, bring us in a safe distance from them, outside of the sonic radius of their voices, so to speak."[47]

This insight is certainly true of the sports media, which will devote around the clock coverage to professional sports of all kinds while restricting airtime for athletes with intellectual disabilities to a few patronizing moments, if any time at all. A research project by Special Olympics sought to discover the influence media has had on the general population's perception of people with intellectual disabilities. "A study spanning four decades and involving thousands of newspaper, television and film depictions found an increasingly narrow portrayal of people with intellectual disabilities. The characters often were depicted as 'vulnerable,' a 'victim' and/or a person worthy of pity."[48]

43. Ibid.

44. Spaemann, *Persons*, 244; italics original.

45. Song, "Fragility and Grace," 241.

46. Wannenwetsch, "Angels with Clipped Wings," 191.

47. Ibid., 192.

48. Special Olympics, "Changing Attitudes: Changing the World."

The study also suggests, as I have here, that whether it is the Olympics or the Special Olympics makes no difference in the level of human striving seen in any sports contest. "Athletic competition provides a unique venue to view the full spectrum of human emotions. Spectators witness unique and remarkable stories of perseverance, dedication and challenges overcome."[49]

These features are experiences of a human activity that calls us to share our lives with one another in a relational, dependent way. It is in recognizing the personhood of others that simultaneously brings about an enriched realization of our own humanity. Wannenwetsch writes,

> Human beings however, cannot recognize their kin, cannot recognize "personhood", apart from having to *become* themselves what they recognize in others . . . As such it may be described as an act of inclusion. Yet the one to be included is not the disabled but the "moral agent" herself, who is to step into the realm of responsible humanity by recognizing her belonging with her kin.[50]

Wannenwetsch's paradigm shift in the way society should view those with disabilities has far reaching implications. In the context of sport this suggests that the practices and attitudes of athletes with disabilities should shift our understanding of sport from one of *citius, altius, fortius* and the incessant desire to win and break records to a theoretical framework centered on community and the shared experience of striving for excellence. We may say the difference is between an emphasis on one of two of sport's characteristics, *agôn* and *arête*. Mainstream sports culture unequivocally endorses the concept of *agôn*, or competition, while the theory I am proposing shifts the primary focus to that of *arête*, or a striving for excellence.

In the same way that recognizing their humanity brings us more in tune with our own, I would suggest that Special Olympics is representative of the paradigm for all athletics. Special Olympians are not "lesser" athletes to be pitied by patting them on the back and saying "nice try." They embody the spirit of sportsmanship as co-competitors striving to accomplish the objectives of the sport. Their striving is representative of and a reminder of humanity's finitude.

In a symbolic sense those with disabilities are, as Wannenwetsch states, angels with clipped wings. They are messengers calling us to refocus the motivations of our athletic endeavors from attempting to surpass humanity's physical limitations to embracing those limits that unite us. These aspirations to do one's best, in sport or any other activity, form a common bond among all who would participate, regardless of one's level of athletic ability.

49. Ibid.

50. Wannenwetsch, "Angels with Clipped Wings," 196; italics original.

Rather than seeing sport as a never ending quest for the expansion of human abilities Christian theology challenges us to appreciate the activity itself as an expression of our common nature and finitude. "The reality that Christians believe in as one indestructibly marked by resurrection of the Crucified, has nothing to fear but everything to gain from the angelic mission of the disabled, as they challenge us to recognize our shared humanity of dependency and hope."[51]

This realization not only alters the way we perceive those with disabilities but it also informs our opinions on the use of biotechnology in sport. "The cure for the adulteration of sports, a cultural disease that is already far along, will require much more than the banishment of steroids and other performance-enhancing drugs. It will require a revival—for contemporary Americans, difficult to achieve—of the athletic ideal, seen as a manifestation of the mysterious powers that make us human."[52]

With the emphasis on these "mysterious powers" it is not surprising that Special Olympics is the world's largest sports organization that does not have an official policy against performance enhancing drugs. The reason is not because they are permissive of their use but because the operating framework of sport employed by the organization denies any need for biotechnological enhancements.

Aesthetic Value in Sport

Kass and Cohen again are helpful when they argue that "by using these technological means to transcend the limits of our natures, we deform the character of human desire and aspiration, settling for externally gauged achievements that are less and less the fruits of our own individual striving and cultivated finite gifts."[53] Some would interject that these enhancements will never lead us beyond our finitude. Biotechnology, they argue, does not exclude the realization of our finite gifts but instead helps to refine them. Steroid use may take athletic ability to the next level, which would result in an even greater appreciation for the aesthetic dimension to an athlete's accomplishments. To address this claim we must look more closely at the role of aesthetic appreciation in sport.

The display of athletic talent tends to evoke the spectator's highest aesthetic approval but as the athletes themselves will admit, there is always room for improvement. But is it reasonable to think that doping

51. Ibid., 197.
52. Kass and Cohen, "For the Love of the Game."
53. Ibid.

would improve the aesthetic quality of sport or only the results? In what sense would enhancements make better the seamless grace and rhythm of techniques performed by elite athletes? What fan of football (soccer) is not awestruck by the beauty and grace of the Goal of the Century? The title, given by the *Fédération Internationale de Football Association* (FIFA) as the greatest goal ever scored in a World Cup tournament, was credited to Diego Maradona of Argentina.

This goal was given the award because the voters recognized and appreciated the incredible athleticism and talent required for such a feat. In other words, it received credit for being among the most aesthetically moving events in World Cup history. Even those who twenty years later still remember the defeat it brought to the English can appreciate the play's majesty.

Opposing team member Gary Lineker admired the goal that ultimately cost his team the 1986 World Cup quarter finals match. Lineker would later confess it was "probably the one and only time in my whole career I felt like applauding the opposition scoring a goal."[54] Even though Maradona's career is plagued by morally dubious behavior the goal in reference taken independently from the player's off-field character nevertheless holds tremendous aesthetic worth.[55]

There is no doubt that the entire sporting world is filled with aesthetic value. Fans and athletes from any sport can point to countless examples of aestheticism. The precision of a serve in tennis, the grace of swinging a golf club, as well as the technique of the Fosbury flop in the high jump are just a few of the skills that call for aesthetic appreciation.

However, there are several problems with viewing sport as a purely aesthetic exercise, not the least of which is the subjective nature of such appreciation. Someone who doesn't understand the game of golf may not appreciate or even notice the intricate details of selecting the right club and hitting the ball in the right place with the right amount of force. To them it may be simply swinging a stick at a ball. The high jump appears as nothing more than awkwardly jumping over a bar. More significant is the problem associated with making the most physically dominant athletes the normative case for what the human body should be like. In this section I will reject the idea that the aestheticism of elite level athletes is sport's highest value. While praiseworthy in its own right and an example of the abilities the human body is capable of it should not become the standard for defining good

54. BBC, "Maradona Predicts English Success."

55. Maradona was a cocaine addict for more than twenty years and was banned from several competitions as a result of testing positive. He also was dismissed from the 1994 World Cup tournament for testing positive for ephedrine. See BBC, "Maradona Set to Coach Argentina."

sport. As we will see there is a distinction between the appreciation we have for natural giftedness and effort. I will make the case that what is needed in our appreciation of sports performance is something like a combination of admiration for giftedness and effort.

The paradigm of the modern sports culture neglects the importance of these two qualities. We are right to admire the abilities of elite athletes for both the natural talents they display and the effort put into preparation and performance. Striving is a common theme available to all athletes. We all can relate to one another in regards to putting forth the effort needed to be our best. But for most of us our best effort falls far short of the abilities of other athletes. It is good to value the natural giftedness of athletes who can do things we simply cannot. When we honor the talents displayed by elite athletes we recognize in them something not present in ourselves, giftedness. Unfortunately, we often fail to appreciate it as a gift and honor their abilities only insofar as they lead to victory. This is especially true in the case of effort. The sports culture often gets so caught up in admiring the beautiful performances of the most successful athletes that it neglects the aspect of sport that commonly unites all of humanity in sport. We cannot fail to admire the effort of athletes to compete with the recognition of our human limitations.

Aestheticism and Categories of Sport

David Best has made substantial contributions to the area of sport and aestheticism. His thoughts will be helpful in further analyzing to what extent the aesthetic beauty of athletic performances may be considered a defining quality of sport. Best explains sport in terms of two distinct categories with fundamentally unique emphases. He labels them purposive and aesthetic. There are games in which a winner is determined by empirical measurement. The first person to cross the finish line wins. Then there are competitions that are judged as in figure skating. Athletes perform their routine and the winner is the one whom the judges credit with the highest scores.

Best defines the categories in terms of means and ends rather than rules. Measured sports are those that focus on the outcome or the end. In this sense they have an external end, or are purposive. In the purposive sports,

> the *manner* of achievement of the primary purpose is of little or no significance as long as it comes within the rules. For example, from the competitive point of view it is far more important for a football or hockey team *that* a goal is scored than *how* it is scored. In very many sports of this kind the overriding

consideration is the achievement of an external end, since that is the mark of success. In such sports the aesthetic is incidental.[56]

This is not to say aesthetic sports have no purpose. That is a common misconception associated with talk of aesthetic value. Best clarifies that this does not mean that "an activity can be said to be of some point or value only if it can be assessed in relation to its success in attaining some purpose external to itself towards which it is directed."[57] Aesthetic sports have purposes internal toward which they are directed, namely, the means to performing the sporting activity. Everything depends upon how one achieves the goal or as Best describes it, "the purpose cannot be considered apart from the manner of achieving it."[58]

Is this a justifiable distinction? Clearly there is some weight to the position but the distinction is not as clearly marked as Best would suggest. If such a division is to be accepted it must overcome two challenges. First, it is difficult to see why scoring a basket is considered an external goal of basketball while landing a double salto is an intrinsic end of gymnastics. Both must be performed within pre-defined rules and both are most effectively achieved by the athlete aligning his or her body in a certain way.

It is true that the manner of performance on the floor exercise is significantly more important than how the ball goes through the hoop in basketball. It does not matter whether the shot was beautifully executed or sloppily thrown at the goal. As long as it passes through the hoop the basket counts. The goal of basketball is to put the ball through the basket in any way that does not violate the rules of the sport. On the other hand it may be argued that basketball allows for more creative, artistic expression whereas gymnastics are judged on specific technical and mechanical execution. Furthermore, aesthetic sports, like gymnastics, also must operate with the rules and have standards by which they are judged.

Best admits that there may be a very limited sense in which aesthetic sports have an externally identifiable aim though he suggests it is better understood as "setting a framework within which the performer has the opportunity to reveal his expertise in moving gracefully than as an externally identifiable aim."[59] What is unclear on this point is how this is categorically different from the objectives of a purposive sport like basketball.

He then goes on to make a claim about aesthetic value in purposive sports that contributes to this confusion. "Our aesthetic acclaim is reserved

56. Best, "The Aesthetic in Sport," 199; italics original.

57. Ibid.

58. Ibid., 202.

59. Ibid., 204.

for him who achieves [the principal aim of the sport] with maximum economy and efficiency of effort."[60] What then is the difference between purposive and aesthetic sports? Best concludes that the difference lies in successfully achieving the goal of a particular sport. In purposive sports there is "an objectively specifiable framework . . . one which does not require the sort of judgment to assess achievement which is necessary in the aesthetic sports."[61]

The difference comes down to degrees of judgment about the ends of sports. Both types have intrinsic goals with one sport placing more emphasis on means than the other. The so-called aesthetic sports are more restricted in how successfully attaining the sport's objectives is judged. This relies heavily on using mechanical criteria to make the distinction. Since aesthetic qualities are prominent in both types we ought to conclude that aestheticism is not a distinguishing mark for types of sport. For the aim of purposive sports cannot be "considered apart from the manner of achieving it" either. At best the aesthetic should measure degrees of performance within sport, not create separate classifications of sport.

Best's account is insufficient in that even aesthetic sports have an "objectively specifiable framework." Again, they are perhaps more subjectively measured but these judgments are based on a standard, (i.e., a framework) for an ideal performance. A gymnast's routine is scored in terms of deductions for flaws in the execution of a particular move, which lends itself to Best's description of aesthetic sports being concerned with the means to the sport's aims. But this does not seem to be sufficient enough evidence to justify a distinction between types of sport as Best suggests.

Moreover, Lesley Wright illustrates the danger in too much emphasis on the aesthetic sports. "Focusing on those kinds of sports may make it look as if, providing those criteria are fulfilled, the performance will necessarily have aesthetic value."[62] This is not so, Wright argues, since it is possible to explain a gymnastics routine purely in technical terms. Yet there is an internal inconsistency in Wright's position since part of the technical scorecard for gymnastics includes points for the degree of difficulty of the routine being performed. This implicitly signifies a level of performance that requires the athlete to execute unique gymnastic acts. Even if they are not done perfectly there will still be some level of aesthetic appreciation to be found

60. Ibid.

61. Ibid.

62. Wright, "Aesthetic Implicitness in Sport and the Role of Aesthetic Concepts," 87.

in the performance. Therefore, Wright is incorrect to suggest a sport like gymnastics is capable of being explained purely in technical terms.

This leads to my second objection to Best's position. His claims suggest the dangerous notion that means do not matter for many sports. While he does not specifically state that means are unimportant, the context within which he is writing does not allow for a discussion of means other than as a signpost for labeling types of sport. It would be unfair to say Best disregards the means in purposive sports from an ethical standpoint. He is speaking strictly in terms of aesthetics when he says means are less important in purposive sports.

The question then becomes to what extent a culture that increasingly views sport as a spectacle will continue to value the means. It is doubtful that all concern for how a victory is achieved will become irrelevant. One of the highest moments in watching a sport is when we witness an athlete perform a specific act that can only be attributed to their well cultivated talents. In basketball for instance, the ball that is thrown carelessly at the hoop does not merit the same admiration as does the perfect technique of a jump shot. Even though both may result in a basket we typically attribute the former to luck and the latter to talent.

The Beauty of Giftedness and Effort

It is not just in admiring the way athletes perform that we find aesthetic appeal but in recognizing their abilities as a form of giftedness. Michael Sandel writes in his *The Case against Perfection* that spectators can distinguish between athletic effort and giftedness. He demonstrates the relevance of the means in a sport by drawing on the issue of biotechnological enhancements. He asks his reader to compare two of America's greatest baseball players of all time, Pete Rose and Joe DiMaggio. Rose, even though he was "not blessed with great natural gifts" excelled in baseball "through effort and striving, grit and determination."[63]

On the other hand, there are players like "Joe DiMaggio, whose excellence consists in the grace and effortlessness with which they display their gifts."[64] Sandel then questions which type of player fans would be most outraged about if it was discovered both used performance enhancing drugs. He concludes that most would be more offended by the naturally gifted player.

The reason is that even though Western society highly values effort and accomplishments of our own, sport is about excellence. "And excellence

63. Sandel, *The Case against Perfection*, 27.
64. Ibid.

consists at least partly in the display of natural talents and gifts that are no doing of the athlete who possesses them."[65] He is not speaking specifically of aesthetic value when he refers to giftedness but the connection is not difficult to make. Sandel draws attention to the intrinsic admiration for *how* an athlete competes but more to the point with *how easy* it seems for them.

I am not as convinced of Sandel's conclusion as he is.[66] Setting effort in contradistinction to giftedness does not provide a helpful illustration for identifying athletic excellence, primarily because giftedness lacks aesthetic value in a context void of effort and striving. Aesthetic appreciation is most readily given to those who achieve the objective(s) of sport in the most efficient and effort-less ways and perhaps this is why, as Sandel argues, the one to whom we gave greater admiration, (i.e., Joe DiMaggio) would also stir up more offence.

He argues that enhancements corrupt the most beautiful aspect of sport, the development of an athlete's natural gifts. "If effort were the highest athletic ideal, then the sin of enhancement would be the evasion of training and hard work. But effort isn't everything."[67] He goes on to argue that no matter how hard one works there are still those athletes whose natural abilities, when properly developed are more worthy of our praise.

> The real problem with genetically altered athletes is that they corrupt athletic competition as a human activity that honors the cultivation and display of natural talents. From this standpoint, enhancement can be seen as the ultimate expression of the ethic of effort and willfulness, a kind of high-tech striving. The ethic of willfulness and the biotechnological powers it now enlists are both arrayed against the claims of giftedness.[68]

While I agree with Sandel's critique of performance-enhanced athletics, I also am cautious about the way he develops his "ethic of effort" argument. I am skeptical of his reliance on a natural and unnatural distinction. He draws the conclusion that enhancement technologies are the "ultimate expression" of society's ethic of effort. He contrasts this with what he sees as sport's ultimate purpose, the cultivation of one's natural abilities. However,

65. Ibid., 28.

66. I am greatly indebted to Sandel's work on this topic as I believe he generally is correct in his assessment of the potential problems with biotechnological pursuits of perfection, particularly in reference to sport. However, altering the specific aspect of his argument I am critical of here would actually strengthen his overall position rather than diminish it as it would bypass the unnecessary, and unhelpful, discussion of natural/unnatural distinction.

67. Ibid., 29.

68. Ibid.

as I pointed out in my assessment of the current ethical debate, arguing from a position of natural and unnatural enhancements encounters a number of seemingly irresolvable conflicts. As we saw, it can be reasonably argued that many substances currently prohibited do not provide any more "unnatural" means of improving one's performance than that which is allowed, (i.e., how are exercise and diet supplements or the equipment we use natural expressions of effort but steroids are unnatural expressions?)

Part of my reservation lies in the attempt to completely separate giftedness from effort. Even the most naturally gifted athletes appeal to the spectator only after their gifts have been developed through effort. We admire those who make sport look easy but often forget the countless hours of practice and training they put in to make it appear so. Giving precedence to the gifted reduces the aesthetic appreciation for the effort. Effort is not everything but neither is giftedness. To be sure, outrage is justified when we learn of talented athletes who have tested positive for banned substances. On the other hand there also are numerous cases of "wasted talent" that suggest fans have reason to be similarly disappointed by a lack of effort. Perhaps more offence is taken in the case of the former but that is likely due in part to the deception of the doped athlete. Deception typically invokes more outrage than does laziness.

I am also concerned that Sandel's emphasis on the giftedness of athletes does not escape the sports culture's paradigm I am seeking to replace. His position places normative value on the abilities of the gifted by virtue of their natural talents. From this position it is very easy to conclude that those who lack such gifts are not as worthy of our admiration.

High regard is due for one's talents but not at the expense of one's effort. It should not be a matter of respecting *either* giftedness *or* effort. Both elements are worthy of our praise and, I think Sandel would agree, the majority of public admiration is because of the athlete's balance of giftedness and effort. Again, we can appeal to athletes with intellectual and physical disabilities to instruct us in honoring the role of effort and human striving. The natural gifts of Special Olympians, purely in terms of athletic ability, are obviously not comparable to those of the world's most physically elite athletes. Contrary to the account Sandel seems to present, it is not primarily the display of physical talent that makes an athletic performance admirable. To be sure, it is a commendable aspect of sport but should not be the chief source of praise.

To say the purpose of sport is contained in the display of an athlete's physical giftedness excludes, or at least reduces, one's admiration for athletes who lack the same level of giftedness yet in spite of that are determined to become better athletes. As a result, excellence comes to be defined not simply as a display of natural talents but a display of the best natural talents human beings have to offer. Take for example children playing a sport. Most likely it is not the best performance of athletic achievement, nor do very many of the children, if any, display natural talent. But there is still a very real sense in which excellence is achievable. The same is true in amateur or non-organized sport just as it is in para-Olympics or Special Olympics. The output of athletic achievement will not produce the same measurements that professional or Olympic athletes would provide but excellence is still frequently attained on various levels of sport.[69]

Still, Sandel is correct to argue that lacking a proper sense of appreciation for one's raw athletic gifts leads to a more obvious form of the "sport as spectacle" mentality. When we fail to appreciate our gifts within the confines of our physical limitations and begin to seek ways of transcending our finitude we replace gratefulness with greediness. As Sandel claims, turning sport into spectacle, "illustrates how performance-enhancing technologies, genetic or otherwise, can erode the part of athletic and artistic performance that celebrates natural talents and gifts."[70] Without question giftedness is something to be celebrated but not at the expense of our admiration for striving. While we rightly admire Joe DiMaggio's natural grace for making the game of baseball look easy we also rightly admire Pete Rose for his relentless determination to be the best ball player he could be.[71]

This does raise the question of what exactly we mean by excellence and how it is determined in sport. In fact, it may be argued that the account I have just given of excellence in the non-professional sporting venues is flawed by definition. Since what is meant by excellence, as it is commonly used, is the state of surpassing others or being superior in some respect. That means, some may argue, that athletic excellence should be determined by the absolute best achievements human beings are capable of. The supreme

69. I do not wish to give the illusion that para-Olympics or Special Olympics are the same as children's sports. To do so would be patronizing and naive. Many para or Special Olympians are capable of athletic accomplishments far beyond that of most amateur competitors. I simply wish to point out that various levels of athletic activity exist that do not meet the standards by which excellence has come to be determined in the modern sports culture.

70. Ibid., 44.

71. My view is that Sandel speaks out of turn when he assumes most would be more outraged by learning that the graceful player has been doping. Since the graceful player has a natural giftedness for the sport it is still conceivable that he could make it to the elite level of competition anyway. Whereas the determined player lacks those special talents, he presumably plays at that level *only because of* biotechnological enhancements. However, in both cases the athlete has engaged in deceptively subverting the equally admirable aspects of sport, giftedness and effort.

achievement, of course, is an act of perfection. In the last section I will look at the notion of perfection in athletic competition and see how it is different from excellence.

Distinguishing Perfection from Excellence

Acts of Athletic Perfection

When thinking of athletic perfection Nadia Comăneci's performance at the 1976 Olympics in Montreal certainly comes to mind. She was the first gymnast in Olympic history to score a perfect ten, a mark she would earn a total of seven times at the Games. Seldom in history is a whole performance considered perfect. Rarely do teams have a perfect season. Most pitchers in baseball, even at the professional level, will never pitch a perfect game. Quarterbacks in American football fall short of perfection completing on average only about sixty percent of their passes. Perfection seems to be an idea athletes constantly pursue but virtually never achieve.

Joseph Kupfer appreciates the pursuit of overall perfection but draws attention to athletes who perform a specific act perfectly. "Perfection as negation" is the term Kupfer gives to "the way nullity provides a determinate limit and outcome, one which cannot be improved upon and so is complete in itself."[72] In other words, perfection takes on its maximum aesthetic value in an act when that act is performed with finality and without the possibility of response from the opponent. It is interesting to note that Kupfer's idea marginalizes the effort and giftedness distinction focusing on the act itself rather than how it is done.

In baseball a home run is an act of perfection as negation. The ball is hit beyond the field of play and therefore does not allow the fielder an opportunity to make a play. A batter's objective in baseball is to get on base and ultimately circle the infield touching all the bases and return home to score a run, all the while not being forced out by any one of the fielders. It is possible to achieve this objective in a number of ways. The batter could be walked and over several subsequent batters move around the bases and score. The batter could hit the ball but only make it to one of the bases and rely on following batters to drive in the run.

The supreme method of achieving the batter's objective, however, is to hit a home run and thereby complete the task in one step. There are no opportunities for additional plays to contribute to achieving the batter's goal.

72. Kupfer, "Perfection as Negation in the Aesthetics of Sport," 18.

The talent needed to avoid these other steps is the object of appreciation Kupfer is referring to.

The difficulty of hitting the ball a long way deserves admiration in its own right but hitting it far enough for a home run removes any chance for the fielder to make a play and that is an additional aesthetic value for Kupfer. These are the events that stand out to modern spectators. "They are absolute, pure events in games of gradation, degree, and accretion."[73] In baseball he contrasts the perfection of batting with the perfection of pitching. Striking out the batter demonstrates the mastery a pitcher has over a batter on that particular occasion.

He suggests that some strike outs are not perfect. He compares a batter watching strike three cross the plate and a batter who swings and misses at the third strike. He even adds the batter who swings and foul tips the ball for strike three. All of these examples are strike outs but it is the swing and complete miss that summons the highest degree of appreciation for Kupfer. He says "the austere beauty of the untouched ball is compromised even though the result for the game is exactly the same."[74]

It may be argued that he is guilty of equating perfection with dominance. In fact, he consents to this accusation when he says "the negation in question is that of domination, of overpowering the opponent so completely that he or she is incapable of even a minimal response."[75] One might question the soundness of this statement's implications. Does overpowering an opponent necessarily command greater aesthetic appreciation than outsmarting or outlasting an opponent? He refers to the service ace in tennis as an example of perfection as negation. Does the ace necessarily hold more value than a lengthy volley that comes to an end only after one athlete proves to have greater endurance? Overwhelming an opponent is not *ipso facto* more aesthetically valuable than any other method of achieving the goal of a given athletic performance.

Many, like Kupfer himself, may see the overpowering victory as the highest aesthetic value but this is not necessarily the case for everyone. The fact that it is true of a majority of sporting spectators suggests there is at least some descriptive worth to Kupfer's claims. Fans tend to be more excited about a home run than a base hit. Basketball fans tend to cheer more loudly after witnessing the sport's most dominating move in the slam dunk than they do when a player simply lays the ball through the hoop.

73. Ibid., 28.
74. Ibid., 22.
75. Ibid., 23.

Yet, Kupfer's idea of perfection as negation faces contextual challenges. He refers to specific events within a larger game. Even conceding his point about domination still presents the problem of comparing seemingly identical events within the larger picture. Which is more aesthetically valuable, a pitcher who throws a strikeout late in the game when the score is tied or a pitcher who throws a strikeout in a game where the two teams are separated by six runs? Is a service ace more valuable when it is the match point? These are questions Kupfer does not address.[76] They are important points though because they illustrate the great diversity of aesthetic appreciation throughout sports.

Kupfer recognizes that while we do see the value of perfect performances we would not want them every play. Where would the excitement be in a tennis match if every serve was an ace? "It is as if in the piling up of negating feats, their distinctive nature might bleed away and they would seem hardly different from the incrementality of abundance. A level of austerity in negation itself therefore seems necessary for negation to retain its sparkle."[77] These are Kupfer's concluding words on perfection as negation and it is only here that he arrives at an aspect of aestheticism in sport he neglected throughout the rest of his paper.

One of the most beautiful aspects of sport is the fact that it is not perfect. There are perfect plays, to be sure, but without the faults and mistakes and even the ordinary plays that make up the game there is no reason to admire the perfection. Kupfer is right to suggest that the perfect acts stand out but it is only in the context of the rest of the game that they do so. The aestheticism of sport finds itself within the narrative of social practices as the athlete attempts to achieve the standards of excellence in a particular sport. Wright concurs when she says, "There is a connection, if only a contingent one, between skilful performance and aesthetic quality, and it is exactly this quality that, in part, gives sport its intrinsic value. For while these qualities are, in one sense, a byproduct of achieving ends that demand skilful means, they do help to explain the intrinsic satisfaction sport can give us."[78]

It is important that Wright gives this statement the qualification "in part" because there is more to sport than its aesthetic quality. However, for many spectators it is the sport's aestheticism that draws their attention.

---

76. Kupfer does consider perfection of a whole game in what he questionably calls non-competitive sports like golf and bowling where perfection is made up of a series of individual acts. Throwing the ball perfectly twelve times results in a score of 300, a perfect game in bowling. He does not offer any ideas as to what a perfect game would look like in team sports like American football or basketball.

77. Ibid., 29.

78. Wright, "Aesthetic Implicitness," 90.

Aesthetic appreciation for the act itself becomes easily assimilated into the quantification and record obsessed culture of sport. The fan's reverence is saved for the athlete who displays acts of perfection. There is a tendency to value perfect acts to the extent that anything less than perfection in sport becomes mundane in the eyes of the spectator. Home runs, hat tricks, and Hail Marys become the standards by which spectators judge their appreciation. Remarkable feats of athleticism are then weighed against previous remarkable feats as the routine quickly fades from memory.[79]

A Christian View of Excellence

It is common to hear conversations among fans that are critical of a particular player on a professional sports team, degrading that player for a "terrible performance" or being an "awful batter." How quickly these critics forget that by the very nature of being in a professional league the athlete who is now the target of their cynicism is among the most elite participants of the sport. This further shows how pervasive the culture of sport is even among those indirectly involved. If an athlete does not heavily contribute to the production of wins he or she is labeled inept, regardless of the fact that he or she has excelled far beyond the abilities of most athletes in the world. In an attitude consumed by the desire to win perfection becomes the supreme standard for determining athletic excellence. Perfection becomes synonymous with excellence. Anything less than perfection cannot be considered excellent and is therefore a deficient form of what sport *ought* to look like.

Christians can distinguish themselves from the sports culture by showing appreciation for the athlete's ability even when not all the performances are perfect. The culture of sport recognizes as praiseworthy only the flawless acts that lead to victory. Yet Christians realize it is not the celebration of physical perfection that is of utmost importance. Sport finds its meaning in the recognition of human limitations and the striving for excellence in the goals of the activity itself. It is here that we express gratitude and admiration to God who gives the gift of sport.

79. This is perhaps a point of distinction in American and British sports cultures. American sports fans seem to place more of an emphasis on quantification, records, and dominating acts of athletics (such as a home run in baseball) than do their British counterparts. This is likely attributable to the combination of cultural differences and the different natures of the games each society favors. For example, football (soccer), a fan favorite in the United Kingdom, may see only one or two goals scored in a typical match where basketball, among the most popular of American sports, will seldom see a team score less than sixty points in a single game.

As Shirl Hoffman notes, "gleaning the spiritual fruits sports have to offer is only possible if they are approached with an aesthetic disposition, with a keen eye focused on the broad array of emotions and attitudes they evoke."[80] He is right to connect the aesthetic with the emotions and attitudes rather than with the apparent giftedness or results a competitor is able to exhibit.

It also should be recognized that athletes do not participate in sport merely because it allows them to express their giftedness. Indeed many participants are not gifted. It seems appropriate when we talk of giftedness that elite athletes come to mind rather than amateurs. There are gifted amateurs, many of whom never rise to the elite levels for one reason or another and we ought to admire the aesthetic qualities they display as well. It is safe to say the vast majority of those engaging in sports we would not consider gifted or at least not in any sense that draws the same profound admiration currently found in elite level events.

As a result it is clear that the level of talent does not compose an essential component of sport. The praise of athletic beauty is interpreted, or read into, the activity by spectators in variously meaningful ways. Therefore, the greater aesthetic appreciation for the achievements of elite athletes does not make performance at those levels the normative case by which all other levels are measured.

Backyard games, Special Olympics and other amateur sporting events will not reach the same level of talent and physical accomplishments as is found on the elite stage but to suggest that they should, or that they in some way are inferior forms of sport is to acquiesce to the sports culture's current paradigm that overvalues the themes of winning, dominance and physical perfection. These non-elite games are just as meaningful forms of human activity and are not excluded from achieving the standards of excellence found within sport. Sport is not about the athletic results one is able to achieve or the victories collected. It is the pursuit of excellence at all levels of ability that reveals to us who we are as created human beings. Excellence involves a striving to be better, whatever one's current level of ability. It is this striving in sport, the effort of being human, that stands to be most depreciated in the current culture of competitive sport. The biggest, strongest and fastest athletes are not the standard by which all other athletes ought to be measured. Instead, the recognition of sport's human essence challenges us to embrace humanity's vulnerability.

As I asserted at the beginning of this chapter, much of the human element of sport has been replaced by a focus on the results of athletic achievements. A Christian theology of sport demands we recognize the human

---

80. Hoffman, *Good Game*, 287.

essence of sport as part of God's created order. We must shift our attention back to the humanity of the performance itself. The beauty of sport is captured in the means of athletic accomplishments, not in purely in their results. However, simply observing the beauty of a performance is not enough since we cannot truly appreciate the performance unless we recognize the frailty of our physical human condition. It is the acceptance of our weakness that makes athletic power and speed most meaningful.

The normative element of athletic achievement is not in the results of that achievement but in the degree to which one strives for excellence. This is the uniting factor that brings all athletes together. Recognizing our physical limitations shifts the focus away from perfection and exposes our human finitude. As Christian athletes and spectators we rightly embrace this vulnerability as it reminds us of both our reliance on our creator and the whole of human equality.

6

Recovering the Spirit of Play in Sport

THE PREVIOUS TWO CHAPTERS sought to reduce the importance Christians ought to place on winning but also cautioned us not to demonize winning altogether. Being human is at the core of the phenomenon we call sport but so is winning. After all, if it is not about winning, then why do we keep score? If not victory, what it is an athlete is striving for? Certainly, as we have just seen, striving is an intrinsic quality of the activity that seeks no further goal than itself. Yet in talking about striving and effort we must be careful not to forget a third basic component to a Christian theology of sport.

By way of review, the first tenet was that sport is not fundamentally incompatible with Christian moral principles. The second claimed that the beauty of sport hangs in the tension between recognizing human vulnerability and striving for excellence and that these two elements reveal to us a need for God as well as equality with each other. The third step toward a Christian ethic of sport is to recover the spirit of play within athletic competition. As we have seen throughout this thesis, the modern sports culture is obsessed with winning at all costs. This attitude often results in behavior that is inconsistent with Christian morality. In addition to recognizing sport's human essence Christians must recover the spirit of play when we participate.

In this chapter I will suggest that the concept of play is a requirement for the way Christians ought to participate in sport. To develop this idea further there are several components we must explore. First, we need to explain what we mean by play. We will look at several characteristics that help us identify play as well as clarify serious from non-serious attitudes in play. Then we will look at attempts to distinguish between the concepts of play, games and sport and conclude that sport is fundamentally an expression of play. In making the distinction between these three ideas some have attempted to define sport based upon the rules that govern the activity. A significant challenge this idea faces is bringing together the various accounts of meaning and value attributed to sport in different social settings.

I will suggest this problem is addressed by identifying the unifying concept of play found throughout all types of sport. In this third section I will argue that play is a basic good of human flourishing that makes our desire to participate in sport an intelligible action rooted in our shared human nature. The notion of basic goods is articulated by John Finnis and provides a foundation for seeing Christian involvement in sport as a form of human flourishing.[1] This stands in contrast to the attitude of popular sports culture, which tends to take the results of sport too seriously while not taking the nature of sport seriously enough.

Identifying Play

What are the values we find in sport that make it an activity worth pursuing? In chapter four we examined several external benefits sport provides including social, health, and moral values. Each of these can be present in sport to greater or lesser degrees but as we saw sport often results in the diminishment of these values. We also saw that these are external goods that do not necessarily speak to the value of sport as an autotelic activity. MacIntyre was helpful in providing a framework for conceptualizing sport in terms of social practices that draws distinctions between internal and external goods of the activity.

The Nature of Play in Sport

Play is an activity that knows no limitations of age, gender, race or culture. It is an essential aspect to the human condition. An understanding of play is crucial to a theory of sport, especially when considering the moral aspect of sport. It could be argued that if sport is nothing more than play then it cannot be considered a serious enterprise. Sport, then being only irrelevant play, lacks any authoritative or pedagogical qualities for the moral life. This is not to say that child's play lacks value in itself but that it lacks the ability to instruct one in how to live well. There are serious problems with the "it's just a game" theory that will be addressed later in this chapter. What follows is a consideration of the concept of play and, more specifically, the role play has

1. Finnis, *Natural Law and Natural Rights*.

in developing a Christian ethic of sport. I will reject the idea that play, and by extension sport, is an inconsequential activity. Contrary to this notion I will suggest play can be and should be taken seriously. In order to develop this argument more fully we must first as what is meant by play.

Theories of play are relatively new, having received systematic treatment only since the middle part of the twentieth century. Pioneering the field was Johan Huizinga, whose seminal work *Homo Ludens* (1970), offers a detailed analysis of the term *play*.[2] Modern theories are indebted to the originality of Huizinga's development of highly specific characteristics of play. Similarly, Roger Caillois offered a significant contribution to the understanding of play in his work *Man, Play and Games*.[3] This section details the meaning of play as found in the ideas of these two crucial thinkers.

Publishing the work twenty years after Huizinga, Caillois's book finds its beginnings in a reply to *Homo Ludens*. The first chapter offers a critique of Huizinga's groundbreaking work on the definition of play, though there is more synthesis than criticism. In fact, the definitions put forward by each individual are remarkably similar. This discussion will predominately focus on Huizinga's definition and will be augmented as necessary by Caillois. When Caillois is silent in this discussion it is not because he has nothing to say but simply for the reason that he is in agreement with Huizinga. Play, then, is summarized in Huizinga's analysis as such,

> We might call [play] a free activity standing quite consciously outside "ordinary" life as being "not serious," but at the same time absorbing the player intensely and utterly. It is an activity connected with no material interest, and no profit can be gained by it. It proceeds within its own proper boundaries of time and space according to fixed rules and in an orderly manner. It promotes the formation of social groupings which tend to surround themselves with secrecy and to stress their difference from the common world by disguise or other means.[4]

This outline of a theory of play may be dissected into six sections. The first characteristic of play is that it is a free activity. That is, play necessarily requires its participants to engage in the act voluntarily. Two people may be involved in an activity, say a board game. One is freely choosing to participate while the other is being forced or coerced into the game. The latter person, according to Huizinga's definition, is not really involved in play but

---

2. Huizinga, *Homo Ludens*.
3. Caillois, *Man, Play and Games*.
4. Huizinga, *Homo Ludens*, 32.

something different entirely. Play "is never imposed by physical necessity or moral duty. It is never a task. It is done at leisure, during 'free time.'"[5]

This is an appealing argument for defining play but as will be shown throughout this section this characteristic offers little help in exclusively identifying sport. For instance, is it accurate to claim that a businessperson is not *playing* golf when his only reason for doing so is because his boss required him to take a perspective client on an outing? Surely, we would say he is in fact playing golf, even if he would rather not be on the golf course or if he was doing it for the wrong reasons. Huizinga's account of play requires him to claim the businessman is not playing golf. If that is the case then what are we to say he is doing?

Saying he is "playing" golf is simply to say that we have no easier descriptor of his actions. He is "playing" insofar as that is what we call it when someone goes through the motions associated with golf, (i.e., hitting the ball with the club). He is not playing in the true sense of the word as Huizinga explains it. He has not immersed himself in the activity for the activity's sake. He is merely going through the motions for some other end. Play can only be engaged in when it is done voluntarily. This applies to the end of play as well as the beginning. It is only play when one freely enters and freely leaves the activity at will. Clearly, an activity cannot be considered play if one is forced to do it.

Caillois adds a characteristic at this point that Huizinga neglects. If play is free it must also be uncertain. "An outcome known in advance, with no possibility of error or surprise, clearly leading to an inescapable result, is incompatible with the nature of play."[6] The enjoyment of play would lose its impact if the end were revealed. Indeed, if it is possible to known the result beforehand the activity simply is not play. The extent to which chance, or luck, influences our appreciation of the performance of athletes is a discussion for a later chapter.

Huizinga's second feature of play is that it involves a clear distinction from "the real world." This is closely connected to the first characteristic in that play is a voluntary removal of oneself from the obligations of social reality, albeit a temporary removal. Huizinga compares this characteristic to a child's pretending. It is set apart from the normal. "Not being 'ordinary' life, [play] stands outside the immediate satisfaction of wants and appetites, indeed it interrupts the appetitive process."[7] Huizinga points to play's role as an interlude in daily life. Play "produces many of the fundamental forms

---

5. Ibid., 26.

6. Caillois, *Man, Play and Games*, 7.

7. Huizinga, *Homo Ludens*, 27.

of social life" and civilization "arises *in* and *as* play, and never leaves it."[8] The difficulty with Huizinga's account of civilization being "played" is summarized by Schirato as inconsistent. "What is implied here is that play is a disposition that inhabits not just people and places but, as Huizinga admits, world-views and institutions that are entirely antithetical to it."[9]

How does this concept of play relate to sport? In what sense is a sprinter pretending? She involves no elements of fantasy. The sport she is participating in requires little more than empirical measurements of distance and time. It is difficult to see how imaginary and disinterested elements pertain to most sports since sport is measured by the real world's physical laws. Schirato concurs that the "material and historical contexts of ordinary life are both what is being escaped from, and the sites of escape."[10]

There is, however, something to be said for play, in general as well as in sport, being distinct from the ordinary world. Athletes often say that when they are performing they think of nothing else. In this sense, the rest of the world, the "real" world, gives way to the play world. Also, within sport there are rules that must be followed that categorically distinguish the activity from the "real" world. The question then becomes why this is altogether separate from the ordinary world and not merely a distinguished part of it?

In an attempt to reconcile this Huizinga relies on the fluidity of play and seriousness. "The consciousness of play being 'only a pretend' does not by any means prevent it from proceeding with the utmost seriousness, with an absorption, a devotion that passes into rapture and temporarily at least, completely abolishes that troublesome 'only' feeling."[11] So then pretend does not exclusively refer to a child's imagination. It is better described in what Allen Guttmann refers to as the autotelic nature of play.[12] This means play has its own goals or purposes that distinguish it from other activities in the world. This is something Huizinga himself recognizes when he states that play is "a temporary activity satisfying in itself and ending there."[13] In other words, play serves its own purpose irrespective of the rest of the world.

Thus to answer one of the fundamental questions posed at the beginning of the discussion, play can in fact be serious. This comes as little surprise even to the most casual sports fans. Any spectator is well aware of the seriousness of defeating a rival opponent. Play can be more than immature

8. Ibid., 198; italics original.

9. Schirato, *Understanding Sports Culture*, 9.

10. Ibid., 9.

11. Huizinga, *Homo Ludens.*, 27.

12. Guttmann, "Rules of the Game," 24.

13. Huizinga, *Homo Ludens*, 27.

fun. Thus the volatility of the intersection between seriousness and play provides a prima facie account for an intense treatment of the meaning of play and sport.

The third attribute of play for Huizinga is that it lacks an interest in material gain. The idea that there is no profit to be gained by play does not necessarily allude to problems of commercialization. After a contest between two opponents both parties start over. The next match begins on level ground. Huizinga's point is that the victor in the previous match does not carry over any measurable element that provides a benefit in the second meeting. However, one might wonder what could be said for the confidence of having already defeated the opponent or the vengeance mentality of the first round loser. Ultimately, his line of reasoning is that in the same way that one is not really playing if forced to do the activity, one is not playing if the incentive is material or biological gain. "As a sacred activity play naturally contributes to the well-being of the group, but in quite another way and by other means that the acquisition of the necessities of life."[14]

Caillois summarized another difficulty with this characteristic when he claimed, "Games of chance played for money have practically no place in Huizinga's work."[15] Gambling would be excluded from Huizinga's definition of play but in all respects gambling and other games of chance qualify as play. Huizinga makes no attempt to reconcile this issue and thus Caillois rightly calls into question this definitional characteristic. Agreeing in principle to the unproductiveness of play he qualifies Huizinga's position by saying play creates "neither goods, nor wealth, nor new elements of any kind; and, except for the exchange of property among the players, ending in a situation identical to that prevailing at the beginning of the game."[16] This means that even though a winner gains money by playing poker and the loser forfeits money. The result is a balance for the whole of the game in which nothing new has been produced.

The fourth formal characteristic is that play works itself out within set constraints of time and space. The separation from "ordinary" life is momentary. In some cases, time and space are predefined as in a soccer match with specific field dimensions and the duration measured by a game clock. In other cases, it is open to the playing individual such as a child pretending to be a pirate. He may think himself a pirate all afternoon or may quickly become bored and cease pretending (playing) after only a few minutes. It was mentioned earlier that play may not be all that different from other

14. Ibid., 28.
15. Caillois, *Man, Play, and Games*, 5.
16. Ibid., 10.

activities such as business sales. This characteristic of play goes a consider-able distance in proving the contrary. For the businessman, work is not re-stricted to the highly articulated time and space limitations that the sprinter is. Additionally, as Guttmann indicates "People work because they have to; they play because they want to."[17] We must be careful not to get ahead of ourselves here. The relationship between work and play is an idea we will return to later. Now our focus should be specifically on the nature of play.

Huizinga's point becomes clear when we see a group of school children racing across the schoolyard. They have created another reality, within the "real" world, in which they obey its unique rules for running a race. That world ends when recess is over and classes resume. The same is true for footballers. They enter the pitch and for a specified period of time are trans-ported to a unique universe where the rules of the sport hold supreme. For that time their actions are guided by those rules. When the match is over that world disappears and they return to their "ordinary" lives.

It is worth noting that Caillois does not give this feature its own status. Rather, he uses the limitedness of play to bridge the separateness and the rule-bound aspects of play. "The confused and intricate laws of ordinary life are replaced in this fixed space and for this given time, by precise, arbitrary, unexceptionable rules that must be accepted as such and that govern the correct playing of the game."[18] For Caillois, the time and space constraints represent underlying assumptions of play rather than meriting a distinct characteristic.

Huizinga offers as a fifth characteristic of play, the element of order. A central tenet of play is the idea of rules. We will return to a fuller critique of rules later in the chapter. For now, to illustrate Huizinga's point the reader should note that "All play has its rules. They determine what 'holds' in the temporary world circumscribed by play. The rules of a game are absolutely binding and allow no doubt."[19]

This can best be seen in the example of what Huizinga calls the spoil-sport. Unlike the cheat, the spoil-sport intentionally breaks or ignores the rules. The cheat still pretends to play the game and at least acknowledges the characteristics of play already discussed. Huizinga does not expand on this claim but his argument suggests those who reject the rules destroy play whereas the deceitful ones who cheat cripple the play world.

---

17. Guttmann, "Rules of the Game," 24. This may be an oversimplification. I would agree with Huizinga and others who have identified us as *Homo Ludens* and would say that since playing is part of our nature that we "have" to play just like we "have" to work.

18. Caillois, *Man, Play and Games*, 7.

19. Huizinga, *Homo Ludens*, 30.

Schmitz adds, "Cheating in play is the counterpart of sin in the moral order. It seeks the good of victory without conforming to the spirit of the game and the rules under which alone it is possible to posses it."[20] What is important here is that rules are considered to be the unaccompanied mediator of games. In other words it could be said that cheaters are not involved in play and therefore not seeking that basic good that the activity is designed to achieve. They are in fact pursuing something less laudable and therefore perverting the purpose of the activity.

Caillois offers a more detailed account of the function of rules in play. Huizinga rightly draws attention to the involvement of rules in play but makes the mistake, Caillois argues, of attributing rules and order categorically to play. That is, for Huizinga "all play has its rules" and those rules are "absolutely binding and allow no doubt."[21] Caillois suggests that there are many games without rules. "No fixed or rigid rules exist for playing . . . games, in general, which presuppose free improvisation."[22] Furthermore, he separates two features of play that are mutually exclusive of each other. "Games", he says, "are not ruled and make-believe. Rather they are ruled *or* make-believe."[23] Yet even make-believe games are governed by rules. There are certain implicit rules in a child's imaginary game of, say, cops and robbers.

This overlap also exists in adult games such as sport. As Thornstein Veblen has pointed out, "Sports share this characteristic of make-believe with the games and exploits to which children, especially boys, are habitually inclined. Make-believe does not enter in the same proportion into all sports, but it is present in a very appreciable degree in all."[24]

What is agreed upon is that when rules are broken (rule-based) play is robbed of its illusion. *Illusion* being a fitting term in that it comes from the Latin *inlusio*, which means "in-play". Referring back to the second characteristic of play we see that as a distinct activity from the real world the idea of play as illusion complements this premise. As an "other-world" activity play is corrupted by disregarding its defining rules. Schmitz tells his readers that while play transcends the real world it still must adhere to the natural laws of the world and yet still is capable of running counter to real space and time.[25] The imagination allows one to wonder through strange lands and travel back in time while never actually leaving the room.

20. Schmitz, "Sport and Play: Suspension of the Ordinary," 27.

21. Huizinga, *Homo Ludens*, 30.

22. Caillois, *Man, Play, and Games*, 8.

23. Ibid., 9; italics original.

24. Veblen, *The Theory of the Leisure Class*, 256.

25. Schmitz, "Sport and Play," 28.

The involvement of the group represents the sixth and final fundamental characteristic of play developed by Huizinga. Play often results in the formation of communities that continue beyond the limited time of play. "The feeling of being 'apart together' in an exceptional situation, of sharing something important, of mutually withdrawing from the rest of the world and rejecting the usual norms, retains its magic beyond the duration of the individual game."[26] The truth of this trait is obvious and I will argue later that the development of these communities plays a significant role in our theological understanding of sport.

The problem facing us now is how this characteristic is distinct of play. Huizinga does not specifically make this claim but given his overall project of defining the play element in culture it is fair to assume the six characteristics he points to offer, in his estimation, a distinct understanding of play. This final quality offers no such distinction. As social beings we form communities wherever our interests may lie. Doctors practicing medicine are not *playing* but they form communities such as medical associations. Meteorologists, psychologists and politicians are among the many others that do the same but none of these practices qualify as play.

We have attempted to explain the flaws and strengths of the characterization of play. It has proven to be a sufficient starting point for developing a theory of sport. Many of these characteristics, as well as their criticisms, help amend our initial thoughts about what it means to play. Play is a free activity with uncertain and unproductive results, which provides a separation from the "real world" either by its rule-based autotelic nature or in an entirely imaginative creation of space, time and activity. It has also been noted that play is a fluid concept in games. Kretchmar notes that one can "fall in and out of play many times" in the same game.[27] Some games are "played" with utmost importance while others are "played" in a completely trivial, care-free manner. Many times these different attitudes occur in the same type of game. It is also possible to have both elements present in the same game.

Allowing for either its presence or its absence helps our understanding of the nature of play but how do these elements of play, games and sport relate to one another? A Christian theology of sport would be remiss if it did not address the subtleties of the connection between these three concepts. In the next section I will show that many athletic activities provide numerous possible relationships between the three, but ultimately sport is best expressed within the spirit of play.

26. Huizinga, *Homo Ludens*, 31.
27. Kretchmar, *Practical Philosophy of Sport*, 212.

The Role of Play and Games in Sport

It is imprudent to attempt a definition of sport without considering Bernard Suits and his account of games. This section will explore the elements of sport in Suits's account as well as some theories that see his attempt to define sport as problematic. Suits has written a substantially on the nature of games and sport. Throughout his career he attempted to explain what one means when using the term sport. His position has shifted significantly with regard to the relationship between games and sport but he has remained consistent with his framework for defining a game.

The Elements of Games

Suits explains that a game requires four elements. First, a game needs to have a prelusory goal. By that he means, "A specific achievable state of affairs."[28] There must be a clear purpose to the event and that purpose must have a feasible end. An activity in which contestants attempt to jump over buildings is not a sport since it cannot be done. More realistically, attempting to race to a specific point and be the first one to reach the finish line is an example of a prelusory goal.

The second element is the means by which athletes are to obtain the prelusory goal. Not only is the goal important it is equally important how one achieves that goal. The goal of boxing is to knock your opponent down for ten seconds. Suits clarifies that although one way to accomplish this is to "shoot [your opponent] through the head," that "this is obviously not a means to winning the match."[29] The goal must be such that one has a reasonable claim at victory or being declared the winner.

The next facet of games governs the means to the goal. Suits argues for what has been termed a formalist position, which explains that breaking the rules means the rule breaker is not actually participating in that sport. In other words, rules are a necessary part of defining sport. A definition of sport cannot be specified without accounting for the rules specific to that sport. Recognizing the potential difficulties with this method of defining sport he spells out two types of rules. There are constitutive rules and rules of skill (also called regulative rules). "To break a rule of skill is usually to fail, at least to that extent, to play the game well, but to break a constitutive rule is to fail to play the game at all."[30]

28. Suits, "The Elements of Sport," 9.
29. Ibid., 9.
30. Ibid., 9.

There must be a distinction in rule types. To illustrate this use the following example. Fouling an opponent in basketball is against the rules. Yet when someone breaks that rule, as happens quite frequently throughout a game, one would not say that athlete is not playing basketball. In fact, the game allows for that rule to be broken in that each player is allowed to make a specified number of fouls before being prohibited from playing the remainder of the game. Furthermore, in certain situations fouls are encouraged as a means of gaining an advantage over the opponent.

Therefore a foul is a regulative rule. It is a rule within the sport that helps to regulate how that sport is to be played. Constitutive rules, on the other hand, are rules that "set out all the conditions which must be met in playing the game (though not, of course, in playing the game skilfully.)" Suits continues, "We may define constitutive rules as rules which prohibit use of the most efficient means for reaching a pre-lusory goal."[31] The purpose of rules is to make the sport difficult. It is this challenge that makes the sport the activity that it is. Constitutive rules place obstacles in the athlete's path to reaching the prelusory goal. These rules define playing the sport. Regulative rules define playing the sport *well*.

A fourth element Suits presents as required for an activity to be a game is a lusory attitude. According to Suits, "the attitude of the game-player must be an element in game-playing because there has to be an explanation of that curious state of affairs where-in one adopts rules which require him to employ worse rather than better means for reaching an end."[32] Therefore, according to Suits the four elements of a game combine to give us this definition, "My conclusion is that to play a game is to engage in activity directed towards bringing about a specific state of affairs, using only means permitted by rules, where the rules prohibit more efficient in favour of less efficient means, and where such rules are accepted just because they make possible such activity."[33]

The essence of this element is the idea of volunteering for such an activity that is more challenging than it should be. The attitude of the athlete is essential to the game because it is the athlete's willingness to compete by the rules that makes the activity a game.

31. Ibid., 10.
32. Ibid.
33. Suits, *The Grasshopper*, 34.

Definitional Requirements of Sport

Suits's early work on sport and games argued that sports are essentially games. The differences are small enough that Suits refuses to call sport a species of the genus games. "The distinguishing characteristics of sport are more peripheral, more arbitrary, and more contingent than are the differences required to define a species."[34] It follows then that the above definition of game applies to sport as well. Sport also must meet the same four qualifications of games. They are 1) the goal, 2) the means of achieving the goal, 3) the rules, and 4) the lusory attitude. By way of clarification, he did not claim that all games are sports. But any game that contains these four specific requirements is to be considered a sport. Suits initially defines sport as any game (as defined by the four elements), which is a game of physical skill with a wide following and a certain level of stability.[35]

The purpose here is not to offer an extended analysis of this definition though it is worth mentioning the latter two qualifications are extremely suspect. Intuition tells us that sport requires the exercise of a specific set of skills and that those skills should be physical but why must a sport have a wide following? Additionally, what constitutes a wide following? It is implausible to set a specific number of followers to qualify a game as a sport. Similarly, it does not seem practical to set a specific time period to elapse before the game is given sport status. While his definition of sport needs serious amendments his definition of games is more thorough. We will look closely at criticisms aimed toward Suits's definition of games in a following section. The question at hand is the relation of sport, games and play.

After publishing "The Elements of Sport," Suits presented another paper that criticized his own previous work. In "The Tricky Triad" he admits that his assumption that all sports are games was wrong. He held fast to his definition of games but offered a modified account of sport and play. Suits draws a Venn diagram to represent his theory. Each field is represented by a circle that overlaps with the others. Certain areas are reserved exclusively for one field while others overlap at certain points with only one other so that, for example, some activities constitute play but not games (recall Huizinga's pretend world of a child), some games but not sport (non-physical activities), others sport but not play (presumably, professional sports). Each of the three fields also overlaps both of the others, resulting in an activity that is at the same time play, game *and* sport. This results in seven categories

---

34. Suits, "Elements of Sport," 11.
35. Ibid.

or types of activity in this "tricky triad, (i.e., games and play, games and sport, sport and play, etc.).

Some of these make perfect sense while others are difficult to conceptualize. It is plain enough that one can play a game that is not sport but what is one to make of, say, sport that is not play or game? Suits proposes that this area of sport is where we find professional athletic performances. This, the core of Suits's newly found distinction, suggests that sports are of two kinds, which he refers to as rule-based contests and judged performances. It is the performances that he focuses on here. Games function by their predetermined rules and are subsequently measured objectively by those rules. Competitions such as gymnastics are *judged* and are thereby "no more games than are other judged competitive events such as beauty contests and pie-baking competitions."[36] Yet gymnastics and the like have physical components that qualify them as sport. So for Suits, judged athletic performances are sport and games that meet his four requirements are also sport but each is of a very different kind.

Is the division Suits maintains between sport and game justified? The answer must surely be negative. The reason is that it seems perfectly feasible to cast performances, such as gymnastics or mountain climbing, in the light of Suits's own definition of games. These sports have unnecessary obstacles with certain means or rules to achieve a specified pre-lusory goal and this is done with a lusory attitude. To be sure, the outcome of the competition is judged rather than empirically measured but both operate within a framework of rules, even if performance events rely less on those rules during competition than do refereed sports.

Klaus Meier offers a response to Suits in which he advocates precisely this point. Suits description of performance events does in fact meet his definitional requirements for a game.[37] Meier redraws the Venn diagram in such a way that sport is encompassed entirely within games. Play intersects with the others individually and collectively. This eliminates sport that is not game or play, as well as sport and play that are not games.

I find Meier's arrangement to be more persuasive since he excludes the possibility of sport being entirely separated from games. This model also is more conducive to the centrality of play in a Christian understanding of sport I will advance in the present work. Meier concludes, "if games or sports are pursued voluntarily and for intrinsic reasons, they are also play

36. Suits, "Tricky Triad," 3.
37. Meier, "Triad Trickery," 31.

forms; if they are pursued involuntarily or engaged in predominately for extrinsic rewards, they are not play forms."[38]

The Deficient Project of Defining Sport

Through his works discussed here Suits has contributed a considerable amount to dialogue over the nature of sport and many subsequent works are indebted to him. Obviously however, there also exists a number of criticisms of his conclusions. The recent work by Graham McFee is one of the more detailed accounts.

McFee points out that the problem with definitions is that they need to be an exact fit for the object or activity they describe. This means definitions can be proven wrong in one of two ways. A definition of sport (or anything else for that matter) can be proven wrong if it excludes activities that should be included or excludes activities that should be included. McFee faults Suits's definition on both accounts. To exemplify this McFee questions the necessity of Suits's use of "unnecessary obstacles". In a game of chess he asks what obstacles are unnecessary leading to checkmate over an opponent?[39] Conversely, there also may be games in which every obstacle is necessary.

The difficulty, as McFee puts it, is that the concept of a definition that encompasses all possibilities is inconceivable based on the fact that there is an infinite number of possibilities throughout the sporting activity in question. While this claim may be guilty of splitting hairs it is successful insofar as it points to the predicament of establishing the essence of an activity understood by a definition based solely on the rules of that activity. McFee is arguing that this type of predicament is inevitable for the formalist position.

Furthermore, many activities, which are not games, involve voluntary actions to overcome unnecessary obstacles. McFee employs the counter example of mountain climbing. A shepherd climbing a mountain to tend to the herd has a specific reason for climbing the mountain but a mountaineer does so with no other purpose. In the truest sense he is climbing voluntarily but, McFee contends, "mountaineering does not, at first blush, seem like a game."[40]

He certainly could turn the climbing into a game but his climbing does not necessarily constitute a game, as McFee believes Suits's definition would require. Suits might insist the shepherd is participating in the sport of mountain climbing but according to McFee that means Suits's argument would require returning to his own definition of sport. Furthermore, McFee

38. Ibid., 32.
39. McFee, *Sport, Rules and Values*, 25.
40. Ibid., 25.

claims that "simply by setting for myself some unnecessarily high limits to some task I thereby transform that task into a game."[41] McFee's purpose here is not to discredit mountain climbing as a sport but to point out what he sees as inconsistencies in Suits's circular definition of sport. For games (and by extension sports) are defined by prelusory goals and means which, in order to be defined, require an understanding of games.

The problem with McFee's criticism of Suits is that he takes each of Suits's elements individually. He makes the mistake of separating the four principles of a game where Suits intends for them all to work together. To see this more clearly take the example of a chair. If one were to take each leg of that chair independently it could easily be argued that this piece of wood is insufficient to build the foundation of a chair. In order for the chair to function it requires all four legs. Remove any one of them and the chair is unusable. Suits proposes the same concept for a game. Subtract any one of the four elements from the others and the activity ceases to be a game.

McFee rightly believes that the fundamental problem with attempts at definitions is that finding even one counter-example disproves the definition entirely. Take for instance McFee's counter-example of mountaineering. In an effort to invalidate Suits's contention about games involving voluntary efforts to overcome unnecessary obstacles McFee suggests that a mountaineer is attempting to overcome unnecessary obstacles (he does not need to climb the mountain) but it is not a game. Therefore, McFee says, Suits's definition of sport must be inaccurate. The question needs to be asked, however, why this mountaineer is climbing the mountain. If he is doing it to herd the sheep atop the mountain then it is clearly not a game. If he is voluntarily climbing the mountain with the purpose of reaching the top by unnecessary means, (i.e., not being taken to the top by helicopter) for the pure enjoyment of climbing a mountain, one might say, for *fun*, then would the activity not contain all four elements Suits depicts?

McFee recognizes the possibility of refuting his counter–example but maintains his position based on the belief that there could always be another counter-example possible. Again, this assumes the counter-examples would challenge the four defining qualities of a game independently. What surfaces then is the strength of these interlocked qualities in that it is unlikely a counter-example could be given that either precludes a game or includes a non-game activity in Suits's definition of a game when all four aspects are knit together.

Even if McFee's assessment of the four elements is incorrect he still can point to the philosophical troubles facing attempts at defining sport. In

41. Ibid., 25.

fact, he suggests that Suits is misguided in his attempt to define sport at all. McFee believes a definition of sport is neither possible nor desirable.[42] There are two reasons for this. First, defining sport seems a bit superfluous since one can understand something without being able to adequately define it. For example, we all know what *time* is yet one can offer no exact definition within the stipulations set out earlier of exclusion and inclusion.

Wittgenstein most famously makes this definitional point in what he refers to as *language-games*.[43] We use language to name an object or activity, in this case sport, and it is in naming it that others can learn what the term means. Also called primitive language, this method of learning is how children learn to speak their native language. We are able to know what an object is without an ostensive definition of that object. He says, "if you look at them [games] you will not see something that is common to *all*, but similarities, relationships, and a whole series of them at that."[44] Rather than assuming a common feature if we "look and see" we find that games share a "family resemblance." Indeed, "'games' form a family."[45] A family has members who share certain features with some but not others, while still others share a different set of features but all are still in the same family. Some may have the same facial features while others share unique dispositions.

Wittgenstein is helpful on this point about games forming a family though I disagree when he says there is nothing common to *all* games. The fact that games are able to be grouped together in a family suggests there is something that makes them all relate to one another. In the next section I will show that the common element of play may be found in all games and it is this uniting component to sporting activity that allows us to move beyond cultural values to a shared, basic aspect of human nature.

The second reason McFee rejects a definition of sport is that we must have some knowledge of what something is prior to being given a definition of it to test if that definition is accurate. By this he means definitions cannot actually contribute to knowledge except perhaps in knowledge of the meaning of a term. But McFee finds no use in definitions for understanding the activity itself. It may be objected that no prerequisite knowledge is necessary to understand the object being described. All that is required is to know what the describer is pointing to. This may help us understand the object but it does not provide a clear definition unless we already have some previous knowledge of the object's function. Wittgenstein notes that pointing to

42. Ibid., 22.
43. Wittgenstein, *Philosophical Investigations*, §7.
44. Ibid., §66; italics original.
45. Ibid., §67.

a piece of wood and naming it the "king" does not tell one anything of value unless "he has already played other games, or has watched other people playing and 'understood'—*and similar things.*"[46]

Since McFee rejects the importance of Suits's definitional project, it rightly may be asked, what does he consider sport to be? For McFee, "the best method of explaining what we mean by sport in a particular context may be to exemplify it: for example, by cricket."[47] Does this answer the question of what sport is without the subsequent requirement of a definition? McFee believes it does and it is made possible by having a right understanding of rules within the activity. The fact that McFee is critical of Suits's formal use of rules to define sport has been addressed already but what remains is to look at the distinctions made between types of rules.

The dichotomization of rules in sport has been sharply criticized. This certainly seems to be a fair subject for investigation since much of Suits's position hinges on these two types of rules. If the dichotomy were found guilty of possessing the inconsistencies it is accused of then rules, in effect, would be rendered useless in defining sport and Suits's theory would crumble. But is such guilt to be found? If the dichotomy is to remain helpful it must withstand the scrutiny of anti-formalists.

A significant difficulty with defining a sport by its rules is the logical conclusion that when an athlete violates the rules he or she ceases to participate in that sport since the action is no longer within the definitional scope of the sport. More succinctly can two sports that share the same constitutive rules but differ in regulative rules be the *same* sport? A conventional example is drawn from D'Agostino. Let the sport of football (soccer) be divided into two categories; G and G`. G represents football as is commonly played and G` represents football in which the handball rule has been removed. Can they both still be called football? D'Agostino suggests the formalist must accept these as the same game since the constitutive rules of both are the same. Constitutive rules, being those that establish the goals of the game, are the same for both versions of football. The regulative rules are the ones that invoke penalties rather than contribute to a definition of a game. Regulative rules, as we have seen, are those that guide specific actions within the context of the constitutive rules. Since there is a penalty for a handball violation it is considered a regulative rule. That means the two games with vastly different regulative rules still share mutual principles that constitute the game. For D'Agostino this seems to be a ridiculous position to hold. It runs contrary to "compelling commonsense intuitions about the

46. Ibid., §31; italics original.
47. McFee, *Sports, Rules and Values,* 27.

'identity of games.'"[48] This is indeed a major problem for formalism since it is difficult to distinguish which types of rules are constitutive and which are regulative.

Attached to this is the additional problem of penalties being rendered irrelevant. It may be asked what right there is to penalize a player for a rule violation if that violation effectively means the athlete is no longer playing *that* sport. The formalist at this point in the argument might remind us of the distinction between constitutive and regulative rules. A considerable difficulty in doing so is discerning which category a specific rule belongs to. D'Agostino points out that "it is possible to treat the rules of a game as if each rule were unequivocally either constitutive or regulative, but not both, and to do so without conceptual or explanatory loss."[49]

The arbitrariness of the typology of rules presents a substantial challenge to the formalist position. Furthermore, in agreement with McFee's position, D'Agostino believes the formalist neglects contextualization. A formalist account simply allows for what is permissible and what is not. Enriching the scope of rules, D'Agostino contends, requires a distinction between what is permissible and what is acceptable. To see this distinction he suggests rules be understood in the context of the ethos of games. The ethos of a game considers the "unofficial, implicit, empirically determinable conventions which govern official interpretations of the formal rules."[50] This position not only allows for a greater appreciation for the game but offers a more substantial account for why in, say basketball, fouls are acceptable but not permitted.

Likewise, McFee suggests the separation of constitutive and regulative rules is not entirely unhelpful. "Our method of reinstating a broadly constitutive/regulative distinction comes to this: that these are uses of rules, which different contexts bring to the fore . . . So something like the regulative/constitutive distinction is maintained but for *uses* of rules, not the rules themselves (although sometimes, for convenience or economy, we will speak of constitutive and regulative *rules*)."[51]

Seeing how we understand some rules to make up the constitution of games and other to regulate our actions within the games helps us to recognize the need for our submission to a moral authority if we are going to properly participate in sport. However, we have not yet addressed the nature of these normative rules. In the final section of this chapter I will

48. D'Agostino, "The Ethos of Games," 46.

49. Ibid., 45.

50. Ibid., 47.

51. McFee, *Sports, Rules and Values*, 44.

describe two approaches to accounting for sport's moral normativity. The first sees individual cultures as the only possible source of moral authority. While cultural interpretations are clearly evident I will suggest there is a deeper level of normativity that Christian theology recognizes as a universal standard for human nature. In identifying play as a basic good I will suggest sport can ultimately be an expression of this element of God's created order.

Shared Values of Sport: Play as a Basic Good

Rules, Sport, and Cultural Values

It should also be noted that D'Agostino's position is compatible at some level with formalism. In fact, he suggests that formalism may be correct if it is supplemented by a recognition of the importance of the ethos of games.[52] One formalist who has attempted to do this is William Morgan. As a formalist he must accept the conclusion of D'Agostino's example that G and G` are the same game, differing only in the regulative rule of handball. Morgan believes the proper response is to view these examples in two different social contexts.

He invites his readers to imagine these games are practiced in a culture that deeply respects football and all its rules (both constitutive and regulative). In this context, "That respect bodes well for the rules of both games in which one would expect not only that the rules of G and G` would be strictly observed, and that the strategic practice of bending and breaking rules would be considered altogether taboo, but that even those instances not directly covered by a regulative rule, in the case of 'handball' in G`, would be avoided out of sheer deference to the game itself."[53] Morgan continues, "to respect the game itself is to respect just those aspects of it (soccer) that make it the particular game of skill that it is."[54]

He then places these games in a social setting where strategic rule breaking is commonly practiced to gain certain advantages. If the penalties for handball are removed there is little doubt that athletes will take advantage of handball opportunities as frequently as possible. The difference in these two instances is "owed to the changed social context, which preempts any claim that the rules will be absolutely obeyed."[55]

---

52. D'Agostino, "Ethos of Games," 48.
53. Morgan, "The Logical Incompatibility Thesis and Rules," 53.
54. Ibid., 53.
55. Ibid., 54.

Morgan accepts D'Agostino's summation of "constitutive rules as game-defining rules, and regulative rules as penalty-invoking rules."[56] But he further clarifies that constitutive rules are also regulative since they set boundaries for what is and is not permissible within competition. This obviously casts doubt on the definitive distinction between regulative and constitutive rules and thus renders the distinction ineffective for identifying two unique games. Predictably, Morgan concedes that they are the same game only that the latter is a defective instance of the game G (in this case, football). Since the regulative rules enforce the constitutive rules of a particular game the games G and G` can be consistently identified as the same game.

It is worth questioning whether Morgan has overcome the objections to formalism or whether he has articulated a new theory that simply better disguises its problems. This conclusion he arrives at may lead one to believe there is a quasi-platonic ideal of soccer. That there is a perfect form of some specific sport and when it is not played precisely by this ideal it is a defective game. The concern here is over how it is we go about determining this ideal sport. Without doubt, if such an ideal is to be found it must derive from the social context in which the game is practiced. Morgan concurs, "When we prick the rational core of a practice like sport, we find not something natural, pure, inviolate, or necessary—not an essence—but something social, impure, and contingent."[57]

Therefore, Morgan argues that a platonic form of sport does not seem to be the mould in which we develop a theory of sport. There is not one specific form of sport that is universally accepted but a multitude of sporting games that evolve with culture. Any attempt to isolate sport purely by a formal account of its rules is too shallow. Instead, Morgan asserts sport is only identifiable through its deep seeded connections with a given society. Clearly, many societies accept the same game, such as football, but this is done within that society, often as a means to social enrichment via other cultures. That is, sport is an avenue for intercultural exchange as we learn about one another by watching and participating in the games each culture plays.

Just as we cannot identify a game without appealing to the social dimensions of that game we cannot identify a game merely by its social dimensions. Paraphrasing Habermas, Morgan argues that rejecting the formal rules of sport as "the standard of legitimation" deprives us "of the one relevant critical standard by which we can explain the corruption of all reasonable standards about games and sports."[58] Therefore, social traditions

56. Ibid., 53.
57. Morgan, *Leftist Theories of Sport*, 216.
58. Morgan, "Logical Incompatibility," 60.

complement the rules of a game rather than replace them. Attempting to discard the formal rules is "neither a simple nor an innocuous capitulation to convention but one purchased at considerable cost, not the least of which is the surrender of a certain critical capacity that I think is crucial to an understanding and appreciation of games."[59]

Describing sport as identifiable only within a social context and only workable within a set of normative rules illuminates what makes sport so important to society. Caillois notes, "to a certain degree a civilization and its content may be characterized by its games."[60] Sport not only represents a path to life's leisure element but also serves a didactic function for a given culture's social values. The two frameworks adhere together to present a moral fertility through which a society may demonstrate and develop culturally significant moral values.

Allen Guttmann states that sociological insights may be gained from "careful attention to the games a society emphasizes" but at the same time recognizes that "the 'same' game is likely to vary greatly in meaning from one cultural context to another."[61] Moreover, the same game may have various meanings for people within the same cultural context. It may be tempting here to conclude that a singularity of meaning in sport is flawed because there is no common element to all games but a variety of meanings in sport. To complicate matters it is evident that different civilizations throughout history have valued different sports in different ways. Even contemporary societies honor values in sport to a greater or lesser degree than each other.

Yet just because each society values different sports and provides varied moral interpretations of the games it honors does not mean there is no common theme underlying all sport. We are able to share the fundamental quality of play while at the same time express a diversity of meanings and values in the sports we play. This element of play is an essential expression common to all human beings and is what John Finnis calls a basic good. After exploring what is meant by basic goods I will conclude the chapter by showing how Christian theology interprets the role of play in sport as a key element to pursuing human flourishing.

Play as a Basic Good

When sport is done for the purpose of exercise, teaching values, or any other external reason it becomes a means to some other end. Some ends are

59. Ibid.

60. Ibid., 83.

61. Guttmann, *From Ritual to Record*, 11.

more praiseworthy than others as we saw with Special Olympics. The Muscular Christianity movement also promoted several commendable external goods in sport such as the development of character. The moral growth of an athlete is a positive outcome of sport, to be sure. But it is not the reason we participate in sports. One does not decide to play sports to become a better person although that may be the outcome.

Unfortunately, sometimes the opposite result occurs. Arrogance and greed enter in and individuals end up worse than before. Some are overcome by the temptation to cheat and as a result unfairness persists. Friendships can be ruined. If moral formation is the reason we engage in sport then often times we fail to achieve its purpose. Sport also leads many to risk physical and mental injuries. So if we think sport is about health then we miss the point yet again.

What then is the point? Perhaps a more focused question would be to ask, if sport is not about winning or any other external good what is it we are striving *for*? Why does every civilization in the world participate in some form of physically challenging leisure activity? One response may be to say that none of these respective goods are *the* reason we participate in sport. These values are parts of the whole of sport. We don't play in sports for one of these reasons but to know the joy of all of them collectively.

From this perspective sport is comprised of several constituent goods. Obviously, athletes experience some degree of these goods during the activity but this is still the wrong way of viewing the purpose of sport. Whether it is one of these goods or a combination of them that make up the value of the activity, this approach still fails to capture the intrinsic value in sport.

Another response would be to identify sport's essential worth in the notion of play as a basic or natural good. That is, sport is enjoyed purely for its own worth, with no further end than itself. Taking this starting point allows one to value the external goods as products of sport without mistakenly turning sport into a means to something else. They are the typical *result* of sport not the *reason* for sport. When we fail to move beyond these extrinsic goods we miss out on the good of what many call sport's purest form, the love of the game.

Helpful in constructing this approach to sport is part of John Finnis' work on natural law. Finnis believes there are seven self-evident, universal goods that are helpful in evaluating various reasons for action.[62] He describes these seven goods as "basic" goods in that they are not derived from other goods. They are first-order or primary goods, each of which is desir-

---

62. The seven basic goods are 1) Life, 2) Knowledge, 3) Play, 4) Aesthetic experience, 5) Sociability, 6) Practical reasonableness, and 7) Religion.

able for its own sake. He articulates this idea of basic goods most specifically through two chapters in his book *Natural Law and Natural Rights*. In one chapter he details the basic good of knowledge while the latter is concerned with listing other basic goods, including the good of play.[63]

Finnis offers five key tenets to support his idea of basic goods. My intention here is to briefly describe the good of play within this aspect of Finnis' natural law framework and to offer my own comments on how this framework shapes the theology of sport presented in the rest of this chapter.

The first component of a basic good is that there is a basic inclination to pursue this aspect of human well-being for no reason outside of the good itself. To remove any confusion over what this means Finnis issues several points of clarification describing what basic goods do not entail. To begin with, not all forms of a particular basic good are equal. For example, he notes the knowledge of certain propositions about natural law is generally better than the knowledge of how much ink was used to print those propositions in a book.

Likewise, basic goods are not equally valuable to every person, at all times, in all circumstances. Individuals from different situations or periods of their lives may value specific basic goods differently. The good of friendship may be more relevant to some people while others may be more drawn to aesthetic experience.[64] This allows for the complexity of human experiences while identifying those goods that the pursuit of "makes intelligible (though not necessarily reasonable-all-things-considered) any particular instance of the human activity and commitment involved in such pursuit."[65]

Nor is one of the basic goods more important than any of the others. While there are several goods to be pursued, Finnis explains that no basic good is to be considered a supreme good that is fundamentally more important than any other. It also is important to note that Finnis does not see basic goods as moral values. Rather they are pre-moral goods that simply ascribe intelligible meaning to one's actions. Finally, basic goods are not means to

63. Finnis uses knowledge as an example for describing the basic goods. Readers of Finnis will notice that "knowledge" is given a full chapter while "play" and the other five basic goods are awarded little more than a paragraph. He clearly states the reason for this is not because knowledge is somehow more important than the other basic goods but simply out of preference. I do not offer a criticism of Finnis for treating play so briefly. On the contrary, he is to be commended for being one of the few voices to give play such an important status.

64. The choice of friendship and aesthetic experience as examples was intentional. Both are important components of sport, as is play, thus strengthening the case for the good of sport as an activity that actively promotes the pursuit of no less than three of these basic goods.

65. Finnis, *Natural Law*, 62.

some other end but are valued for their own sake. Any good (A) that is sought as a means to another good (B) cannot be basic as (A)'s value may be reduced to an instrumental value in the pursuit of (B).

By definition, to be a basic good the object considered must be sought for its own sake and its value cannot be derived from or reducible to any other good. The pursuit of intrinsically intelligible goods is irreducibly basic. According to Finnis, they provide a foundation for reasonable discourse and explanation of actions. They "distinguish sound from unsound practical thinking and which, when all brought to bear, provide the criteria for distinguishing between acts that (always or in particular circumstances) are reasonable-all-things-considered (and not merely relative-to-a-particular purpose) and acts that are unreasonable-all-things-considered."[66]

The second tenet is that a basic good be described in terms of practical principles that provide a foundation for action. Statements like "play is good" or "play is something to be desired" serve to justify the realization of that value. Moreover, participating in the pursuit of that value should have a broadening effect as, "it suggests new horizons for human activity."[67] Thus, practical principles serve to promote those goods worth pursuing, which are not derived from other goods.

Thirdly, a basic good must have the characteristic of being self-evidently good. This epistemological qualification does not require an appeal to assumptions about human nature nor does it mean that everyone naturally recognizes to the same extent the value of a basic good. The principle that a basic good is "worth pursuing is not somehow innate, inscribed on the mind at birth. On the contrary, the value of truth becomes obvious only to one who has experienced the [basic good] . . ."[68]

Finnis' claim to experiential understanding of a good is analogous to the account given by Alasdair MacIntyre in which he explains the internal goods of a social practice. Recall that for MacIntyre, internal goods "can only be identified and recognized by the experience of participating in the practice in question."[69] For MacIntyre, as well as Finnis, only when someone has experienced the internal good are they then qualified to be a judge as to its value.

Drawing the comparison between MacIntyre and Finnis on this point should not be carried too far. One may be tempted to equate Finnis' basic goods with MacIntyre's internal goods though there is an important reason

66. Ibid., 23.

67. Ibid., 63.

68. Ibid., 65.

69. MacIntyre, *After Virtue*, 188–89.

for not doing so. The types of goods described by each theorist are fundamentally different in kind. Finnis is describing irreducibly basic goods of a more abstract nature, such as knowledge, play, and religion. These ideas serve as building blocks for human fulfillment and describe values sought for their own sake. MacIntyre is utilizing the notion of internal goods to explain specific actions or concepts within an activity. Therefore, while MacIntyre is describing what is intrinsically good about an activity, Finnis is providing the principles that make the activity intelligible.

Their mutual assertion that one must first experience the good before gaining an adequate understanding and appreciation for its value should not translate into viewing all pursuits of basic goods as social practices. Recall that MacIntyre's account of practices requires the exercise of certain moral virtues to realize the goods internal to the practice. Finnis is providing *a priori* reasons for action that do not entail assertions of morality. The statement "Play is worth pursuing" says nothing of the morality of particular actions or the modes of achieving that good.

Instead, he is labeling those values that are naturally desirable as ends in themselves. This is the penultimate claim about basic goods. They are what he refers to as objects of desire. Does this suggest that Finnis believes basic goods like play are good because they are desirable? He rejects this idea on the grounds of a distinction between "a principle's lack of derivation with a lack of justification or lack of objectivity."[70]

Finnis' epistemological foundationalism advocates these basic goods as self-evident justification for the goods from which all successive goods are derived. Play is not good simply because we want to do it. Our desire to play, as well as the pursuit of any other basic value, is not responsible for the good in play. Quite the opposite is true. Play, because it is good in itself, produces the desire in human beings to attain it. He condenses his arguments for the self-evidence and desirability of basic goods in the following way. "I am contending only (i) that if one attends carefully and honestly to the relevant human possibilities one can understand, without reasoning from any other judgment, that the realization of those possibilities is, as such, good and desirable for the human person; and (ii) that one's understanding needs no further justification."[71]

The final qualification of a basic good is that any skepticism against it is indefensible. On this point he provides little commentary concerning the other basic goods. In the example given, knowledge does not need further justification since any claim against the good of knowledge would be

70. Finnis, *Natural Law,* 70.
71. Ibid., 73.

self-refuting. For the other basic goods, it is simply a matter of a lack of sufficient reason to doubt their intrinsic value. "If a proposition *seems* to be correct *and* could never be coherently denied, we are certainly justified in affirming it and in considering that what we are affirming is indeed objectively the case."[72]

The proposition in this case is that play is fundamentally both good and desirable in and of itself. Finnis argues that play is a "large and irreducible element in human culture" with vast potential to be experienced in a number of ways including "solitary or social, intellectual or physical, strenuous or relaxed, highly structured or relatively informal, conventional or ad hoc in its pattern."[73]

As was said in the introduction, without the spirit of play being at the centre of our involvement in sport we overlook the deeper significance of the activity. Sport without play does not mean that it is no longer sport but it might suggest that our priorities in sport are misplaced upon the results of sport, (i.e., winning, health benefits, etc.) rather than on the act of playing. This is not to say that because play is a good to be pursued that sport done without play is necessarily bad. Rather my point is that when we ignore the playfulness of sport we fail to appreciate its fundamental quality and thereby do not experience sport in its fullest sense. The ability to play is an innate capacity given to us by God.

This also does not mean we cannot play in seriousness though it is worth cautioning that the earnestness of our sport must not be confused with competitive self interest. When we disregard sport as a gift, as often happens in the "win at all costs" doctrine, we fail to participate in sport in the way God intended. The inability to enjoy sport in a spirit of play comes as a result of taking the external awards of sport too seriously. When this happens and our focus is on the benefits we gain from sport rather than taking pleasure in our play as God's good gift we take ourselves too seriously as well.

The purpose of this chapter has been to identify play as a requirement for the way Christians ought to participate in sport. The contemporary sports culture has replaced the leisure of sport with the intense desire for victory and, a far more serious indictment, so have many Christians. A Christian theology of sport calls us to recover the spirit of play as we enjoy sport for the sake of leisure.

72. Ibid., 75; emphasis original.
73. Ibid., 87.

7

The Christian Athlete in
Relationship with God

THE CHRISTIAN PERSPECTIVE I advocate here maintains that play, as a basic human good, serves its own ends as an autotelic activity. In taking the three steps toward a Christian ethic of sport we have developed a richer understanding of the nature of sport and its purpose. When our understanding of sport is informed by Christian theology instead of popular sports culture we gain a deeper appreciation for the gift of sport. In fact, in this concluding chapter I will suggest that when Christians participate in sport with the principles described above they will see sport as more than a form of entertainment, exercise, or competition. Sport can be an avenue through which Christians express worship and celebration that imparts physical, moral, and spiritual auxiliary benefits to those who participate.

Contrary to the view expressed by some Christians, notably the Puritans, play is more than a means of rest and preparation for work. To say that play is merely an activity in service of work is to devalue the significance of play as a fundamental component of human flourishing.

This chapter will address three ideas. The first is the relationship of work and play and how that impacts the notion of playful sport articulated in the previous chapter. The second returns to answer the initial question of what Christian theology might contribute to the discussion of biotechnological enhancements in sport. The third summarizes the argument and suggests that Christians have an opportunity to worship God through enjoying his gift of sport by offering our gratitude and praise to him as we recognize the need to rely on God's grace as we play.

Work and Leisure in Christian Perspective

The three key areas where sport is said to offer benefits to its participants certainly hold elements of truth. Clearly, it is good for a society to promote health, social unity, and morally upstanding citizens. But as we have already pointed out these qualities as Christians have traditionally defended them say nothing about the theological value of sport itself. In this respect Christians have typically been guilty of restricting their view of sport to a utilitarian framework. Arguing for sport's intrinsic quality as a method of pursuing a basic good of human flourishing it becomes necessary to address the key distinction between work and play.

Work and Play

The Puritans, famous for the urgency with which they promoted ideas of hard work, have already been criticized for their over-emphasis on the utility of sport. Leland Ryken offers one such critique when he says, "their defense of leisure was essentially a utilitarian defense. Leisure was good, in their view, because it makes work possible. Leisure was not valued for its own sake (that is, as self-rewarding), or as a celebration of life, or as an enlargement of the human spirit."[1]

This is certainly the case in Richard Baxter's description of leisure as some "delightful exercise" where, in the context of the rest of his work, he places substantially more emphasis on the exercise than on the delight. It is questionable whether Baxter's definition of leisure is attainable or whether it turns leisure into some variation of labor. In his view, play is something necessary to refresh our minds and bodies for service but we are not to enjoy leisure with other ends in mind.

In other words sport is not something to truly enjoy for its own sake. We are to enjoy it, Baxter says, only as much as necessary to renew ourselves for our work. Enjoying it beyond that is sinful. This means our work never fully leaves our mind. We are never fully free from our work to enjoy the blessings God has given us.

There are two reasons this concept is relevant to the ethics of biotechnologically enhanced athletes as well as our more general theological

---

1. Ryken, "The Puritan Ethic and Christian Leisure for Today," 40–41.

inquiry of sport. First, it is important to understand the distinction between work and play. Obviously, engaging in the activity is not enough to make a claim on leisure. What is work to one person may be play to another and vice versa. For most of us, sport is a form of play; a recreational activity we engage in for fun. For some, however, sport is their profession.

Does this disparity negate the point I am trying to make about the unique role of play? It certainly does not. For in sport, as in most professions, both elements are present and it depends on the individual which one is exercised. Finnis notes the transcendent and fluid nature of this basic aspect of human flourishing. "An element of play can enter into any human activity, even the drafting of enactments, but it is always analytically distinguishable from its 'serious' context."[2]

For example, John is a carpenter who builds boats. He then sells his boats to earn a living. For him building boats is a profession. It is his work. Jane also builds boats but does so in her spare time as a hobby. She has no interest in earning a living through building boats. She does it because she enjoys it. To her it is play. Does this mean that John cannot enjoy boat building because, for him, it is work? Of course not, since John may also enjoy building boats. In fact, most people find at least some enjoyment in the work they do so such a sharp distinction between work and play may not always exist.

This is true of sport as well. For most it is a hobby or done just for fun. For the physically elite among us sport may be work, a means of making a living (however lucrative it may appear). However, it is very common to hear professional athletes talk about their love for the game. Often times simply by watching them compete it becomes evident that they are engaged in a form of play. Indeed, it can be a difficult task to distinguish when an athlete is "playing" from when he or she is "working." The individual attitude and sense of pleasure achieved in performing the action is an important element in identifying a distinction between the two.

This presents us with the second reason to stress the work/play relationship. It is to help our understanding of work and play as two frameworks that complement and fulfill each other rather than being fundamentally in conflict. Seeing them as integrated, rather than contrary, parts of life illuminates the fact that changes in one will certainly have implications for the other. Moreover, this conception of play leads one to question whether play is more accurately described as an activity or as an attitude.

---

2. Finnis, *Natural Law and Natural Rights*, 87.

Roger Caillois observed that games "reflect the moral and intellectual values of a culture, as well as contribute to their refinement and development."[3] If Caillois is correct then play has more of a dispositional nature that promotes certain values through its various forms. The moral weight of sport has been sorely neglected, especially in theological circles, due in part to the influence of the Puritan emphasis on work and productivity.

However, I maintain any ethical argument that seeks to identify the boundaries of acceptable and unacceptable practices in sport, such as those surrounding biotechnological enhancements, which does not take into consideration the relationship between work and play, has failed to offer a complete discussion of the issues.

Some may see a sharp contrast between work and play but this is a relatively recent phenomenon. "Probably the concept of leisure as something apart from and opposed to work was unknown until there arose a group in society which did not need to labour in order to ensure its livelihood."[4] Work in these terms refers to the means through which one achieves livelihood. Though we could describe work as labor necessary for survival it is often work that describes people. For in many respects work defines who we are as individuals. One only need think of introductions where one of the first questions in the conversation is to ask the new acquaintance what he or she does for a living. This may be a mere search for common interests to continue discussion but nevertheless we instantly know a good deal about a person by knowing their profession.

But what does the other aspect say of an individual and is it equally as important? The term leisure comes from old French and Latin sources meaning "to be permitted" or "to be free." It has come to be perceived as the absence of work. It is what one does in spare time that is free from the demands of labor. Leisure may yield to work in the sense that without earning a living the means of leisure are not provided for.

Yet it is easy enough to prove leisure to be work's equal in respect of contributing meaning to our lives. In fact, most people regard the important things in life to be outside of work. Henry Durant reminds us that the status of individuals "fixed by the work they do, leaves them unsatisfied" and in search of life's meaning and purpose.[5] This important role belongs to leisure.

However, this may not be painting the right picture for the role of leisure. Durant acknowledges the proper roles of work and leisure are

3. Caillois, *Man, Play and Games*, 27.
4. Durant, *The Problem of Leisure*, 1.
5. Ibid., 31.

complementary not diametrically opposed.[6] For Durant, the problem of
leisure comes when leisure is envisioned within a social class framework in
which it is the supreme aim of the working class. The poor class is tempted
to view the elimination of the necessity for work as life's chief goal. Durant
believes this problem will only be resolved "when leisure is complementary
and not opposed to work."[7]

That the two realms of life should complement one another is true
enough. The problem, however, with Durant's view of leisure is that leisure
is only explicable in terms of social class. Wealthy civilizations, such as the
United States and the United Kingdom, can afford to spend more time and
resources on leisurely activities.

It is true that poorer societies or classes do not have the same carefree
luxuries afforded to the rich and powerful. Individuals must concentrate
all their time and energy to providing for their family. The incessant social
concerns in leisure theory are illustrated by the fact that our technological
world has afforded us the resources and energy to give leisure a greater role
than it previously had. Though as Thorstein Veblen argued this may not be
as true for the less wealthy classes or societies.[8] Yet, every society and class
experiences play in some form or another.

The lack of abundant resources does not mean the poor have no time
for leisure in the broadest sense of the term. Two primary non-work activities celebrated by all communities in the history of humanity are religion
and relationship building. Worshipping the divine and creating a family and
support group of friends have been foundational endeavors to all known
societies irrespective of social class. Aside from religion and community,
leisure assumes many natural forms. Recreational activities range from
enjoying a book to talking with friends to sports. Play pervades the vast
world of activities and is not exclusive to the wealthy and privileged. Nor is
it restricted to activities outside of the workplace.

Yet there seems to be a common misconception that in every case they
cease to be leisurely pursuits if they are done with the goal of earning a
living. "In so far as a pursuit is followed as a means of livelihood it ceases
to be sport, and becomes merely a matter of business."[9] This is stated too
strongly and fails to view play in the way we have described here. It is very
likely that someone may pursue her dream of playing in a professional level
sport league, earn a living by doing so, and still engage in play.

6. Ibid.

7. Ibid.

8. Veblen, *The Theory of the Leisure Class.*

9. Graves, "A Philosophy of Sport," 8.

True, leisure can easily be corrupted and often times she may participate in her sport without the desire to play, for instance having to practice
even when she does not want to. In such cases it is easier to say it is a matter
of business but this does not mean play is incompatible with work. As another example it is plain to see that an academic may pursue the basic good
of knowledge and still be working as a tutor.

The point is to see play, or other basic goods, more in terms of attitudes
and motives than as specific activities. When this happens play cannot be
equally compared with work since they are two very different types of thing.
As we will see, a problem arises when the sphere of play becomes dominated
and controlled by the sphere of work. Unfortunately, this has been the case
for quite some time as the work dominated society has negatively influenced the sports culture.

A society that is driven by production and consumption and ascribes
value in terms of one's functions and achievements spells an ill fate for sport.
When the results of a contest outweigh the performance itself something
valuable has been lost. But sport, as I have argued, is worthwhile (in a moral
sense) if the ways and reasons for our participation are esteemed above the
more tangible results. "The teacher must therefore initiate children into
a particular conception of sport characterised by its internal goods and
their virtuous pursuit eschewing the dominant commercial and selfish
picture of sport."[10]

Josef Pieper on Work and Leisure

Josef Pieper has articulated a Christian perspective of the distinguishing
roles of work and leisure that will be helpful in critiquing the results driven
sports culture. What Pieper means by leisure follows the distinction made
above that sees play as attitude rather than activity. He describes leisure in
terms of the contemplative life. In the classical traditions of Aristotle and
Aquinas he sees the contemplative life as a higher order than the active life,
though attention to both is important to living a good life. I will say more
in a moment about how this philosophical concept of leisure relates to a
Christian conceptualization of proper sport. First it is worth noting the distinction Pieper makes between leisure and work as well as his criticisms of
the work-obsessed society that he was referring to.

He contends "leisure . . . is a mental and spiritual attitude—it is not
simply the result of spare time, a holiday, a weekend or a vacation. It is, in

10. Jones, "Teaching Virtue through Physical Education," 341.

the first place, an attitude of mind, a condition of the soul . . ."[11] He sees leisure not as a break from work, nor is it the absence of work, in the sense of idleness, but instead it is an attitude of the mind.

For Pieper, the utilitarian framework around which modern culture is built is forcing leisure out of the picture, or at least forcing it to assume a role for which it was never intended. Culture promotes the idea that for anything to be of value it must produce a specific measurable outcome. Leisure then has been transformed into an activity that serves as a means to becoming more productive rather than an end in itself. Pieper again points out, "The pause is made for the sake of work and in order to work, and a man is not only refreshed *from* work but *for* work. Leisure is an altogether different matter."[12]

Pieper suggests an understanding that gives leisure far more substantial meaning. "For leisure is a receptive attitude of mind, a contemplative attitude, and it is not only the occasion but also the capacity for steeping oneself in the whole of creation."[13] Leisure is more than a means of preparing for one's workaday world. It must be seen as part and parcel of the created order. Without this understanding, says Pieper, leisure will remain allusive. "Leisure is possible only on the premise that man consents to his own true nature and abides in concord with the meaning of the universe."[14]

The most lucid example Christians have of the type of leisure Pieper is describing comes from the first chapter of Genesis. God, observing that what he had made was good, rested on the seventh day. In the same way humanity is intended to rest in a non-utilitarian way. "In leisure, man too celebrates the end of his work by allowing his inner eye to dwell for a while upon the reality of the Creation."[15]

True leisure is autotelic in that it should be done for its own sake. Instead, modern culture assigns leisure the sole task of rejuvenation so that the worker will then function in a more efficient manner. Even though, as Pieper says, "it gives new strength, mentally and physically, and spiritually too, that is not the point."[16]

Such benefits are, as was noted in the previous chapter, secondary to leisure's purpose. The mental and physical restorative powers of sport do not constitute why one participates, just a result of participation. Pieper ascribes a far deeper, more spiritual reason for leisure. "The point and the

11. Pieper, *Leisure the Basis of Culture*, 46.

12. Ibid., 49.

13. Ibid., 46–47.

14. Ibid., 48.

15. Ibid., 49.

16. Ibid., 50.

justification of leisure are not that the functionary should function fault-lessly and without a breakdown, but that the functionary should continue to be a man—and that means that he should not be wholly absorbed in the clear-cut milieu of his strictly limited function."[17]

Being "wholly absorbed" by one's work in a labor-oriented society makes for a very shallow and incomplete life. Pieper suggests that more reflection is needed if we are going to more fully grasp what it means for human beings to flourish as God intended. "The point [of leisure] is also that he should retain the faculty of grasping the world as a whole and real-izing his full potentialities as an entity meant to reach Wholeness. Because Wholeness is what man strives for, the power to achieve leisure is one of the fundamental powers of the human soul."[18]

Here again it is important to remember that Pieper is referring to lei-sure as an attitude of contemplation, not merely as anything done in one's spare time. In fact, he identifies a crucial distinguishing mark between leisure and idleness. Leisure is different from idleness in that leisure incor-porates a celebrative quality absent from idleness. Pieper believes the most expressive mode of celebration is the festival. Festivals are forms of celebra-tion that affirms "the basic meaningfulness of the universe and a sense of oneness with it, of inclusion within it."[19]

If celebration is the focal point of leisure then a state of mind lacking in celebration necessarily becomes something less than pure leisure. To state this point more positively one could say that a state of mind that includes a conscious affirmation of the meaningfulness of the universe, (i.e., celebra-tion) is participating in something far more meaningful than relaxation and rejuvenation. Pieper argues that "if celebration is the core of leisure, then leisure can only be made possible and justifiable on the same basis as the celebration of a festival. *That basis is divine worship.*"[20]

That idleness is separated from leisure by divine worship is instructive for the Christian view of sport I have sought to put forward. Christians who fail to participate with an attitude of leisure are missing sport's meaningful-ness. With the purpose being an affirmation of God's good gift of sport and our expression of celebration and thanksgiving therein, we do not experi-ence its fullest potential when we become selfishly consumed by the desire to win or other external factors. "The vacancy left by absence of worship is filled by mere killing of time and by boredom, which is directly related to

17. Ibid.

18. Ibid.

19. Ibid., 49.

20. Ibid., 65; italics original.

inability to enjoy leisure; for one can only be bored if the spiritual power to be leisurely has been lost."[21]

Though it remains inaccurate to categorically condemn all sport, perhaps the Puritan critique of sport as idleness is not as far off the mark as many sports enthusiasts would have us believe. The quantification of sport and the obsession with records that Guttmann pointed out has noticeably continued to grow stronger since the Puritans launched their attacks on sport in the sixteenth century. Certainly, the emphasis on mathematization in the seventeenth and eighteenth centuries contributed to the rise of mathematical accounts of sport. Reducing athletic activity to a series of statistics employed as tools for gaining a competitive advantage can be clearly seen in modern sport. An attitude of leisure is plainly absent in the "win at all costs" doctrine that pervades the contemporary sports culture. What is needed is referred to by Pieper as "active leisure" the purpose of which is "to bring back a fundamentally right possession of leisure."[22]

Grace, Gratitude and Worship

Thanksgiving and the Pursuit of Excellence as Expressions of Worship

When applied to sport this spirit of leisure acts as a safeguard against the "win at all costs" mentality. For Christians it will result in an attitude glaringly different from that of the sports culture. In its proper context with leisure at the core of the activity, sport will be a form of worship. "The celebration of divine worship, then is the deepest of the springs by which leisure is fed and continues to be vital—though it must be remembered that leisure embraces everything which, without being *merely* useful, is an essential part of a full human existence."[23]

Embracing sport's autotelic ends by seeking to achieve the standards of excellence intrinsic to the activity captures the human essence of sport and can become an expression of worship. It is important to note that we do not participate in sport *for the sake of* worship. That would nullify the autotelic nature of sport we have suggested here and land us in the instrumentalist camp we rejected. We play sport for sport's own ends. It also does not replace other forms of worship, (i.e., prayer, scriptural readings, musical, etc.) but when played with the Christian distinctives discussed here, Christians

21. Ibid., 69.
22. Ibid., 72.
23. Ibid., 69–70; italics original.

may find themselves in a quasi-liturgical atmosphere—worshipping their creator by means of one of his good creations. "Our playful activity, unlike a verbal confession of faith, becomes a work of art giving allusive testimony to the reality of the Kingdom of God."[24] Christians will do well to remember that the attitudes and behaviors they take into activities like sport ought to be in line with Christian principles.

Not only should the actions of believers be consistent with the doctrines of their faith but the way in which they engage in sport should demonstrate the joy of God's creation. "The quality of our play should be an attractive sign-post that directs and entices others to the richness of God's kingdom. Our play should be imaginative, hilarious, creative expressions of thanksgiving to our good Father."[25]

Thus it becomes evident that the characteristic work of Christian athletes should be a spirit of humility and thankfulness. "As Christians we know the author of every good and perfect gift. Let us resolve that whenever we're enjoying sports, whether playing or watching them, we will thank our extravagantly lavish God who gives us such wonderful gifts."[26] Sadly, this is not always the case. Often times the Christian athlete is influenced by the "sport as spectacle" culture and fails to participate in a humble and grateful way.

When this occurs Christians miss out on one of the key distinguishing aspects of sport in the spirit of play. As Robert Johnston points out, "in play God can, and often does, meet us and commune with us. The result is a new openness to the religious more generally, our experience of the sacred in play serving as a prolegomenon to further encounters with God."[27]

To the earlier discussion that emphasized the communal nature of sport we may add Johnston's claim that sport in the spirit of play reflects another relational dimension. Sport, when engaged for the sole purpose of winning, not only alienates the athlete from other competitors, but removes the possibility of communing with God. Michael Goheen echoes this when he says, "Pursuing athletics with an idolatrous abandon does not allow us the joy of receiving it as one of God's good gifts."[28]

This is not to say that all athletic activity is necessarily a religious act. Nor am I claiming that all aspects of a game are metaphorical representations of religious principles. The point is simply to claim that Christians recognize a more meaningful purpose of sport as an activity given by God. "We are

24. Frey et al., *At Work and Play*, 44.

25. Ibid., 56.

26. Altrogge, *Game Day for the Glory of God*, 102.

27. Johnston, *The Christian at Play*, 80.

28. Goheen, "Delighting in God's Good Gift of Sports and Competition."

created to respond to God in joy, thanksgiving, love, and praise as we receive the whole of our lives as a gift from His hand."[29] It is not merely a reprieve from work or a means to a more physically fit body but an aspect of our lives in which we can honor the giver of life. In the right context sport may become a sacred activity where participants can rejoice in the gift of sport.[30]

Goheen reasserts the created goodness of sport as a gift from God who intends for us to enjoy it freely. It also should serve as a reminder that "every good gift and every perfect gift is from above."[31] He states, "Those things that especially bring delight can be occasions that remind us of this fact, and opportunities to return to God the thanksgiving and praise that is due for every part of our lives."[32]

The Christian narrative of creation identifies sport as an avenue of pursuing human flourishing. It reminds us that participation in sport is a manifestation of human essence. It is an activity in which humans are free to creatively express themselves, display their physical abilities and develop their aspirations to excel. "He created the potential in the creation for humanity to discover, develop, and enjoy them. He delights when we receive them as gifts, honour Him in our use of them, and thank him for them."[33] Moreover, "humanity was given the delightful task of exploring, discovering, and developing the potential God put in the creation in loving communion with Himself."[34]

However, as with everything else the activity of sport has been corrupted and stands in need of redemption. Christians will fail to display a redeemed form of sport if their understanding of the practice is informed by the fallen, sin-tainted world that provides the prevailing sports culture. Envisioning what a redeemed form of sport might look like is no easy task. Goheen equates it with struggling to understand the intended structure of other human activities in a fallen world. "In the same way that we seek to understand the creational structure and order of marriage or emotions so that we might increasingly become wise and conform ourselves to God's design for marriage and emotional response, so we need to struggle to

---

29. Ibid.

30. This is similar to how the same piece of music can be simply a piece of music in one context, but in another it becomes a power worship song.

31. Jas 1:17

32. Goheen, "Delighting in God's Good Gift of Sports and Competition."

33. Ibid.

34. Ibid.

understand the creational structure and order of sports and competition so that we might more and more conform to God's original design."[35]

God's Grace and the Christian Athlete

In so far as sport has become a spectacle of modern culture, consumed by the "win at all costs" mentality it is incompatible with several Christian principles. However, Christians may still engage in sport under an alternative model that identifies a more meaningful experience in the striving for excellence with a spirit of gratitude and praise. Throughout this work I have laid the foundation for a critical analysis of the contemporary ethical debate over the use of biotechnological enhancements in sport. The four primary arguments used in the debate have proven to be unfavorable for arriving at a consensus either for or against their use. I argued that both sides of the argument fail to provide any criteria describing the fundamental purposes of sport.

I then showed how we can begin to develop a theoretical framework by identifying the nature of sport as a social exercise with its own intrinsic goods, which in part make up the essence of the activity. I concluded that sport is best described in terms of Alasdair MacIntyre's theory of social practices that emphasize a cooperative, communal dimension to sport.

MacIntyre's framework differentiates between goods internal and goods external to the practice, which is important to the development of a theory of sport. "But sport . . . is only worthwhile (in a moral sense) if it is pursued in a particular way" says Carwyn Jones who goes on to state that MacIntyre is instructive in developing, "a particular conception of sport characterized by its internal goods and their virtuous pursuit eschewing the dominant commercial and selfish picture of sport."[36]

In order to view sport as a social practice further work was needed that foundationally established sport in the concepts of play and games. Aligning sport with social practices required explaining the significance and types of rules in sport. It was concluded that sport is at the same time serious in that it follows specific rules (both moral and practical) that transcend the practice and non-serious by virtue of the freedom and "other-worldliness" play exhibits. I argued, as Shirl Hoffman does, that "the evangelical sports enthusiast who desires to understand how sport fits into the Christian experience must first recognize it and nurture it as play."[37]

35. Ibid.

36. Jones, "Teaching Virtue through Physical Education," 341.

37. Hoffman, Good Game, 274.

Following this I pointed out that Christian theology's treatment of sport has been negligible. Of the three primary attitudes Christian thinkers have taken toward sport I found that all three insufficiently convey the good of sport, seeking either to condemn it altogether or enlist it merely as a means to some other good. Hoffman reminds us that, "When Christians value sport only as it serves extraneous ends, the experience is diminished in the Christian imagination. Reimagining sport as an autotelic, leisure-based experience means shunning flaccid rhetoric about the sports field as a training ground for character, or as a way of building strong bones and muscles, or as a fertile field for evangelism, or realizing any other practical benefit."[38]

I then began to develop a Christian ethic of sport that is critical of unchecked competition, erroneous views of the human body, and inadequate arguments for sport's moral pedagogy. None of the three theological challenges to sport proved sufficient to forbid Christian involvement in sport. Instead, Christians can be critical of prevalent attitudes in sport that fail to capture sport's essence. They also should keep in mind the extent to which the corruptive influences of the "win at all costs" doctrine can reach. Hoffman argues that, "the first step toward a well-played game will come when Christians appreciate the death-grip that big-time sports have on sports played at any level and when they recognize now this can snuff out the spiritual potential of sports."[39]

At this point in my argument it became necessary to further articulate a Christian perspective of the essence of sport. I have argued that the culture of sports is morally and spiritually bankrupt and stands in need of redemption. The theological understanding of sport I presented called for a paradigm shift in how we approach sport. Rather than degrading sport to nothing more than a spectacle it is enhanced by its essence as humans strive to achieve excellence in full recognition of their finitude. In this context Christians are free to enjoy sport as an activity in pursuit of the basic good of play. "The Christian view," says Hoffman, "sees play as a celebration and affirmation of that which they could never have earned. Play for the Christian is anchored in grace."[40]

An understanding of grace in sports is crucial. All levels of athletic activity display varied forms of God's grace. The need for grace is most pronounced in the recognition of our human limitations. These boundaries are precisely what enhancements of various kinds seek to eliminate. In regards to the debate over biotechnological enhancements, I argue from this

38. Ibid., 267.
39. Ibid., 282.
40. Ibid., 278.

theological response that sport has no need of these enhancements since they fail to enhance the true beauty of sport. Their use is only valuable in so far as they contribute to a less human display of athletic ability. They do not contribute to a game well played; instead only serve to corrupt the autotelic ends of sport.

Therefore, the moral issues surrounding their use that make up the vast majority of the ethical debate are of secondary concern. What is more important, as we have said, is the fundamental attitude with which we approach sport. As Kass and Cohen note, "absent such gratitude for our gifts and the correlative desire to cultivate them honourably to the fullest extent possible, the adulteration of sport will not be overcome, even if the steroid era were to come to an end."[41]

Another way of stating the issue is to say that Christians have (or should have) bigger concerns about the present state of the sports culture than finding a moral distinction between steroid enhancement and dietary enhancement. The argument I have presented here challenges Christians to step back and reevaluate our sporting commitments in light of this alternative framework of sport. In these concluding paragraphs I wish to further point out some ways in which Christians can think through their participation in sport in such a way that clearly distinguishes their behavior from the mainstream sports culture. Hoffman argues that if Christians were to put into practice a form of sport that is more attuned to their religious commitments then categorically different sports might come into existence. "Games designed for the specific purpose of complementing rather than challenging the Christian's better instincts are not likely to look like sports played in most places today. Realistically, this will be possible only where the Christian community controls the shape and purpose of sports and all participants and sponsors agree that games should serve such a purpose."[42]

I would not go quite as far as he does to suggest a separation of Christian from non-Christian games (although Christian games would certainly resemble a more corporate form of liturgical worship). Christian athletes rightly should participate in "secular" games though it undoubtedly will be more difficult to keep in check the blood-thirsty attitudes fostered by the sports culture. Perhaps one point that may be somewhat influential, even on non-Christians in the sports world would be a reminder of the history sport shares with religion. "For Christians who believe that creation conveys, though in a veiled way, God's design for the universe and that the

---

41. Kass and Cohen, "For the Love of the Game."

42. Hoffman, *Good Game*, 279.

Christian's responsibility is to restore sport to its created essence, the fact of sport's religious roots may have some significance."[43]

Hoffman correctly suggests sport's storied past with religious activity presents rich opportunity to display one's Christian faith in sport. "Christians have much to gain from organizing and playing their sports in ways that enable the cultivation and expression of religious meaning."[44] However, sport is void of religious meaning unless it is done in the spirit of play. He states, "Unless sport is approached as a derivative of the God-given play impulse, invested with religious motivations and meaning, and structured in a way to facilitate this religious function, an honest positioning of sport in the context of the Christian life will be difficult, perhaps impossible."[45]

Christ's renewal of creation makes possible a Christian ethic of sport that upholds the rules of the game and encourages a healthy understanding of cooperative competition without compromising the athlete's relationship to other competitors or to his or her spiritual union with God. As a gift from God, sport is designed to point our attention to God. Our behavior in athletic activity should reflect an attitude of praise, worship, and thanksgiving regardless of the outcome of the contest. "God is glorified when athletes, coaches, and spectators respond to his presence and greatness, something just as possible in defeat as in victory."[46]

Sport that glorifies God is found only after the all-consuming desire for personal victory has been lost. If Christians are to glorify God and exhibit Christ-like behavior on and off the field it will be because they have rejected the frame of mind that shapes most of mainstream sports. A Christian response to the ethics of biotechnological enhancements is not primarily concerned with superficial argumentation over cheating or health issues.

Instead we must approach issues in sport from a spirit of gratitude and admiration of the one who created the gift of sport and also has redeemed creation through Christ. Redemptive sport will always be a relational experience between creator and creation. In his refutation of a sacred-secular dichotomy A.W. Tozer comments that "it is not what a man does that determines whether his work is sacred or secular, it is why he does it. The motive is everything."[47] Tozer's motive principle in work finds application in sport as well. Whether or not a Christian athlete engages in sport as a form of worship is dependent upon why she or he is participating. Experiencing

43. Ibid., 269.
44. Ibid.
45. Ibid., 280.
46. Ibid., 272.
47. Tozer, *The Pursuit of God*, 82.

sport to its fullest potential requires the forsaking of selfish gain in exchange for an approach of gratitude and humility, of grace and humanity.

Here we honor God through the exercise of our physical abilities in a manifestation of our being human. Christians are right to refuse any artificial enhancements, biological or otherwise, that weaken the relational dynamic of our dependence on God's grace in our efforts toward excellence. "If we would only be attentive, we would hear Scripture proclaim that our play, like our work, is to be a God-given expression of our humanity."[48]

A Theologically Informed View of Sport and the Ethics of Doping

The purpose of this thesis is to present a theologically informed alternative to common conceptions of sport in contemporary culture, particularly in response to the challenges of doping in athletic competition. The account I have presented is reflective of Christian theological convictions. I have argued that the current ethical discourse surrounding doping insufficiently addresses the problem because it fails to remove itself from the adulterated view of sport that pervades the modern sports culture. The problem of doping in sport is that sport has become mostly about the results of competition and the discussions about the ethical ways of playing sports are similarly structured around results or consequences.

Instead, I have argued that we must remove ourselves from that framework and take a different approach to sport. We must look more fundamentally at the purpose of sport if we are going to adequately respond to future challenges that may or may not threaten the activity as we now know it. Christian contributions to sport are helpful in identifying several qualities of sport that are lacking in contemporary conceptions of sport including the elements of play, worship, admiration, and gratitude but also a recognition of corrupted attitudes in sport such as greed, selfishness, and violence.

If Christians are to take part in the redemption of sport to its intended design they must first reorient the conceptual attitudes of sport from a spectacle of physical elitism and selfish competitive gain to an admiration of our mutual striving for excellence in recognition of our need for grace. In this version victory is reduced to its proper role within the rules of the game. A redemptive attitude in competitive sport does much to dissolve the need or desire for doping to gain a competitive advantage. It also enhances the presentation of the activity's human essence.

48. Johnston, *The Christian at Play*, 143.

However, even accepting this attitude as I have advocated here it has not yet addressed the proposal some advocates of enhancement, like Julian Savulescu, have made that our humanity would be more properly exhibited if we allowed doping rather than prohibiting it. He says, "performance enhancement is not against the spirit of sport; it is the spirit of sport. To choose to be better is to be human."[49] Striving to be better is indeed one of the most noble of all human pursuits but it is worth asking in what sense we become better by employing biotechnology in athletic competition. We become faster and stronger but not necessarily better.

It is doubtful that we become any better human beings. Our effort would not improve. The determination and aspiration to become better would not be enhanced. Instead, any potential value of their use seems to be restricted to the achievement of sport's external aims as dictated by a sports culture where winning and physical elitism reign supreme. This is made evident by the nature of the ethical debate that centers around the competitive benefits derived from their use, (i.e., sport will be more fair, competition will improve, greater accomplishments will result in the growth of spectatorship, etc.).

The sports culture has a deep seated problem that honors performance only insofar as it produces the outcome of winning. Proposals by defendants of doping that enhancements will enable us to more fully experience sport fail to appreciate sport independently of the results those enhancements are believed to provide. Doping only serves to improve the results of our performances not the experience or the performance itself. In this light it would perhaps be better to remove the label "*performance* enhancing substances" and opt instead for "*results* enhancing substances" as this would be a more accurate description of their intended purposes.

When sport becomes an undertaking that makes clear the importance of performance over results and the common good of the activity over the external goods we stand to gain individually, then the use of biotechnological enhancements has little to offer. The spectacle model of sport with its "win at all costs" mentality "will erode the twin possibilities of gratitude and excellence" and all that will be left will be "cartoon heroes and high-tech magic acts, and a life devoted to their soul-deforming amusements."[50] Watson and White bring clarity to the origin of a "win at all costs" attitude that is so prevalent in the modern sport culture. They state,

> In sport, when winning is the primary aim of the athlete or coach, we see the desperate and even bizarre attempts by athletes

49. Savulescu et al., "Why We Should Allow Performance Enhancing Drugs in Sport," 670.

50. Kass and Cohen, "For the Love of the Game."

and coaches to address the angst of their human predicament by doing anything and everything to reach their goal and bolster their identity and sense of significance. It is this driven, single-minded striving to 'win at all costs' that often leads to boasting of achievements, alienation of others (e.g. opponents and family members) and violence and cheating in sport, which we maintain flows from a prideful heart.[51]

As Christian theologians, our considerations of doping, and of sport in general, must surely come to grips with the impact of humanity's deeply fallen nature. Watson and White argue, "From a theological perspective, the principle enemy in this battle in sport is the often deeply seated and unconscious vice of pride; deeply seated in that pride is something that most people, including Christians, fail to see in themselves but hate in others."[52] Even though they were not speaking directly to biotechnology in sport, it seems fair to apply their statement to this present reflection on doping. "Desperate" and "bizarre" surely are accurate descriptions of some doping methods but the deeper implication of this line of thinking is that beyond the auxiliary issues of cheating, coercion, and the like, doping is a serious affront to the Christian practices of humility and friendship. The motivation behind doping is not as innocent as wanting to win the contest. Doping for a competitive advantage both implicitly and explicitly displays egotism incommensurate with the teachings of Christ.

Yet the athlete is not alone in his or her hubris. Spectators in the sports culture complacently approve the extremely competitive environment. Perhaps without even realizing it, the sports culture is so consumed with winning that it serves as an enabler and enthusiast of those individuals who succumb to the vice of pride. As fans, we often cheer for the victorious and look down upon the defeated. As participants, we often will go to any lengths necessary to ensure victory and beckon unto ourselves the approval of our fans. This perpetual cycle can only serve to reinforce the mentality that winning is synonymous with significance. In this paradigm, victory over opponents signifies, not only dominance over other competitors, but greater control over the human condition.

Yet Christians affirm that God's plan of redemption has turned on its head the wisdom and power of this world.[53] The alternative ethic of sport I have proposed is one in which our humanity is enlivened by humility that expresses itself through gratitude to, and communion with, God. Christians

51. Watson and White, "'Winning at All Costs' in Modern Sport," 68.

52. Ibid., 69.

53. 1 Cor 1:25–31.

stand to gain a deeper, selfless, and more meaningful experience in their sports activities when those activities are primarily expressions of thanksgiving and praise rather than self-honoring pursuits. When this happens we recognize the concerns of enhancement not as fundamental problems in themselves but as an outcome of one of the many deeper problems preventing sport from being practiced in a God-honoring way. As Christian fans and participants in sport we would do well to evaluate the extent to which we are involved in the injurious corruption of a "winning at all costs" attitude that is so deeply ingrained in the sports culture. It is my hope that the view presented here toward a theological basis for sport here will contribute not only to the ethical conversation of doping in a formative way but also will challenge those in the Christian tradition to reexamine their commitments to the way sport is commonly practiced.

In this regard, a final comment is necessary concerning a Christian understanding of sport. We have already said that play can be both serious and non-serious. We identified it as a basic component of human flourishing. Play also is a necessary part of sport. We are to be serious in that athletes are commended to do their best and compete well. But Christians also need to remember that God desires our play to be joyous. Sport is an activity we are intended to enjoy freely. In sport we too quickly get caught up in the competition of the moment and forget to be joyful. Play and joy are two elements Christians cannot neglect if we are to restore the nature of sport. Chesterton provides us with an excellent thought about the value of joy in the Christian life at the end of *Orthodoxy*. He says that joy is "the gigantic secret of the Christian."[54] It is a secret because it was one of the few of Jesus' emotions the gospels chose not to show. Chesterton states, "There was some one thing that was too great for God to show us when He walked upon our earth; and I have sometimes fancied that it was His mirth."[55]

As Christians we will do well to display more joy in our sport for the privilege to be able to play rather than discontentment when we do not win. Both seriousness and non-seriousness have their place in sport but at all times we ought to come together to enjoy sport in the spirit of play as we reflect gratitude and grace. The joy comes when the object of our focus as Christian athletes and fans is more consistent with our theological principles than our desire to finish first, though both are important. Here, sport becomes more about the one who gives us the gift of sport and the others with whom we enjoy it than it is about ourselves. For it is somewhere in this union of important and irrelevant—serious and frivolous—that we find the joy of sport and as Lewis said, "Joy is the serious business of Heaven."[56]

54. Chesterton, *Orthodoxy*, 238.

55. Ibid., 299.

56. Lewis, *Letters to Malcolm*, 93.

Bibliography

Agar, Nicholas. *Liberal Eugenics: In Defence of Human Enhancement*. Malden, MA: Blackwell, 2004.

Altrogge, Stephen. *Game Day for the Glory of God: A Guide for Athletes, Fans, and Wannabes*. Wheaton, IL: Crossway, 2008.

Aquinas, Thomas. *Summa Theologica*, II–II.

Aristotle. *Nicomachean Ethics*. Translated by Terence Irwin. Indianapolis: Hackett, 1999.

Associated Press. "Pats' Harrison Suspended for Violating NFL's Drug Policy." http://sports.espn.go.com/nfl/news/story?id=2999994.

———. "Pettitte Admits Using HGH to Recover From an Elbow Injury in 2002." http://sports.espn.go.com/mlb/news/story?id=3156305.

———. "Report: Brent Musburger Talks Steroids." http://sports.espn.go.com/ncf/news/story?id=5656825.

Augustine. *De Musica*. Fathers of the Church 4. Translated by Ludwig Schopp. Washington, DC: Catholic University of America Press, 1947.

———. *The Confessions of Saint Augustine*. Translated by Rex Warner. New York: Penguin Putnam, 2001.

Bäck, Allan. "The Way to Virtue in Sport." *Journal of the Philosophy of Sport* 36 (2009) 217–37.

Bailey, Kenneth E. *Paul through Mediterranean Eyes: Cultural Studies in 1 Corinthians*. Downers Grove, IL: InterVarsity, 2011.

Baker, William J. *Playing with God: Religion and Modern Sport*. Cambridge: Harvard University Press, 2007.

Baxter, Richard. *The Practical Works of Richard Baxter*. Vol 1. London: George Virtue, 1838.

BBC. "Fina Extends Swimsuit Regulations." http://news.bbc.co.uk/sport2/hi/olympic_games/7944084.stm.

———. "Maradona Predicts English Success." http://news.bbc.co.uk/sport2/hi/football/world_cup_2006/4947084.stm.

———. "Maradona Set to Coach Argentina." http://news.bbc.co.uk/sport2/hi/football/internationals/7696408.stm.

Beauchamp, Tom, and James Childress. *Principles of Biomedical Ethics.* 5th ed. New York: Oxford University Press, 2001.

Berkes, Howard. "China's Olympic Swimming Pool: Redefining Fast." http://www.npr.org/templates/story/story.php?storyId=93478073.

Berthelot, Geoffroy, et al. "The Citius End: World Records Progression Announces the Completion of a Brief Ultra-Physiological Quest." *PLoS ONE* 3/2 (2008) e1552 1–5.

———, et al. "Athlete Atypicity on the Edge of Human Achievement: Performance Stagnate after the Last Peak, in 1988." *PLoS ONE* 5/1 (2010) e8800 1–8.

Best, David. "The Aesthetic in Sport." *British Journal of Aesthetics* 14/3 (1974) 197–213.

Boffetti, Jason. "How Richard Rorty Found Religion." *First Things* 143 (May 2004) 24–30.

Bradley, Bill. *Values of the Game.* New York: Broadway, 2000.

Branon, David, ed. *Sports Devotional Bible.* Grand Rapids: Zondervan, 2002.

Calvin, John. *Calvin's Commentaries.* Vol. 20. Grand Rapids: Baker, 2003.

Caillois, Roger. *Man, Play and Games.* Translated by Meyer Barash. London: Thames & Hudson, 1962.

Cawley, John, et. al. "The Impact of State Physical Education Requirements on Youth Physical Activity and Overweight." *Health Economics* 16/12 (2007) 1287–301.

Center for Disease Control. "Health Effects of Cigarette Smoking." http://www.cdc.gov/tobacco/data_statistics/fact_sheets/health_effects/effects_cig_smoking/index.htm.

Center for Reformed Theology and Apologetics. "Westminster Confession, Chapter XVI 'Of Good Works.'" http://www.reformed.org/documents/wcf_with_proofs.

Chesterton, G. K. *Orthodoxy.* Chicago: Moody, 2009.

Chicago Cubs. "Mission Statement." http://chicago.cubs.mlb.com/chc/ticketing/sth/mission_statement.jsp.

D'Agostino, Fred. "The Ethos of Games." In *Philosophic Inquiry in Sport,* edited by William Morgan and Klaus Meier, 63–72. 2nd ed. Champaign, IL: Human Kinetics, 1995.

D'Andrea, Thomas. *Tradition, Rationality, and Virtue: The Thought of Alasdair MacIntyre.* Burlington, VT: Ashgate, 2006.

Daniels, Bruce. *Puritans at Play: Leisure and Recreation in Colonial New England.* New York: St. Martin's, 1995.

Davis, Paul. "Ability, Responsibility, and Admiration in Sport: A Reply to Carr." *Journal of the Philosophy of Sport* 28 (2001) 207–14.

Delattre, Edwin J. "Some Reflections on Success and Failure in Competitive Athletics." *Journal of Philosophy of Sport* 1 (1975) 133–39.

Dick, Frank. *Sports Training Principles.* 5th ed. London: A. & C. Black, 2007.

Durant, Henry. *The Problem of Leisure.* London: Routledge, 1938.

Eassom, Simon, "Sport, Solidarity, and the Expanding Circle." *Journal of the Philosophy of Sport* 24 (1997) 79–98.

Edelman, Robert. *Spartak Moscow: A History of the People's Team in the Worker's State.* Ithaca, NY: Cornell University Press, 2009.

Elias, Norbert, and Eric Dunning. *The Quest for Excitement: Sport and Leisure in the Civilizing Process.* Oxford: Blackwell, 1986.

ESPN the Magazine. "The Body Issue." October 2009.

Farmer, Sam. "NFL Is Taking the Long-term Impact of Concussions Seriously." http://articles.latimes.com/2010/sep/11/sports/la-sp-nfl-concussions-20100912.

Feezell, Randolph. "Sport and the View From Nowhere." *Journal of the Philosophy of Sport* 28 (2001) 1–17.

———. *Sport, Play and Ethical Reflection.* Urbana: University of Illinois Press, 2006.

Fellowship of Christian Athletes. "Beginner's Guide to FCA." http://www.fca.org/vsItemDisplay.lsp&objectID=B01DC373-3310-4311-BA1999095BA3816E&method=display.

Finnis, John. *Natural Law and Natural Rights.* Oxford: Oxford University Press, 1980.

Fost, Norman. "Banning Drugs in Sport: A Skeptical View." *Hastings Center Report* 16/4 (1986) 213–34.

Freud, Sigmund. *Civilization and Its Discontents.* Translated by James Strachey. 1962. Reprinted, New York: Norton, 2005.

Frey, Bradshaw, et al. *At Work and Play: Biblical Insight for Daily Obedience.* Jordan Station, ON: Paideia, 1986.

Frisina, Warren. *The Unity of Knowledge and Action: Toward a Nonrepresentational Theory of Knowledge.* Albany: State University of New York Press, 2002.

Gibson, John. *Performance versus Results: A Critique of Values in Contemporary Sport.* New York: State University of New York Press, 2001.

Giulianotti, Richard. *Sport: A Critical Sociology.* Oxford: Polity, 2005.

Grandjean, Ann. "Diets of Elite Athletes: Has the Discipline of Sports Nutrition Made an Impact?" *Journal of Nutrition* 127/5 (1997) 874S–75.

Graves, H. "A Philosophy of Sport." In *Sport and the Body: A Philosophical Symposium,* edited by Ellen Gerber, 6–15. Philadelphia: Lea & Febiger, 1974.

Goheen, Michael. "Delighting in God's Good Gift of Sports and Competition." Keynote Address, Christian Society for Kinesiology and Leisure Studies Annual Conference. Redeemer College. Ancaster, Ontario, June 5, 2003.

Grivetti, Louis, and Elizabeth Applegate. "From Olympia to Atlanta—A Cultural Historical Perspective on Diet and Athletic Training." *Journal of Nutrition* 127/5 (1997) 860S–85.

Gust, Bruce. "Muscular Christianity Overview." http://muscularchristianityonline.com/study/overview.php.

Guttman, Allen. *From Ritual to Record: The Nature of Modern Sports.* New York: Columbia University Press, 2004.

———. "Rules of the Game." In *The Sport Studies Reader,* edited by Alan Tomlinson. London: Routledge, 2007.

Hauerwas, Stanley and Charles Pinches. *Christians among the Virtues: Theological Conversations with Ancient and Modern Ethics.* Notre Dame: University of Notre Dame Press, 1997.

Habermas, Jürgen. *Theory of Communicative Action.* Vol. 1, *Reason and the Rationality of Society.* Translated by Thomas McCarthy. Boston: Beacon, 1984.

———. *The Philosophical Discourse of Modernity.* Cambridge: MIT Press, 1990.

Hall, Murray. "Christian Ethics in North American Sports." In *Christianity and Leisure: Issues in a Pluralistic Society,* edited by Paul Heintzman, et al., 227–36. Sioux Center, IA: Dort College Press, 2006.

Harris, H. A. *Sport in Greece and Rome.* Aspects of Greek and Roman Life. Ithaca, NY: Cornell University Press, 1972.

Higgs, Robert J. *God in the Stadium: Sports and Religion in America*. Lexington: University of Kentucky Press, 1995.

Hoffman, Shirl James. *Good Game: Christianity and the Culture of Sports*. Waco, TX: Baylor University Press, 2010.

———. "Sports Fanatics." http://www.christianitytoday.com/ct/2010/february/3.20.html?start=5.

Horton, John. *After MacIntyre: Critical Perspectives on the Work of Alasdair MacIntyre*. Notre Dame: University of Notre Dame Press, 1994.

House of Commons Science and Technology Committee. "Human Enhancement Technologies in Sport." http://www.publications.parliament.uk/pa/cm200607/cmselect/cmsctech/67/67.pdf.

Howe, Leslie. "Gamesmanship." *Journal of the Philosophy of Sport* 31 (2004) 212–25.

Hudson, Winthrop. "The Weber Thesis Reexamined." *Church History* 30 (1961) 88–99.

Huizinga, Johan. *Homo Ludens: A Study of the Play Element in Culture*. London: Paladin, 1970.

Hye, Allen. *The Great God Baseball: Religion in Modern Baseball Fiction*. Macon, GA: Mercer University Press, 2004.

Hyland, Drew. "Competition and Friendship." *Journal of the Philosophy of Sport* 5 (1979) 63–70.

Intelligence Squared. "We Should Accept Performance-Enhancing Drugs in Competitive Sports." http://intelligencesquaredus.org/debates/past-debates/item/574-we-should-accept-performance-enhancing-drugs-in-competitive-sports.

International Sports Federation. "Why Sports Missions?" http://www.sportsmissions.com/learn-about-isf/why-sports-missions.

Jackson, Judi. "Introduction to Recreation and Sports Ministry for All Ages." In *Recreation and Sports Ministry: Impacting Postmodern Culture*, edited by John Garner, 181–206. Nashville: Broadman & Holman, 2003.

John Paul II. "Jubilee of Sports People." http://www.vatican.va/holy_father/john_paul_ii/speeches/2000/oct-dec/documents/hf_jp-ii_spe_20001028_jubilsport_en.html.

———. "Address of John Paul II to the Players, Trainers and Directors of Real Madrid, The Champion Soccer Club of Europe." http://www.vatican.va/holy_father/john_paul_ii/speeches/2002/september/documents/hf_jp-ii_spe_20020916_real-madrid-soccer_en.html.

Johnston, Robert. *The Christian at Play*. Grand Rapids: Eerdmans, 1983.

Jones, Carwyn. "Teaching Virtue through Physical Education: Some Comments and Reflections." *Sport, Education and Society* 13 (2008) 337–49.

Kadet, Anne. "Parents Spare No Expense in Children's Sports." http://finance.yahoo.com/news/pf_article_105324.html.

Kass, Leon, and Eric Cohen. "For the Love of the Game: Roger Clemens, Barry Bonds, the Mitchell Report, and the adulteration of American Sports." http://www.tnr.com/article/politics/75137/the-love-the-game.

Keller, Kimberly, et al. "Competition in Church Sport Leagues." In *Christianity and Leisure: Issues in a Pluralistic Society*, edited by Paul Heintzman, et al., 220–26. Sioux Center, IA: Dort College Press, 2006.

Kerrigan, Michael. "Sports in the Christian Life." *Christian Reflection: A Series in Faith and Ethics* 29 (2008) 19–27.

Kilmeade, Brian. *The Games Do Count: America's Best and Brightest on the Power of Sports*. New York: HarperCollins, 2004.

———. *It's How You Play the Game: The Powerful Sports Moments That Taught Lasting Values to America's Finest*. New York: HarperCollins, 2007.

Kix, Paul. "Peaked Performance: The Case That Human Athletes Have Reached Their Limits." http://www.boston.com/bostonglobe/ideas/articles/2011/01/23/peaked_performance/?page=full.

Klaus Meier. "Triad Trickery: Playing with Sport and Games." *Journal of the Philosophy of Sport* 15 (1988) 11–30.

Kluck, Ted. "An Open Letter to ESPN the Magazine." http://www.christianitytoday.com/ct/2009/julyweb-only/130-21.0.html.

Knight, Kelvin. *The MacIntyre Reader*. Oxford: Polity, 1998.

Krattenmaker, Tom. *Onward Christian Athletes: Turning Ballparks Into Pulpits and Players Into Preachers*. New York: Rowman & Littlefield, 2010.

Kretchmar, R. Scott. *Practical Philosophy of Sport*. Champaign, IL: Human Kinetics, 1994.

Kuhse, Helga, and Peter Singer, eds. *Bioethics: An Anthology*. Oxford: Blackwell, 2006.

Kupfer, Joseph. "Perfection as Negation in the Aesthetics of Sport." *Journal of the Philosophy of Sport* 28 (2001) 18–31.

Kyle, Donald. *Sport and Spectacle in the Ancient World*. New York: Blackwell, 2006.

Lasch, Christopher. *The Culture of Narcissism: American Life in an Age of Diminishing Expectations*. New York: Norton, 1979.

Lavin, Michael. "Sports and Drugs: Are the Current Bans Justified?" In *Ethics in Sport*, edited by William Morgan, 263–72. 2nd ed. Champaign, IL: Human Kinetics, 2007.

Lawler, Peter. *Stuck With Virtue: The American Individual and Our Biotechnological Future*. Wilmington, DE: ISI Books, 2005.

Lemak, Larry. "Sports Injury Facts." http://www.sportssafety.org.

Lewis, C.S. *Letters to Malcolm: Chiefly on Prayer*. New York: Mariner, 2002.

———. *Surprised By Joy: The Shape of My Early Life*. Orlando, FL: Houghton Mifflin Harcourt, 1995.

Linville, Greg. "Ethic of Competition in a Church Setting." In *Recreation and Sports Ministry: Impacting Postmodern Culture*, edited by John Garner, 135–60. Nashville: Broadman & Holman, 2003.

Loland, Sigmund. *Fair Play in Sport: A Moral Norm System*. New York: Routledge, 2002.

Lumpkin, Angela et al. *Sports Ethics: Applications for Fair Play*. 3rd ed. New York: McGraw-Hill, 2003.

Lutz, Christopher Stephen. *Tradition in the Ethics of Alasdair MacIntyre: Relativism, Thomism, and Philosophy*. Lanham, MD: Lexington, 2000.

MacIntyre, Alasdair. *After Virtue*. 2nd ed. Notre Dame: University of Notre Dame Press, 1984.

———. *Dependent Rational Animals: Why Human Beings Need the Virtues*. Chicago: Open Court, 1999.

Mahlmann, Christopher. "Transcript of John Furlong's Speech." http://www.valpolife.com/business/staff-development/6205-welcome-to-vancouver-stirring-speech-from-john-furlong.

Mandelbaum, Michael. *The Meaning of Sports: Why Americans Watch Baseball, Football, and Basketball and What They See When They Do*. New York: Public Affairs, 2004.

Mathew, P. G. "Muscular Christianity Sermon Transcript." http://www.gracevalley.org/
    sermon_trans/2007/Muscular_Christianity.html.
Maughan, R. J. et al., eds. *Food, Nutrition and Sports Performance II: The International
    Olympic Committee Consensus on Sports Nutrition.* London: Routledge, 2004.
Maughan, Ronald and Robert Murray. *Sports Drinks: Basic Science and Practical
    Aspects.* Boca Raton, FL: CRC Press, 2000.
McFee, Graham. *Sport, Rules and Values: Philosophical Investigations into the Nature of
    Sport.* London: Routledge, 2004.
———. "Normativity, Justification, and (MacIntyrean) Practices: Some Thoughts on
    Methodology for the Philosophy of Sport." *Journal of the Philosophy of Sport* 31
    (2004) 15–33.
McGrath, Alister. *A Life of John Calvin: A Study in the Shaping of Western Culture.* Ox-
    ford: Blackwell, 1990.
Messiniesi, Xenophon. *History of the Olympic Games.* New York: Drake, 1976.
Miah, Andy. *Genetically Modified Athletes: Biomedical Ethics, Gene Doping and Sport.*
    New York: Routledge, 2004.
———. "Gene Doping: The Shape of Things to Come." In *Genetic Technology and
    Sport,* edited by Claudio Tamburrini and Torbjörn Tännsjö, 42–53. New York:
    Routledge, 2005.
Midgley, Mary. *Heart and Mind: The Varieties of Moral Experience.* New York: St.
    Martin's, 1981.
Milbank, John. *Theology and Social Theory: Beyond Secular Reason.* Oxford: Blackwell,
    2001.
Mitchell, George. "Report to the Commissioner of Baseball of an Independent Investiga-
    tion into the Illegal Use of Steroids and Other Performance Enhancing Substances
    by Players in Major League Baseball." http://files.mlb.com/mitchrpt.pdf.
Moore, David. "For Lindsey Vonn and Maria Riesch, Friendship and Rivalry Blur."
    http://www.usatoday.com/sports/olympics/vancouver/alpine/2010-02-16-
    lindsey-vonn-cover_N.htm.
Moore, G. E. *Principia Ethica.* Cambridge: Cambridge University Press, 1971.
Morgan, Laura. "Enhancing Performance in Sports: What is Morally Permissible?" In
    Sports Ethics: An Anthology, edited by Jan Boxill, 182–88. Oxford: Blackwell, 2003.
Morgan, William. "Are Sports More So Private or Public Practices?: A Critical look at
    Some Recent Rortian Interpretations of Sport." *Journal of the Philosophy of Sport*
    27 (2000) 17–34.
———. "Ethnocentrism and the Social Criticism of Sports: A Response to Roberts."
    Journal of the Philosophy of Sport 25 (1998) 81–102.
———. *Leftist Theories of Sport: A Critique and Reconstruction.* Urbana: University of
    Illinois Press, 1994.
———. "The Logical Incompatibility Thesis and Rules: A Reconstruction of Formalism
    as an Account of Games." In *Philosophic Inquiry in Sport,* edited by William
    Morgan and Klaus Meier, 50–63. 2nd ed. Champaign, IL: Human Kinetics, 1995.
———. "Why the 'View From Nowhere' Gets Us Nowhere in Our Moral Considerations
    of Sports", *Journal of the Philosophy of Sport* 30 (2003) 51–67.
Morris, Leon. *1 Corinthians.* Tyndale New Testament Commentaries. Grand Rapids:
    Eerdmans, 1983.

Murphy, Nancey et al., eds. *Virtues & Practices in the Christian Tradition: Christian Ethics after MacIntyre*. 1997. Reprinted, Notre Dame: University of Notre Dame Press, 2003.

Murray, Thomas. "The Coercive Power of Drugs in Sports." *Hastings Center Report* 13/3 (1983) 24–30.

Nagel, Thomas. *The View from Nowhere*. New York, Oxford University Press, 1986.

National Football League. "Policy on Anabolic Steroids and Related Substances." http://www.scribd.com/doc/28662767/bannedsubstances.

Nietzsche, Friedrich. *The Will to Power*. Translated by Walter Kaufmann. New York: Vintage, 1968.

———. *Thus Spoke Zarathustra: A Book For None and All*. Translated by R. J. Hollingdale. New York: Penguin, 1969.

Novak, Michael. *The Joy of Sports: Endzones, Bases, Baskets, Balls, and the Consecration of the American Spirit*. Lanham, MD: Madison, 1994.

Orwell, George. "The Sporting Spirit." In *Shooting an Elephant and Other Essays*. London: Penguin, 2003.

Page, Holly. *God's Girls in Sports: Guiding Young Women through the Benefits and Pitfalls*. Colorado Springs, CO: Authentic, 2008.

Palmatier, Robert, and Harold Ray. *Dictionary of Sports Idioms*. Lincolnwood, IL: National Textbook, 1993.

Parens, Erik, ed. *Enhancing Human Traits: Ethical and Social Implications*. Washington, DC: Georgetown University Press, 1998.

Pfitzner, Victor. *Paul and the Agon Motif: Traditional Athletic Imagery in the Pauline Literature*. Novum Testament Supplements 16. Leiden: Brill, 1967.

Pieper, Josef. *Leisure, the Basis of Culture*. Translated by Alexander Dru. San Francisco: Ignatius, 2009.

Plunkett Research. "Introduction to the Sports Industry." http://www.plunkettresearch.com/sports%20recreation%20leisure%20market%20research/industry%20overview 4.

President's Council on Bioethics. *Beyond Therapy: Biotechnology and the Pursuit of Happiness* Washington, DC: PCBE, 2003.

Putney, Clifford. *Muscular Christianity: Manhood and Sports in Protestant America, 1880–1920*. Cambridge: Harvard University Press, 2003.

Resnik, David. "The Moral Significance of the Therapy-Enhancement Distinction in Human Genetics." In *Bioethics: An Anthology*, edited by Helga Kuhse and Peter Singer, 209–18. 2nd ed. New York: Blackwell, 2006.

Roberts, Terence. "Sport and Strong Poetry." *Journal of the Philosophy of Sport* 22 (1995) 94–107.

———. "Private Autonomy and Public Morality in Sporting Practices." In *Ethics and Sport*, edited by Mike McNamee and Jim Parry, 240–55. London: Routledge, 1998.

———. "Sporting Practice Protection and Vulgar Ethnocentricity: Why Won't Morgan Go All the Way?" *Journal of the Philosophy of Sport* 25 (1998) 71–81.

Robertson, A. T. *Word Pictures in the New Testament*. Vol. 4. Grand Rapids: Baker, 1931.

Rorty, Richard. *The Consequences of Pragmatism*. Minneapolis: University of Minnesota Press, 1982.

———. *Contingency, Irony, and Solidarity*. New York: Cambridge University Press, 1989.

————. *Objectivity, Relativism, and Truth*. New York: Cambridge University Press, 1991.

————. *Philosophy and the Mirror of Nature*. Princeton: Princeton University Press, 1979.

Roth, Paul. "Politics and Epistemology: Rorty, MacIntyre, and the Ends of Philosophy." *History of the Human Sciences* 2 (1989) 171–91.

Ryken, Leland. *Worldly Saints: The Puritans as They Really Were*. Grand Rapids: Zondervan, 1986.

————. "The Puritan Ethic and Christian Leisure for Today." In *Christianity and Leisure: Issues in a Pluralistic Society*, edited by Paul Heintzman, et al., 32–50. Sioux Center, IA: Dort College Press, 2006.

Rytko, Stanisław. "Preface to the Publication of the Proceedings for 'Church and Sport.'" http://www.vatican.va/roman_curia/pontifical_councils/laity/documents/rc_pc_laity_doc_20051112_prefazione-sport_en.html.

Sandel, Michael. *The Case against Perfection: Ethics in the Age of Genetic Engineering*. Cambridge: Harvard University Press, 2007.

Savulescu, Julian, et al. "Why we should allow performance enhancing drugs in sport." *British Journal of Sports Medicine* 38 (2004) 666–70.

————. "Compulsory Genetic Testing for APOE Epsilon 4 and Boxing." In *Genetic Technology and Sport*, edited by Claudio Tamburrini and Torbjörn Tännsjö, 136–46. New York: Routledge, 2005.

Schirato, Tony. *Understanding Sports Culture*. Understanding Contemporary Culture. London: Sage, 2007.

Schmitz, Kenneth. "Sport and Play: Suspension of the Ordinary." In *Sport and the Body: A Philosophical Symposium*, edited by Ellen Gerber, 22–29. Philadelphia: Lea & Febiger, 1974.

Schneider, Angela and Robert Butcher. "A Philosophical Overview of the Arguments on Banning Doping in Sport." In *Values in Sport: Elitism, Nationalism, Gender Equality, and the Scientific Manufacture of Winners*, edited by Torbjörn Tännsjö and Claudio Tamburrini, 185–99. London: E & FN Spon, 2000.

Schneider, Angela, "Genetic Enhancement of Athletic Performance." In *Genetic Technology and Sport*, edited by Torbjörn Tännsjö and Claudio Tamburrini, 32–41. New York: Routledge, 2005.

Schapiro, Rich. "Mark Spitz: Michael Phelps Couldn't Have Beaten Me." http://www.nydailynews.com/sports/2008olympics/2008/08/20/2008-08-20_mark_spitz_michael_phelps_couldnt_have_b.html.

Sider, Robert, ed. *Christian and Pagan in the Roman Empire: The Witness of Tertullian*. Washington, DC. Catholic University of America Press, 2001.

Simon, Robert. *Fair Play: The Ethics of Sport*. 2nd ed. Boulder, CO: Westview, 2004.

Solc, Josef. *Communicating on the Playing Field*. Longwood, FL: Xulon, 2009.

Song, Robert. *Human Genetics: Fabricating the Future*. Cleveland: Pilgrim, 2002.

————. "Fragility and Grace: Theology and Disability." In *Theology, Disability and the New Genetics: Why Science Needs the Church*, edited by John Swinton and Brian Brock, 234–44. New York: T. & T. Clark, 2007.

Spaemann, Robert. *Persons: The Difference Between "Someone" and "Something."* Translated by Oliver O'Donovan. Oxford: Oxford University Press, 2006.

Special Olympics, "Changing Attitudes: Changing the World: Media's Portrayal of People with Intellectual Disabilities." http://www.specialolympics.org/uploadedFiles/LandingPage/WhatWeDo/Research_Studies_Desciption_Pages/Policy_paper_media_portrayal.pdf.

———. "Special Olympics Mission." http://www.specialolympics.org/mission.aspx.

———. "The History of the Special Olympics." http://www.specialolympics.org/history.aspx.

———. "Sports and Competition at the 2009 World Winter Games." http://www.specialolympics.org/WGU_sports.aspx.

St. John, Warren. *Rammer Jammer Yellow Hammer: A Road Trip into the Heart of Fan Mania.* New York: Random House, 2004.

Stevenson, C. L. *Ethics and Language.* New Haven: Yale University Press, 1960.

Suits, Bernard. *The Grasshopper: Games, Life and Utopia.* Boston: Godine, 1978.

———. "The Elements of Sport." In *Philosophic Inquiry in Sport,* edited by William Morgan and Klaus Meier, 39–48. Champaign, IL: Human Kinetics, 1988.

———. "Tricky Triad: Games, Play, and Sport." *Journal of the Philosophy of Sport* 15 (1988) 1–9.

Swanton, Christine. "Can Nietzsche Be Both an Existentialist and a Virtue Ethicist?" In *Values and Virtues: Aristotelianism in Contemporary Ethics,* edited by Timothy Chappell, 171–88. New York: Oxford University Press, 2006.

Swinton, John, and Brian Brock, eds. *Theology, Disability, and the New Genetics: Why Science Needs the Church.* New York: T. & T. Clark, 2007.

Taylor, Louise. "Premier League Clubs Hit Fans with Massive Price Rises." http://www.guardian.co.uk/football/2008/may/28/premierleague.

Tertullian, *De Spectaculis.* Translated by T. R. Glover. Cambridge: Harvard University Press, 1984.

Tozer, A.W. *The Pursuit of God: Finding the Divine in the Everyday.* Radford, VA: Wilder, 2008.

Tamburrini, Claudio. "After Doping, What? The Morality of the Genetic Engineering of Athletes." In *Sport Technology: History, Philosophy and Policy,* edited by Andy Miah and Simon Eassom, 253–68. Amsterdam: Elsevier Science, 2002.

United Kingdom Anti-Doping. "About UK Anti-Doping." http://www.ukad.org.uk/pages/about-us/.

United States Anti-Doping Agency. "USADA Athlete Handbook." http://www.usada.org/wp-content/uploads/athlete_handbook_2014.pdf.

Veblen, Thornstein. *The Theory of the Leisure Class.* New York: Modern Library, 1934.

Verstraete, Larry. *At the Edge: Daring Acts in Desperate Times.* Toronto: Scholastic Canada, 2009.

Waddington, Ivan, and Andy Smith. *An Introduction to Drugs in Sports: Addicted to Winning?* New York: Routledge, 2009.

Wannenwetsch, Berndt. "Angels with Clipped Wings: The Disabled as Key to the Recognition of Personhood" In *Theology, Disability, and the New Genetics: Why Science Needs the Church,* edited by John Swinton and Brian Brock, 182–200. New York: T. & T. Clark, 2007.

Watson, N. J. "Muscular Christianity in the Modern Age: 'Winning for Christ' or 'Playing for Glory'? In *Sport and Spirituality: An Introduction,* edited by Jim Parry et al., 80–94. London: Routledge, 2007.

Watson, Nick J. and John White. "'Winning at All Costs' in Modern Sport: Reflections on Pride and Humility in the Writings of C. S. Lewis." In *Sport and Spirituality: An Introduction,* edited by Jim Parry et al., 61–79. London: Routledge, 2007.

Weber, Max. *The Protestant Ethic and the Spirit of Capitalism.* Blacksburg, VA: Wilder, 2010.

Weir, Stuart. *What the Book Says about Sport*. Oxford: Bible Reading Fellowship, 2000.

Weisman, Larry. "Super Bowl Tickets are Way over Price of Admission." http://www.usatoday.com/sports/football/nfl/2008-01-29-ticket-prices_N.htm.

Weiss, Paul. *Sport: A Philosophic Inquiry*. Carbondale: Southern Illinois University Press, 1969.

Wells, Samuel. "The Disarming Virtue of Stanley Hauerwas." *Scottish Journal of Theology* 52 (1999) 82–88.

Whitehead, Alfred. *Process and Reality*. New York: Free Press, 1978.

Wittgenstein, Ludwig. *Philosophical Investigations*. 2nd ed. Translated by G. E. M. Anscombe. Oxford: Blackwell, 1958.

World Anti-Doping Agency. "Anti-Doping Community." http://www.wada-ama.org/en/Anti-Doping-Community.

———. "World Anti-Doping Code." https://wada-main-prod.s3.amazonaws.com/resources/files/wada-2015-world-anti-doping-code.pdf.

———. "The Copenhagen Declaration on Anti-Doping in Sport." https://wada-main-prod.s3.amazonaws.com/resources/files/WADA_Copenhagen_Declaration_EN.pdf.

———. "The 2014 Prohibited List." https://wada-main-prod.s3.amazonaws.com/resources/files/WADA-prohibited-list-2014-EN.pdf.

———. "Therapeutic Use Exemptions Guidelines." https://wada-main-prod.s3.amazonaws.com/resources/files/wada_guidelines_tue_2014_v7.0_en.pdf, 6.

Wright, Lesley. "Aesthetic Implicitness in Sport and the Role of Aesthetic Concepts." *Journal of the Philosophy of Sport* 30 no. 1 (2003) 83–92.

Wright, N. T. *Paul for Everyone: 1 Corinthians*. London: Society for Promoting Christian Knowledge, 2003.

———. *How God Became King: The Forgotten Story of the Gospels*. New York: Harper-Collins, 2012.

Zirin, Dave. *Bad Sports: How Owners Are Ruining the Games We Love*. New York: Simon & Schuster, 2010.

Zuidema, Marvin. "Athletics from a Christian Perspective." In *Christianity and Leisure: Issues in a Pluralistic Society*, edited by Paul Heintzman, et al., 193–202. Sioux Center, IA: Dort College Press, 2006.

Index

You may also be interested in

The Games People Play
Theology, Religion, and Sport

Robert Ellis

ISBN: 978 0 7188 9371 2

In *The Games People Play*, Robert Ellis constructs a theology
around the global cultural phenomenon of modern sport, paying
particular attention to its British and American manifestations.
Using historical narrative and social analysis to enter the debate
on sport as religion, Ellis shows that modern sport may be said
to have taken on some of the functions previously vested in
organized religion. Through biblical and theological reaction,
he presents a practical theology of sport's appeal and value, with
special attention to the theological concept of transcendence.

Throughout, he draws on original empirical work with sports
participants and spectators. *The Games People Play* addresses
issues often considered problematic in theological discussions
of sport, such as gender, race, consumerism, and the role of the
modern media, as well as problems associated with excessive
competition and performance-enhancing substances.

Available now with more excellent titles in Paperback, Hardback,
PDF and ePub formats from The Lutterworth Press

www.lutterworth.com